MAKING
SCIENCE
OUR OWN

DATE DUE	

MAKING
SCIENCE
OUR OWN

Public Images of Science
1910–1955

Marcel C. LaFollette

The University of Chicago Press

Chicago and London

Marcel LaFollette is a visiting scholar at the National Museum of
American History, Smithsonian Institution.

The University of Chicago Press, Chicago 60637.
The University of Chicago Press, Ltd., London
© 1990 by the University of Chicago
All rights reserved. Published 1990
Printed in the United States of America

99 98 97 96 95 94 93 92 91 90 5 4 3 2 1

Library of Congress Cataloging in Publication Data

LaFollette, Marcel C.
    Making science our own : public images of science, 1910–
1955 /
    Marcel C. LaFollette.
        p.   cm.
    Includes bibliographical references.
    ISBN 0–226–46778–3 (alk. paper). —ISBN 0–226–46779–
1 (pbk. : alk. paper)
    1. Science news—United States—History.   I. Title.
    Q225.L34   1990
    509.73—dc20   89–20555
                                                  CIP
⊗The paper used in this publication meets the minimum
requirements of the American National Standard for Information
Sciences—Permanence of Paper for Printed Library Materials,
ANSI Z39.48–1984.

CONTENTS

PREFACE

Science has been so thoroughly incorporated into American culture that it is hard to imagine life without it. Scientists routinely appear at the side of the President, in the evening television news, and in commercial endorsements; scientific laboratories form the backdrop for movies; and conclusions reached in real laboratories help justify legislation, policies, and personal decisions. At the same time, skepticism of science is also high: many political movements derive their energy from a denial of science's authority, and it is not unusual for local governments to investigate the conduct of private research. Clearly, science has become too important to be ignored, even by those who do not understand it or who reject it.

The ambiguity of current public attitudes did not result, however, from any one event or use of science, such as the atomic bomb or the space program. The prominence of science as a cultural symbol—and scientists as national heroes—arose gradually through the twentieth century, as the research enterprise itself gained political and economic strength. And skepticism grew alongside it. This book traces the construction of those attitudes, examining how science and scientists were presented in mass-circulation magazines over a fifty-year span.

By placing public images in their political context, past and present, I hope to bridge the gap between studies of science in the mass media and the concerns of public policy. What people believe about science—how it is done, who does it, and why—affects their political response. In a democracy, citizens have a right (and obligation) to learn about the institutions, groups, and projects they underwrite or sanction, lest ignorance or emotion alone govern their support. A well-informed and knowledgeable citizenry is especially vital for science because it now depends so heavily upon government subsidy and is affected by federal tax policy, regulatory policy, and national security, as well as by the ebb and flow of normal legislative action. Probing the origins of public attitudes toward science has therefore become important to science policy strategy in all countries.

Are these images exclusive to the United States? Only cross-cultural research, of course, could really answer such a question; but to the extent that scientists around the world have been trained here or have worked with or been influenced by U.S. scientists, these images may also be present elsewhere. Science, of course, possesses certain universal qualities. Facts do not respect national boundaries: chemical theories developed in Calcutta should work just as well in Cleveland. But images do not always reflect reality and what individuals believe about science may be culturally determined. A sensitivity to our own peculiar biases will help us communicate more precisely as the nations of the world attempt to use science and technology to solve common problems of pollution, hunger, violence, and disease.

Although I analyzed a database of popular magazines, I could equally well have examined the content of other media; similar messages about science permeate all modes of cultural expression. American popular magazines interpreted scientific facts and explained scientific issues; they described events and people, providing repeated images of institutional, organized science—how research was conducted, who scientists were, what scientific research produced for society, what role it should play in the future. What was said in their pages found its way into the general political discourse of the era, as well as reflected prior debate. Especially in a democracy, ideas and images flow freely through interconnected media systems, affected by the agents of communication, whether author, editor, producer, or publisher, and by the sources of information (in this case, the scientists). The audience, too, influenced the content. Ideas flowed in more than one direction. Magazine readers selected from what editors presented; and the audiences' feedback (either by letter or pocketbook) shaped subsequent editorial selections. The images and ideas I describe are therefore just as much products of American culture as of American science. The face of science shown here was not only the face that scientists wanted presented but also the one that Americans wanted to see as their own.

Over the past twenty years, my work has been influenced and helped by a number of teachers, advisors, colleagues, and friends. In the late 1960s,

David Manning White recognized that the insights of mass communications research might be fruitfully applied to the special case of science; his encouragement was instrumental in sending me on for graduate study at Indiana University. At Indiana, Trevor Brown, Herbert J. Altschull, John C. Hayes, Ralph Holzinger, Anthony San Pietro, David Smith, John Woodcock, and the late Richard C. Gray advised and guided my research; the Poynter Center for the Study of American Institutions and its director William Lee Miller provided crucial support; and the late Nicholas C. Mullins showed me (and many others) how quantitative analysis could support the concerns of politics, and how academics could also be good citizens. Later, when I was at Harvard University, Harvey Brooks and Gerald Holton encouraged my work on this book, as did also Larry Cohen of MIT. I thank Melvin Kranzberg and many other members of the advisory board of *Science, Technology, & Human Values,* who believed in the social studies of science and in the discussion of science in its social context long before it was fashionable. And I thank my colleagues John C. Burnham and Richard Davies, who read interim drafts of this manuscript and offered invaluable criticisms for revision.

Thank you also to the editorial staff of *Science, Technology, & Human Values,* especially Lisa Buchholz, John Gianvito, and Melinda Thomas, as well as to my students at MIT, whose honest reactions to my ideas consistently pushed me toward clearer expression and understanding. They taught me much about current popular culture (and its images of scientists) that has deepened this book.

I thank the Smithsonian Institution, National Museum of American History, and its Director, Roger Kennedy, for the respite, as a visiting scholar, to finish this book.

True friends are rare; even rarer are those who listen to our puzzles and show us new solutions. Several women, Joan Laws and Holly Stocking among them, have been continual inspirations. Dorinda Hale has laughed and cried with me through the years, with equal fervor. The peripatetic Robert Bird and the elusive Elvis P. supplied the songs that made work easy.

My husband Jeffrey Stine listened to progress reports with undiminished enthusiasm (how *do* you stay so cheerful?), and was always willing to bat ideas around over breakfast, lunch, and dinner, during walks on the shore and runs on the Mall, in a Rockport restaurant, in sight of the Eiffel Tower, and at the Eastern Market fish counter. Thank you, my dear, for keeping *my* eyes on the stars.

Washington, D.C.,
September 1989

1

New Expectations, New Images

The half-century from the 1910s through the 1950s represented a time of exciting rearrangement for the scientific research enterprise in the United States, a period during which its political and social power strengthened, and scientists began to pay attention to their public image. Shifts in who funded research, for how much, and why accompanied upheavals in American political and social relations, in domestic and foreign policy, in the economy, and in the national culture. Science became caught up in—and was sometimes the instrument of—these changes.

Without question, science now occupies an important place in American national life, not only in billion-dollar research and development (R&D) budgets, but also in the direct, visible effects of research knowledge. Ironically, however, the relationship between society and the scientific enterprise has grown not closer but more tense. Most Americans appear to believe—even if it is not true—that they do not and cannot comprehend modern science, and that they do not understand how research is conducted; moreover, they do not trust scientists alone to control the direction or methods of scientific research, and they regard the scientific research community as somehow distanced from the society of which it is, in truth, a part.

The origins of this tension, and its political consequences, can be explained, I believe, by images of science widely shared by American citizens throughout this century and, in particular, by the significant dis-

1

crepancy between what the public expected from science and what science delivered. Shared images in the culture—what Walter Lippmann once characterized in a political context as "the pictures in our heads"[1]—affect public opinions about science and science-related political and social issues over the long term. How then to determine what these shared images have been in this century? How to measure whether they have changed?

Although some historians and sociologists of science have begun to provide detailed glimpses of scientific life in the twentieth century, those descriptions of laboratories or individual careers cannot explain the underlying political support for science; moreover, much of this work still takes an elitist approach and ignores the influence of citizens who, in this democracy, direct government's actions on science. Likewise, we routinely accept as a fashionable truism the argument that there are "two cultures," but we have insufficient information on how any such separation operates; we observe tensions between the citizenry and the scientific establishment, yet we propose few plausible explanations for their existence other than "disillusionment" or "loss of confidence." On occasion, commentators will attribute negative public attitudes to particular events or discoveries (most notably, to the development of nuclear weapons), but much work in the social studies of science—however valuable it may be to our understanding—tends to view the science-society relationship inside out, by analyzing first the forces at work in science and then proceeding to speculate about the cultural impacts. This book approaches that science-society relationship—and the tensions apparent in it—from the perspective of American culture; in particular, I focus on the ideas about science prevalent in mass magazines, using them as representative of the content of all the mass media and as a measure of public sentiment.

Magazines serve as useful mirrors of social attitudes in earlier times. We cannot now test the opinions of residents of Des Moines or Boston in the 1920s, for example, and the statistical data that do exist on political attitudes before the 1940s are limited. Compared to today's sophisticated analyses, the opinion polls of fifty years ago seem primitive and simplistic; they also rarely addressed issues related to scientific research. Certain mass media content, however, sharply reflects past public attitudes; for in the American democracy, with a free press and marketplace sensitivity, commercial success and audience acceptance go hand in hand. In this book, I have assumed the existence of just such a direct (if complex, interactive, and imperfect) relationship between what people believed about science generally and what they learned about science from the mass media.

This concept of the "dual role" of the media is well-established in communications science: the media routinely present new images for the audience's consideration and publicize ideas current elsewhere in American society. People also develop impressions about public issues in more than one way; as communications research shows, attitudes are both "based on mass-mediated representations of political events and of developing, distal public response" and "filtered through the social influences of their immediate personal surroundings."[2]

These impressions take on special significance for subjects as complex as science. The words *science* and *scientist,* for example, evoke strong mental images, but not necessarily the same for everyone. Think "scientists," what do you see? Think "science," what characteristics come to mind? In one person, the terms may recall vivid pictures from a mixture of sources—perhaps Nobel laureates photographed at press conferences, perhaps clever fictional characters from a movie or novel. For another, the words may revive unhappy memories of school laboratories and their inhabitants. In each person's mind, the images formed over a lifetime blend together. Complex and multifaceted, based on both fact and fancy, these ideas are continually revised through education and experience as well as through exposure to the images reproduced in the mass media.

Descriptions of science were especially vivid in the popular periodicals of early twentieth-century America. Curled up by the fireside, teenagers could learn about the latest exploits of physicists and chemists; their parents could read how research could help win a war or cure disease. Until the rise of television in the late 1950s, mass magazines such as *The Saturday Evening Post* and *Cosmopolitan* were information sources about the world of science that were easily accessible to millions of readers in all parts of the country and from all walks of life.

Moreover, these sources possessed considerable credibility, even if their goals were partially entertainment. Nonfiction magazine articles purported to present truth, not supposition, when they gave informative (and usually sympathetic) interpretations of current research. Journalists would characterize even the opinions of scientists as fact, rather than as gossip or biased interpretation.

The format of presentation varied, but all these mass-market publications strove to combine information and entertainment. Science could easily fit both these goals. Some articles described *science as culture,* announcing new discoveries or summarizing scientific knowledge about the natural world; others presented *science as technique* or *science as power,* educating readers about the institution of science, about how research was conducted, and about how it was organized and financed.[3] Articles included extensive discussions of who scientists were, what they did, why they did it, and what values they cherished.

These media descriptions played an unusually important role in shaping cultural attitudes because science was actually quite segregated from ordinary life. Researchers performed their experiments and calculations in laboratories or isolated observatories, away from the scrutiny of nonscientists (and sometimes away from their colleagues). Scientists peppered their communications with multisyllabic terms and abstract concepts; they whisked away the curtain of technical incomprehensibility only when the research was complete and the discoveries announced. Like a foreign city never visited, scientific research could therefore easily appear mysterious and intimidating to a nonscientist. The magazines' intimate format, however, allowed readers to "observe" mysterious experiments or to "overhear" scientists' conversations—all while sitting safely as home. The journalists could visit the scientists' lairs and bring back accounts of what was going on, could even translate for the inhabitants. The social separation of the work of science, as well as the technicality of the language, magnified the importance of these media accounts.

When shared by other members of the public, cultural beliefs disseminated through the mass media helped to shape the role of science in American life as well as affect Americans' attitudes toward and actions on science. Stereotypes in the mass media drew readers' attention to salient aspects of research, and thereby guided and influenced political support for research.[4] What Americans believed about science determined what they expected of it. What they believed about scientists affected what they allowed scientists to do. What they wanted from science eventually determined whether they paid for it. By categorizing the images most prevalent in twentieth-century culture, we may shed some light on how those ideas influenced the modern social and political context for science.

This book analyzes a particular group of such accounts—nonfiction magazine articles on science and scientists from the 1910s to the mid-1950s—and does so from a macroscopic perspective, viewing mass-market magazines as a large communications system, related to other contemporary systems such as radio and newspapers, but subject to independent study. Moreover (since this was not a study of editorial or reportorial practices), I have analyzed the content apart from the decision-making of those who produced it.

My approach rests on a number of assumptions about public communication. First, in a free marketplace of ideas, there is a direct relationship between the popularity of a concept—as demonstrated by its frequent appearance in the mass media—and how well it matches the audience's own beliefs about that concept. An assertion's repeated presence in mass-circulation periodicals owned by many different publishers diminishes the probability that the editors or publishers made any coordinated effort to promote certain images. Editors chose to describe science so that each description would make sense to their readers, would fit with that audiences' general beliefs about science, and therefore enhance the publication's marketability.

Communication, Kurt Lang and Gladys Engel Lang remind us, "is above all concerned with meanings," some created, some embedded in the culture, but all of which "exist in the form of mental images."[5] For such abstract terms as *science,* these mental images also helped audiences to discern the *implications* of repeated messages about science that permeated contemporary social and political discourse. The mass media carried out, therefore, both a reporting function, as they described what scientific research had proved or what scientists were doing, and a "poll-taking" function, as they shared ideas of science present elsewhere in the culture.[6]

Throughout this book, I have also tried to be mindful of the fact that mass communication involves the transmission of signals—whether via the electronic impulses from a television camera or via a magazine's printed pages—and that these signals pass through channels that are by no means neutral filters for information: they can create bias.[7] In communicating scientific information, all participants—authors, editors, staff, even the scientists who supplied information—shaped the details of magazine articles according to their own beliefs about science. Moreover, the meanings that were transmitted depended upon how users processed the signals. For science, prior knowledge and education (or lack of it) could determine that reaction, especially if an audience lacked the appropriate technical vocabulary.

What Lang and Lang call *mutuality*—"reciprocal adjustments" by communicator and audience—also affected the overall display of images and messages over time.[8] For mass magazines, the interplay between circulation, sales, and reader interest influenced the importance that editors assigned to science and thereby determined the proportion of content allocated to the topic. Although the attention to science (the proportion of total magazine content that discussed science) varied slightly among magazine types, the images of science and scientists did not differ significantly among the magazines studied, indicating that the images must have had deep roots in American culture.

Some General Themes

Twentieth-century Americans shared not one public image of science but many, as reflected in the multiple uses of the word. Scientists and journalists alike used the term *science* interchangeably to refer to the research process, the body of knowledge, *and* the professional community of scientists; moreover, they often anthropomorphized the concept, making science into a living, growing thing that could "do" things, could "act," could even "assert." In truth, of course, a writer could only describe what *individuals* did, how they acted, what they asserted; but underlying the factual description was always the implication that there was some powerful entity called *science*—with a mysterious and unstoppable life of its own.

Stereotypical "scientists," on the other hand, possessed many characteristics more appropriately applied to machines and, as a group, they had a mysterious uniformity. Throughout decades of magazine discussions, writers would measure each interview subject against some mythical "average scientist"—male, white, brilliant, energetic, rational, and dispassionate. Specialties and even occupations blurred under one common identifier: biologists, psychologists, research engineers, and logicians all became "scientists."

Recurring images reinforced identifiable themes. "Scientists" chipped away relentlessly at tradition and ignorance, for example, and were intelligent enough to solve *any* problem. "Science" continually rejected old philosophies and proposed new ones. Every modern scientist reportedly had an "ungovernable instinct to extend the boundaries of knowledge."[9] Only scientific truth remained "the same yesterday, to-day, and forever."[10]

The cornucopia of research had no end, no limits. Scientists cited each new development (even those created by engineers) as proof that science would bring more. No matter how arcane a research topic appeared, it just might lead to industrial progress. Throughout the decades, a rosy halo surrounded science, an image of good intentions and good will, an image purportedly worthy of unquestioning public trust.

A single magazine article could contain dozens of different assertions about science or about a specific research project; it could examine research from several perspectives—political, economic, and philosophical. Images available to readers were thus exceedingly complex in their composition, yet important images remained remarkably consistent across time. In the 1950s, authors (nonscientists and scientists alike) used the same descriptive phrases as had authors in 1910. Modulations, when they did occur, were subtle, such as the shift from an "active" energetic image to a "passive" cerebral one (discussed in Chapter 4). Consistency far outweighed change—despite science's own dramatic transformation during the same period.

What did change significantly from decade to decade was the intensity of attention that magazines in general paid to science. Given the recent history of science, one might reasonably expect magazine coverage to have risen steadily from the 1910s through the 1950s, in tune with the spectacular discoveries and larger research budgets. Popular folklore in fact describes science in the twentieth century as booming—more scientists, more successes, more money, and (by implication) more media attention. In mass-market magazines, however, there was no steady rise in science coverage; instead, the statistical measures of coverage discussed in Chapters 2 and 3 show regular patterns of increased and decreased attention to science (as measured by the average number of articles published per year), patterns that coincided with whether scientists were authors or subjects of interviews. This finding, in particular, raises some provocative questions related to the history of science and science policy, as recounted briefly in the remainder of this chapter.

Historical Background: Cultural Images and Science Policy

The period on which this book focuses—from the 1910s through the mid-1950s—was not only a time of significant growth of science in the United States but also the time when the model for current science policy was drafted.[11] Before World War I, scientific research (especially basic or undirected research) was modestly funded, oriented around the individual investigator, and regarded as culturally important but not universally relevant to national politics; after 1945, U.S. science moved to an era of million-dollar research budgets, multiple-investigator teams, and intensive federal support for even seemingly arcane research topics. The word *science* entered the modern political lexicon. Mass-media content from this time of change indicates what many Americans during those decades believed about the function and value of scientific research.

The magazines presented science to their readers not in isolation but as an integral part of modern life which affected and sometimes usurped the traditional authority of morality, social custom, and politics. As science popularizer Edwin E. Slosson explained, such forums wanted to show "How a Single Scientific Discovery May Influence Politics, Finances, Industry, Social Ideals, the Drift of Population, and the Balance of Power."[12] Coverage of science was not limited to straightforward accounts of what researchers had discovered about the natural world or to expansions on scientific "facts"; instead, writers addressed science's social and political context as well.

At the beginning of the twentieth century, scientific research sometimes seemed a private matter.[13] Most individual investigators derived their support from industry or university employers, rather than from the state or federal government.[14] By the 1920s, however, there were signs of change. Such giants of nineteenth-century science as Charles Darwin and Thomas Huxley still stood, aloof and elite, as the conventional models for scientists, but new heroes were also emerging. A few bright young scientists linked their careers to practical American mercantilism, and many of the establishment spokesmen for science assumed dress and manners that belied conventional stereotypes of intellectuals as awkward or unfashionable.

Some changes in funding and organization resulted inevitably from war. Although science had long been considered useful to the military, relatively few scientists participated in military-sponsored research prior to World War I.[15] In the early days of that conflict, therefore, the magazines tended to characterize scientists as eager outsiders, as newly hired hands to the purposes of government and national need. This attitude permeated scientists' popular writings as well. In 1917, the Chairman of the National Research Council, astronomer George Ellery Hale, interpreted for *Scribner's* readers a new social function for science: "How Men of Science Will Help in Our War."[16] The "uninformed" might dismiss basic research as of "purely academic interest," Hale wrote, but "the most practical leaders of industrial research" exalt it as "the source from which all progress springs."[17] He hammered home the connection between research and industrial productivity: Pure science was "the bedrock of progress." "None recognizes this so clearly as those industrial leaders who have profited greatly from discoveries in pure science ultimately adapted to practical end," he asserted. To Hale and many other leaders of the scientific community, the usefulness of *some* research served as sufficient evidence that *all* should be publicly supported. At a time when the federal government supported relatively little university or other basic research, such arguments signaled a budding effort to persuade society of science's value to national needs.

Occasionally, the practical uses of science attracted unwanted criticism, however, as happened with chemistry in the 1910s. Before World War I, German industry had had a virtual monopoly on patents and international trade in chemistry. When hostilities eliminated most trade exchanges, the United States experienced shortages of some chemicals, and a few popular writers tried to pin the blame on U.S. chemists. The chemists, they implied, should somehow have anticipated the problem and were obliged therefore to "explain" why the shortages occurred: "What are you going to do about it? . . . What is the matter with American chemistry, anyway?"[18] Such criticism diminished as industrial chemists began to develop substitutes for the German products. Some writers portrayed American chemistry as a new partner with business and commerce; other praised chemistry's contribution to the war effort.[19]

This publicity rebounded after the war, for chemists had also helped to design such horrible new weapons as mustard gas. One journalist explained later that "On the whole the man in the street did not think much at all about chemistry before the war"; but after the war "he thought of it only as making poison gas or dyes."[20] Journalists began to call the conflict "the chemists' war."[21] And chemists discovered that although nationalism could bring praise for local benefits, people assigned blame more broadly: when things went wrong, it was not necessarily the fault of either "German chemists" or "Allied chemists" but, instead, of *the* chemists."

During this time, science also played an important symbolic role in some political ideologies, such as progressivism and technocracy.[22] Belief in progress became a central article of "the dominant American faith"; life was getting better and, with skill (and science), it might be possible to speed up the process.[23] The popularity of Frederick W. Taylor's "scientific management" idea, for example, gained strength from science's image as the ultimate reliable authority. To proponents of these and other sociopolitical movements, scientific and engineering knowledge (aided by a technocratic emphasis on efficiency) appeared able to solve every problem, to supply an answer to every question.[24]

Because scientific research had instigated, either directly or indirectly, many visible social improvements, the link between scientific knowledge and its application became a crucial element of science's image. "With every year that passes," *The Saturday Evening Post* editorialized, "it becomes harder and harder to draw the dividing line between pure science and applied science; and rash is he who is ready to declare that any given addition to the body of human knowledge is not, and never will be, of any practical use."[25] As American industry thrived, engineers, inventors, and managers translated the basic researchers' insights and knowledge into practical action, and scientists often received the credit. Each new product and social improvement brought praise to scientists, no matter how little they had actually contributed to its development.

The blurring of the connection between undirected research and technological application, and the conflation of the images of science and technology, contributed to a blurring of responsibility. Traditionally, science discovered the keys; technology unlocked the doors. What lay behind those doors was, unfortunately, not always what either scientists or society anticipated—or wanted.

Concern about their public image led some scientists to become more involved in political action, therefore. Following World War I, leaders in the scientific community sought substantial federal funding for basic research and, believing that a well-crafted, positive image would help to attract the necessary public support, attempted to found a popular science magazine.[26] Plans for the magazine were at first proposed independently in 1916 by groups of influential scientists within the National Academy of

Sciences, the American Association for the Advancement of Science, and the American Chemical Society, but all these projects failed for two reasons. First, several publications such as *Popular Science Monthly* (and its legatee *Scientific Monthly*) already dominated the market. And second, many other scientists vigorously opposed such sanctioned popularization efforts, arguing that they would divert energy and resources away from research.[27]

During World War I, similar attitudes had kept U.S. scientists from coordinated attempts to elicit public "sympathy and support" for their war-related research; nevertheless, a small group of scientific leaders remained convinced that to attract public sympathy, research must be seen as an *American* activity.[28] Projecting messages about scientific solidarity, about science's usefulness, and about science's importance to the *national* interest, they believed, would improve science's overall public image as well as increase scientists' own sense of community.

A few years later, therefore, another group of scientists, convinced that the political value of popularized writings on science could influence political support, revived the effort to establish a scientist-sponsored popular science magazine. Once again, the effort failed. This time, however, the discussions paved the way for the establishment in 1920 of Science Service, a nonprofit syndicate, to distribute "general news of science."[29] Initially financed by newspaper publisher E. W. Scripps, the service was later sponsored by the American Association for the Advancement of Science and the National Research Council, and it represents a turning point for scientists' open and formalized participation in public communications efforts. Its avowed purpose was to promote a positive image of science. The founding editor, chemist and writer Edwin E. Slosson, declared that the Service would not "indulge in propaganda unless it be propaganda to urge the value of research and the usefulness of science."[30] By the mid-1930s, the Service was meeting a subscription list of over 100 newspapers and reaching about one-fifth of the U.S. reading public.[31]

Similar motives lay behind the successful proposals to make the wartime National Research Council (NRC) a permanent institution. Years after the NRC became a quasi-independent federal agency, George Ellery Hale candidly observed that one of the "prime purposes" of the new Washington, D.C., building to house the NRC and its parent organization, the National Academy of Sciences, was to symbolize scientific progress and "the importance of research" to all who visited or worked in that city.[32]

Publications and buildings may have been tangible symbols of scientists' rising prominence in American life, but the best expression of power was money. Ever richer research budgets beckoned to the entrepreneurial scientist. Private universities, foundations, or industry sponsored most basic research at this time, and compared to the bounty of today's laboratories, the budgets were modest. Industrial laboratories experienced almost threefold growth in the 1920s; but basic research funding, outside of a few industrial operations such as that of General Electric, did not keep pace with applied research.[33] Many scientists objected on principle to linking the future of scientific research to federal largess, believing, as one historian has noted, that "the advancement of scientific theory required an autonomy not at the mercy of government purposes, popular passions, or utilitarian needs."[34] This suspicion of government funding motivated another contemporary political activity of the scientists, the campaign for a National Research Endowment ("A National Fund for the Support of Research in Pure Science").[35] Aimed at creating a $20-million fund for "research having no necessary commercial value," the campaign, headed by Hale, Robert A. Millikan, and other prominent scientists, ran from 1926 through 1930.[36] Their efforts failed—in part because of the Great Depression, but also because the scientific community could not attract crucial industrial donors (who preferred to invest "in their own company laboratories, where technologically promising discoveries could be patented before they were published").[37] The failure of this campaign convinced many scientists that they lacked sufficient deep social respect to attract public support of "the best science for its own sake."[38]

Various political proposals for using scientific advice (from the short-lived Science Advisory Board of the 1930s to the Science Committee of the Natural Resources Board) brought a few more scientists into the political mainstream.[39] Although these efforts also failed in their ultimate goals, they set the stage for post-1945 actions in that, as historian Carroll Pursell has shown, they "strained and sometimes broke the old patterns of scientific organization, support, and relationships."[40] In part because the scientists participated less in popularization efforts in the 1930s (see the discussion in Chapter 3), they gained little new political clout during this time; and in many respects, the scientific establishment lost ground in its effort to portray science as a national political force. The depression itself dispelled the popular notion that "progress could result only from the free union of science and industry,"[41] and there was little national coordination of the research done throughout the country, which contributed to a perception of irrelevance. During this time, magazine writers rarely described science in terms that assumed automatic usefulness for all research. One of the events that helped to change this perception was, again, a war.

The Manhattan Project to design and build an atomic bomb during World War II represented an extraordinary conjunction of world events with an ongoing stream of scientific research. Physics in the 1930s had already been moving in the direction of "controlling" the atom. Had there been no war, the research would undoubtedly have proceeded, albeit more slowly and cautiously. Instead, the war (and especially the news of Nazi atrocities and rumors of a German atomic bomb project[42]) provided a special impetus to scientists' participation in what was for them an unusual arrangement: a cooperative, nationally-coordinated, government-funded research project involving hundreds of the best researchers and directed toward the creation of a single product. Although many chemists had engaged in government-sponsored team research during World War I (some of them in uniform), the Manhattan Project was different—by several orders of magnitude—from how most other scientists had ever conducted their research. The invention of an atomic bomb changed world politics. The project to design it changed how U.S. scientists worked and how they thought about themselves—their sense of social responsibility, their beliefs about how research should be funded, and their overt acceptance of a connection to government policies and politics. These changes eventually influenced public images of science as well.

In the 1910s, mass-magazine articles routinely implied that scientists cared little about national politics or about the social context of their work. Journalists treated scientific accountability as a private matter, one of professional or perhaps institutional integrity, but not of *social* responsibility. This early twentieth-century image of scientists laboring independently in an ivy-covered tower of research may have been exaggerated and inaccurate—scientists were indeed human, and many were doing research on contemporary social problems—but it was not *wrong*. By and large, most scientists then did not themselves admit that research should be controlled by any agenda but the scientific one.[43]

After World War II, the image changed to one exhibiting a new sense of the inevitability of research. Society might not like every result of the scientists' work; but we "cannot stay the victory of the laboratory," one journalist wrote.[44] There was also a new sense of the political usefulness of science. In late 1944, that same writer described what science's political role would be like when the war ended: Researchers in chemistry were said to be "building a new world where no old rules hold."[45] "We are in the midst of a chemical revolution," he observed, "and we have to reckon with chemical values." To thwart scientific progress would be to thwart postwar expansion and economic redevelopment worldwide. This author's solution expressed a wholesale confidence in science common in other popular discussions: "At the present time we are taking a political approach to problems . . . that will arise in postwar years. We would be on much safer ground if we took a chemical approach."[46]

Concurrent with this sense of inevitability was an image of science's two faces, a realization that each new advance carried the potential for *both* benefit and harm. Acknowledgment of this ambiguity formed a less significant part of public discourse early in this century, but grew during the 1930s and 1940s. Sometimes the risk of new knowledge appeared clear: the chemical weapons used during World War I had killed friends as well as enemies. Sometimes the link was less obvious: advances in physics had made possible the internal combustion engine, and the automobiles using such engines gave people new mobility; but no one appeared to blame "physicists" because these "infernal engines" also polluted the air, created new forms of sudden death, and required additional government expenditures for highway maintenance and traffic signals.

A related aspect of the assessment of risks and harms involved estimates of how long it took for a scientific idea to be used in technology, and hence involved beliefs about who was responsible for the misapplication of scientific knowledge. Early in the century, magazine articles portrayed scientists as aloof from the effects of their work. Writers provided elaborate but secondhand explanations of just how useful the seemingly useless work might be, but the scientists themselves explained little. Some change in this image occurred after World War II, even if the reasoning seemed faulty. As Jean-Jacques Salomon has observed, the Manhattan Project demonstrated "that the time-lag between theoretical research and practical applications could be prodigiously shortened, if people were prepared to pay the price in men, money and logistics"; but few journalists of the time, when citing the project as an example of what scientists could do, acknowledged that it represented a mobilization of effort only possible in a democratic society during wartime.[47]

New discussions of scientific responsibility also appeared in postwar coverage as scientists sought to justify their actions against new criticisms. Physicist J. Robert Oppenheimer, speaking in 1947 to science and engineering students, asserted that "it must be clear to all of us how very modest [the scientist's] assumption of responsibility can be, how very ineffective it has been in the past, how necessarily ineffective it will surely be in the future."[48] Although many prominent scientists, like Oppenheimer, still insisted in public that researchers could not bear the responsibility for all uses of their research, the Manhattan Project had indeed forged a different impression. As the years passed, fewer and fewer journalists accepted the scientists' qualification of "modest" responsibility. To the contrary, journalists began to assess society's stake in the practice of science even more openly. Scientists enthusiastically took credit for the advances of beneficial technologies, but the mass media began quietly to hold them accountable for any harmful effects. Scientists could not escape the link between what they did at Los Alamos and what happened at Hiroshima. To the nonscientist, one seemed undeniably the result of the other.

Postwar debate over federal research funding helped to bring these

and other policy-related questions to public attention. As the war was ending, a number of scientists and politicians began to discuss continuance of
the wartime science-government relationship. The depression of the 1930s
had depleted many university science budgets; no one wanted to give up
the riches of the Manhattan Project and return to prewar funding levels.[49]
So the postwar planners agreed that the federal government should create
some central agency to channel funding into basic research; they disagreed, however, about the institutional structure of the agency and about
who would exercise political control over the research (and to what extent).[50]

Two well-defined positions on this question emerged, with groups of
prominent scientists and politicians promoting each side and each group
exploiting representative ideas of science. Vannevar Bush, who had been
director of the wartime Office of Scientific Research and Development and
a principal science advisor to the president, argued for a model of "loose"
federal control. Pleading for a different model of support were such men
as Senator Harley Kilgore (whose Congressional hearings helped to stimulate the debate), Presidential Assistant John R. Steelman, and scientists
Harold C. Urey, Edward U. Condon, and Harlow Shapley.

Bush articulated his position in a report to the President published
in 1945, *Science—The Endless Frontier,* which outlined a plan for orga-
nizing science after the war. In brief, Bush and his advising committees
proposed that the federal government adopt a significant role in funding
basic research but that scientists' traditional independence in matters of
research agenda, procedures, and communication be preserved. The initial
plan called for relatively modest financing. To insure that "the best science
be supported," the scientists, through advisory groups and a system of
review by scientific peers, were to be regarded as the experts on how funds
should be used and how research should be conducted.[51] Wartime controls
on some scientific and technical information were to be lifted in an effort
to encourage "the healthy competitive scientific spirit so necessary for expansion of the frontiers of scientific knowledge."[52] Scientific progress,
Bush wrote, results from "the free play of free intellects, working on subjects of their own choice, in the manner dictated by their curiosity for
exploration of the unknown."[53]

Those in opposition did not quarrel with the general idea of federal
support of science. Basic researchers had clearly proved their usefulness
to the nation, and some type of support was in order. The opposition did,
however, argue that the arrangements should follow traditional political
requirements for review and accountability. The director of the proposed
agency, for example, was to be appointed by and politically responsible to
the president, as was true for other federal departments. Bureaucrats (not

scientists) were to monitor the research system. And government security regulations on scientific communication (especially in the areas relating to atomic physics) should continue to be applied as necessary to protect military secrets. A report issued in 1947 from a White House group headed by John Steelman made it perfectly clear that Bush's opponents did not fear science, were not proposing moratoria or needless restrictions on science, and were not attempting to "slow down" science. Instead, they worried about the long-term implications of the proposed political relationship. They simply did not believe that scientific research was a sufficiently special activity to justify departure from "traditions of democratic government or from tested principles of administrative organization," including principles of close accountability and avoidance of the concentration of power.[54]

Ultimately, a model for federal funding emerged which, with varying influence in different agencies, sided with the Bush forces and allocated significant control to the organized scientific community. That model prevailed because, in fact, it embodied the prevalent cultural images of science. The images underpinning the political justifications for the Bush model represented entirely natural choices, common views at the time. Bush employed metaphors and ideas that epitomized Americans' trust in and expectations of science and scientists, while the Steelman forces drew on suspicions and uneasiness that represented at that time only a minority view.

In the forty years since the Bush report, the balance has shifted. In congressional hearings, even politicians supportive of science and growth may be heard voicing demands for accountability and restrictions in terms that echo Steelman's rhetoric, not Bush's. Science is now conducted within a regulatory environment.[55] Restrictions in just one part of science, biomedical research, demonstrate the pervasiveness of legislated control throughout organized science. Concern in the 1960s over the use of human subjects in research led to the development of a federal regulatory system to oversee that use; concern in the 1980s over how animals are treated when used in research has already resulted in new regulations, and estimates of future compliance costs run as high as $1 billion; furthermore, controversy over whether scientists should use human fetal tissue in their research has already stopped some projects in biomedicine.[56] Most of these and similar federal restrictions have been implemented only since the late 1960s, yet regulation has proceeded with a political sureness of a type that usually indicates strong grounding in public opinion and tight consistency with social beliefs. What fuels this regulation? Opinion polls and other cultural barometers do not reveal widespread antiscience feelings among the majority of the American public.[57] People admire famous scientists.

They support funding for research. They flock to science museums in ever-growing numbers. They may even *like* science. The wholesale rejection of science predicted by some analysts in the 1970s has simply not material-ized.[58] Nevertheless, as demonstrated by the extent of regulation, the American public also does not fully trust either scientists or scientific in-stitutions, especially in regard to how research should be conducted.

Examining these seeming contradictions in the light of the popular image of science since 1900 helps to explain what happened. The popular image early in the century was strong and self-assured but less entwined with national interests. When other oracles, such as religion or political ideology, failed to supply sufficient hope of better times, science could be (and was) substituted as an instrument of faith. Science's record of positive achievement throughout the century and the scientists' incessant promises of infinite progress reinforced its social authority. When journalists hailed each new discovery as a "whisper of salvation,"[59] the public naturally ex-pected more. These expectations—unquestioning and ill-informed—dressed scientists in a mantle of mystery and endowed them with almost supernatural attributes. The overall image was not negative, and the level of concern low.

The images of science present in the Bush report and similar policy statements represented an inaccurate, idealistic view of science, how-ever—a view that could not be sustained. The view ignored how science was really done, it exaggerated what scientists could really accomplish, and it miscommunicated what scientists were really like. It proposed an impractical, improbable array of promises; it made assumptions of good behavior that were simply incompatible with human nature; and it advo-cated programs that flew in the face of basic democratic ideas about whose interests should govern—those of the special interest group or those of the public. As Jean-Jacques Salomon so astutely observes, in the twentieth century scientific researchers "aspired" to win state support while holding their institutions "at arm's length"; they wanted funding but also wanted to maintain control over their own affairs.[60] Bush's supporters won politi-cal acceptance for their model at a time when science's public image, rose-colored and energetic, rode high on the success of wartime service; but like most inconsistent ideals, the autonomy model was inherently politi-cally unstable. Something had to shift, and adjustments had to be made. Society could, of course, have lost faith in science, and as a result govern-ment funding would have declined. Instead, Americans needed science; they continued their strong economic support of research but simply in-creased the accompanying regulation; they continued to admire experts but began to remove science's special political privileges.[61]

Although each generalized image of science described in this book played some role in influencing and informing twentieth-century science policy, these images' most important effect was cumulative. After decades of contradictory messages, Americans appear to have acknowledged a significant difference between what they want science to be and what they are told science is doing. In the early part of the century, popularized science articles reflected little difference. With time, however, the discrepancy has increased. Americans may still have wanted to believe that science alone fueled technological progress and that all technological progress was good, for that was an attractive illusion; and they may have listened politely while the research community pled for political autonomy and "modest" responsibility. They could not, however, ignore the problems unleashed or unsolved by research.

No single negative image led to the current political reassessments of science. Citizens and politicians alike have simply reacted, with characteristic American pragmatism, to decades of mismatch between positive messages and negative effects, between an idealized expectation of benefit and the reality of unpredicted harm, between the scientists' endless promises and the public's unfulfilled desires.

2

Mass-Circulation Magazines
and the Popularization of Science

As instruments of education and entertainment, fact and fiction, the mass media help to shape public beliefs and knowledge about all sorts of things, but they are most influential when describing places, people, and events outside their readers' everyday experiences. At such times, the audience must trust the accounts of those who have "been there," just as they respond to travel writers who visit exotic places, meet elusive people, and experience unusual situations. For few subjects has this translation and information function been as important as for science, in part because the nature of research seems so alien to everyday experience, and in part because the mass media do not offer neutral channels for transmitting information about science.

Science is also not a "visible" occupation. Ordinary people may readily observe carpenters, lawyers, or nurses at work; but even in a technologically advanced country such as the United States, few people ever watch scientists working in any stage of the research process—data-gathering, experimenting, calculating, or writing. Throughout this century, most scientific research has been conducted in private laboratories or offices, away from routine public scrutiny. Americans have primarily, if not exclusively, learned about science and scientists in school or through the news and entertainment media.

Traditional schoolroom instruction, however, has presented a carefully controlled, restricted view of research.[1] Even today, primary- and secondary-school science classes in the United States still concentrate on scientific "facts," theories, and principles, or favor stylized instruction in experimental methods. School learning may serve as a "filter" for later assimilation of mass media content, but even the best educational experience has provided people with far less information about the nature of science than they have routinely received through the mass media during their lifetimes.[2] In addition, early in this century, schoolroom instruction did not emphasize the connection of scientific knowledge to social and political issues—an approach current in the educational efforts of the 1960s and 1970s but not widely adopted until then.

In the early twentieth century, the channels for informal, out-of-school learning about science included many options, each with identifiable advantages and limitations.[3] The print media—books, newspapers, and magazines—constituted the principal channels both for science news and for popular entertainment with science themes. U.S. newspapers carried articles on science and scientists and reported on discoveries and scientific meetings.[4] In the late 1910s and 1920s, the scientific associations, recognizing the importance of science "news," began hiring public relations directors and setting up news services.[5] Other media also played important roles in communicating scientific information to the public. Well-known scientists gave public lectures in urban areas and on the Chautauqua circuit, for example, but such forums were limited in both appeal and audience size. Natural history museums helped people to visualize scientific information and sought to educate children and adults alike within an entertaining format, but their messages too were limited to description and simple explanation. Until well after World War II, most science museums adopted passive styles of presentation, such as "cabinets of curios" or dioramas, with little accompanying discussion of science in its social context and little audience engagement.[6]

Competition for these forums came in force in the 1920s. The development of radio and radio networks allowed the most soft-spoken science professors to lecture to millions.[7] Radio plays and the movies also brought new dimensions to the dramatic presentation of science; now, ever-larger audiences could hear and see scientists, real and imaginary.[8] By the late 1940s, commercial television broadcasts offered new opportunities for serious as well as frivolous discussions of science, but in the early decades of American commercial television, science shows constituted only a minor portion of the content.[9]

Whatever the mode of communication, each article, book, or script about science included information about how research was conducted and described scientists' physical attributes, character traits, and personal motives. Each included assertions about the goals or purposes of research, and each description and assertion, whether presented as fiction or nonfiction, either complemented or contradicted the audience's prior assumptions about typical science and scientists. Public images of science, because of their consistent appearance in the mass media, thus reflected the aggregated, collective, undifferentiated ideas that general audiences shared about science and scientists.

This book draws its conclusions from a study of how one type of communications channel, popular magazines, presented science to mass audiences of Americans from the 1910s to the 1950s, but I believe firmly that these conclusions apply as well to other mass media of the same period and similar audience. Quantitative studies of the science content of other media (and my own studies of U.S. television in the 1970s and 1980s, for example) have not revealed starkly different popular images.

Nonfiction articles from general-content mass magazines sought both to inform and entertain their readers. Articles had to seem useful to a reader's life yet present information in a lively and attention-holding format, often with substantial illustration. The relationship between audience, writer/editor, and sources of scientific information that was involved in creating these magazine articles resembled those relationships found elsewhere in American commercial mass media. As I shall discuss later in this chapter, the internal consistency of both my statistical conclusions and the content analysis of images, even for magazines of different editorial positions and different publishers, indicates that these images were, in fact, widely accepted in the national culture and not unique to any particular communications source.

Editorial Policies

Because their success and survival depended on maintaining strong circulations, and because the feedback from increased (or canceled) subscriptions could be seen in a matter of months, general-content, mass-circulation magazines serve as especially sensitive indicators of what their readers believed (or wanted to believe) about science. To maintain a large, stable circulation base, a magazine's editorial policy had to be "responsive to the interests, values and sensibilities" of its readers.[10] "If a magazine is to be popular," *The Saturday Evening Post* wrote in 1910, "it must understand and meet the wishes of the public."[11]

Publications for a mass market usually met those wishes by monitoring what was current and what was new and then balancing their coverage of both. A magazine could not present images that conflicted wildly with its current subscribers' images of the people, institutions, or ideas discussed, lest it confuse or repel readers. Research in commercial mass magazines of this period shows clearly that they tended to "perpetuate what they perceived as the accepted social and cultural standards of the majority," rather than innovative or radical notions.[12] Publishers had to entice subscribers into continuing purchases, however, so each issue had to appear to be at once new, yet familiar and comfortable.[13] Fiction writers could indulge in wild and improbable imaginings, of course, but nonfiction content, although it might initially shock or surprise, ultimately had to conform to readers' underlying assumptions about how the world worked (or, in the case of scientific research, how research was ordinarily done). Significant shifts in editorial outlook occurred only over the course of many years, reflecting widespread changes in political and social thought. On occasion, a publisher convinced of the existence of an emerging new market of subscribers with different "interests, values and sensibilities" might alter content slightly in order to attract those readers.

The consistency of the magazines' content over many years also reflected American journalism's inclination to reinforce the social and political status quo.[14] Mass magazines, because they were profit-generating activities, required a stable society for their financial well-being. This is not to say that coverage of science was unrelentingly conservative. Journalistic traditions of social and political criticism, and each magazine's desire to stir its readers' simmering passions, of course, played crucial roles in content choice; but a commercial mass-circulation magazine could not afford to ignore either the political realities or the basic economics of publishing, and content stability usually reflected such managerial choices.

For most mass-circulation magazines, the principal administrative model involved a publisher (or more likely a publishing company) who owned the magazine, made the profit or underwrote the loss, set the publication's general identity, and appointed the editor or editors. Each magazine's financial operating formula included different proportions of income from investment underwriters, advertising, and subscriptions. Some periodical publishers, for example, relied more on advertising than subscription income, in order to keep subscription prices low and circulation high; but the content of successful magazines always had to be acceptable to sufficient advertisers (or backers) *and* audience to survive. Mass-market publishing was ultimately an act of merchandising.[15]

Radical content changes were therefore rare. Editors of the biggest, most successful publications included familiar features along with new ideas and made each selection according to some tried and true editorial formula.[16] General-content magazines, such as *The Saturday Evening Post*, thrived on a predictable mix of topics and articles. Ray Long, editor of *Cosmopolitan* for thirteen years, in describing his philosophy of editing, emphasized just such a match between his tastes and those of his readers.

I happen to be an average American who has the opportunity to read a tremendous number of manuscripts. From these I select the stories I like, publish them within the covers of a magazine, and through the facilities of our circulation department, put that magazine where people may see it; and there are enough other average Americans who like to read the same thing that I like to read to buy the magazine in sufficient quantities to make me worthy of my salary.[17]

When readers ceased to agree with editorial choices, then an editor changed the criteria—or stopped being editor. Successful editors knew what their subscribers had wanted to read in the past, and anticipated what they would find interesting in the future. Even though they trusted their own tastes, editors did not select content in isolation from their audiences' concerns. As a *Post* editorial observed in 1910, "Some editors of popular periodicals may believe that they are leading and that the people are following. . . . It is a harmless delusion and it carries its own corrective."[18]

Choosing editorial material for a magazine involved more than just selecting favorite topics and authors, however; each article contained implicit or explicit messages—or images—about the topic, to which editors had to be sensitive. Economist Kenneth E. Boulding, writing about how abstract images are communicated in a culture, has compared the mass communicator's role to that of a cartographer: both depend on feedback from their audiences. "A map maker who puts out an inaccurate map," Boulding writes, "will soon have this fact called to his attention by people who use the map and who find that it violates their spatial image derived from personal experience."[19] American popular magazines assumed similar but even more powerful roles when describing science to their readers for, to most of the general public, science was an unknown, as remote as Katmandu. The messages had to fit not just with readers' knowledge or direct experience (since this may have been limited) but also with their beliefs about science—*even if those beliefs were inaccurate*. This point holds special importance for the images of science, because, as I shall discuss, the messages did not simply assert what science was but also predicted what it would do. Roland Marchand, in a study of magazine advertising in the 1920s and 1930s, contends that readers did not actually want advertisements, for example, to reflect their real lives or to show society as it really was; instead, they "preferred an image of 'life as it ought to be, life in the millennium.' "[20] Or, as historian Nathan Reingold acerbicly writes, "Mass culture, like dreams, sometimes discloses suppressed beliefs."[21]

Magazine editors, in commissioning or selecting articles, also acted as partners with the writers in shaping the images. A writer took what he or she had learned from a source and then summarized, refined, and altered the information to suit a specific readership.[22] The editor packaged that article and its set of images with articles on all sorts of things, from politics to romance to gardening, and presented the completed issue to the reader.

At this point of repackaging, the messages—especially when they involved abstract scientific concepts—were subject to subtle influence and interpretation. The editors' and journalists' own attitudes toward a topic rather naturally affected their choices; as a result, they became "agents of creation" of certain images and emphases. Some articles became the lead articles in an issue; some received special illustration highlighting certain themes. As part of this process, consistent "patterns of cognition, interpretation, and presentation, of selection, emphasis, and exclusion"—what sociologist Todd Gitlin calls media *frames*—affected how each person in the editorial chain organized and repackaged information.[23] Each unconsciously selected his or her own version of reality. Each editor then applied the publication's particular editorial policy—with its own set of assumptions about the value of science—and selected an issue's content.[24]

When constructing or choosing an article on science, journalists and editors became also "agents of transmission," because they were unusually dependent upon their sources. Science was as much an unknown territory to the magazine journalists of the early twentieth century as it was to their readers. To produce their copy, the writers relied on facts and ideas that had already been filtered through the formal scientific communication process or that scientists had translated for them. Few American journalists had had sufficient scientific training to enable them to comprehend the content of technical journals or scientific meetings and then to select the central ideas and translate them on their own. Even fewer editors had the expertise to evaluate a journalist's success at such translation.

When we examine the images of science widely present in mass-circulation periodicals, we are attempting therefore to measure ideas constructed through a complex decision-making process that was influenced by its need to match cultural expectations. Images of science, in particular, were affected more by long-term cultural change than by hasty shifts in public attitudes or editorial fashion. Unlike the reputations of movie stars (which success or scandal might affect in a matter of weeks), or unlike public support for a political program (which could change back and forth), the public images of science moved like indolent dinosaurs. When change occurred in those images, it was measurable but exceedingly slow.

The Content Analysis—A Brief Look

To study the images of science and scientists in the mass media, I chose a group of eleven U.S. magazines that were nationally circulated and moderately priced, had high circulation within their periodical classification, were published without interruption over a substantial part of the period to be studied, and included high-quality, nonfiction articles on a broad range of subjects. These magazines were also well-documented by such historians of American periodicals as Frank Luther Mott, and their circulation figures and publishing records could be easily certified through the *N. W. Ayer and Son's Directory of Newspapers and Periodicals* for each year of the study. Table 2.1 lists the magazines sampled for the content analysis and the inclusive sampling periods.

The analysis focused on magazines directed at general audiences, rather than science magazines intended for audiences attentive to science, such as *Popular Science Monthly* or *Scientific American*. The general-circulation periodicals addressed all aspects of current affairs, literary, social, and political; science was just one part of a full range of content. They were not magazines directed at specific audiences, as were women's magazines such as *Ladies' Home Journal* or the political or ethnic journals. The images presented in these eleven magazines were thus more likely to represent those shared by a majority of middle-class Americans, male and female, from many different ethnic backgrounds, geographical locations, and occupations.[25]

The general-circulation periodicals were, in fact, among the principal sources of entertainment-based messages about science available at the time. From 1910 to 1955, the combined monthly circulations of these periodicals ranged from 3.2 million to almost 12 million.[26] Middle-class Americans routinely monitored more than one communications medium, of course. A *Collier's* reader from the 1930s, for example, may have listened to the radio, read newspapers, read the current best-sellers, and subscribed to more than one magazine.[27]

The statistical data on content quoted throughout this book come from an analysis of articles in a 39.9% stratified random sample of the

Table 2.1   Magazines Sampled for the Study, with Inclusive Sampling Periods

The American Magazine (1910 through 1955)
The American Mercury (1924 through 1955)
The Atlantic Monthly (1910 through 1955)
The Century Illustrated Monthly Magazine (1910 through 1930)
Collier's, The National Weekly (1910 through 1955)
Cosmopolitan (1910 through 1955)
Everybody's Magazine (1910 through 1929)
Harper's Monthly Magazine (1910 through 1955)
Scribner's Magazine (1910 through 1939)
The Saturday Evening Post (1910 through 1955)
The World's Work (1910 through 1932)

eleven magazines.[28] Of the 8,300 issues that these magazines published between January 1910 and December 1955, I examined the contents of 3,316, locating a total of 687 articles.

Although I also read editorials, columns, and similar content to check for editorial consistency, the statistical analysis included only three types of *nonfiction* articles: (1) biographies of or interviews with scientists; (2) articles that described, analyzed, discussed, or criticized science in general or a scientific development or field in particular; and (3) articles written by scientists, in which the author's credentials as a scientist were clearly identified and relevant to the topic discussed (as was almost always the case). In every article included in the sample, *science* or *scientists* was the author's principal subject; but the topic was broadly defined to include articles on (a) science as a social institution (e.g., education of scientists, research organization, funding, or communication); (b) scientific research methods and equipment; (c) the knowledge or data collected through scientific research; and (d) science as a philosophical approach to life (as in a "scientific way of thinking"). Such classification included articles on engineering research, for example, but excluded articles on the construction of dams; it included knowledge from biomedical research but excluded articles on the ordinary practice or practitioners of medicine.

The study did not analyze the images present in the magazines' fiction content. Although some studies of "science fiction" (that is, fiction with futuristic or fantastic themes involving science or scientists) have found exaggerated images of scientists in the negative traits attached to scientists who are villains, a brief analysis of magazine short stories containing scientist characters did not convince me that fiction content necessarily contained images of scientists different from those in the nonfiction.[29]

There were 687 nonfiction articles about science or scientists published in the sampled issues.[30] As Chapters 4 through 10 will show, the image of science present in these articles showed remarkable consistency in the characteristics measured. Changes, when they occurred, were more apt to be across time than among types of articles or among magazines.[31] Any differences between magazines appear to have been related more to changes in the editorship or to publishing problems than to a publication's editorial policy of approval or disapproval of science. By way of background, then, let us look at the factors that for these particular magazines might have influenced the attention they paid to science.

Price and Content—How Science Fit the Formula

Because many of the great mass-circulation magazines in the United States were founded after 1910, or changed format or direction about then and, likewise, because many ceased publication or changed content after 1950, this study encompasses a time important to the history of American magazine publishing as well as to the history of science.[32] Around 1900, the economics and editorial outlook of mainstream American magazine publishing underwent dramatic changes that affected how and why general magazines included articles on science. In a flurry of competition, publishers reduced the price of many of the best general magazines to ten or fifteen cents and, as Frank Luther Mott has observed, editors also began to lock up "their ivory towers and [come] down into the marketplace."[33] Over the next fifty years, the general magazines successfully appealed to millions of middle-class Americans, and most sustained sufficient circulation and advertising to maintain a low price. They achieved much of their success through varied content, timeliness, fresh editorial presentation, high standards for production and illustration, and a sense of topics related to national unity. During periods of economic prosperity, the magazines were a bargain; in the late 1920s, for example, a dime could buy a two-hundred-page issue of *The Saturday Evening Post*.[34] Even in periods of economic recession, the magazines offered affordable, reusable entertainment for millions.

In the 1950s, a combination of forces—rising postal rates, competition from television, "frantic" circulation wars, and changes in how Americans used magazines to fulfill their information and entertainment needs—combined to reorient the American magazine market. Although the magazine industry survived and, in many ways, is healthier today, eventually, more specialized publications supplanted the general-content weeklies. As the history of this period shows, with the death of *Collier's*, *The Saturday Evening Post*, *Look*, and *Life*, "the general interest mass audience magazine group simply ceased to exist in the United States."[35] Periodicals that had helped to bind the nation's culture together were supplanted by electronic media as both the topics of conversation and the reflectors of current social and political trends.

Among the thousands of U.S. periodicals published between 1910 and the mid-1950s, two types—general-interest "family" magazines and general-interest public affairs/literary magazines—served the greatest number of households. Magazines such as *The Saturday Evening Post* and *Cosmopolitan* addressed any subject deemed suitable for the American family; a single issue might include short features, columns, romantic fiction, cartoons, detective stories, and poetry as well as political editorials. Illustrations, especially in color, enlivened the text; photo-essays on public figures and celebrities were common. The family publications unashamedly aimed to entertain as well as to provide "mild and easy instruction"; their political allegiances, although by no means consistent over the period studied, were rarely controversial, neither extreme left nor extreme right.[36]

Magazines that emphasized literature and public affairs favored a more serious tone and makeup, usually eschewing photographs, cartoons, and romantic fiction. As *World's Work* observed of its sister publications at the time, these periodicals focused on "the present activities of the world" and interpreted "contemporary life" for their readers, usually from a well-defined but mainstream political perspective.[37] Although not strictly aimed at the entire family, the public-affairs magazines attracted well-educated, middle-class readers, and the same affluent household might subscribe to *The Saturday Evening Post* and *Harper's Monthly*. Despite their different orientations, both types of magazines took active interest in American politics and the assessment of current social proposals. During their heyday, one analyst writes, "Events that people talked seriously about at the national level more often than not had their origins in weekly magazines"; they filled a need somewhere between the immediacy of newspapers and the reflective "hindsight" of the book.[38] And, although the format and frequency of presentation changed from decade to decade, both types of magazines showed remarkable collective consistency in the images of science chosen for presentation.[39]

Serving Families—General-Content Magazines

To many social historians, antique collectors, and nostalgia buffs, *The Saturday Evening Post* seems the epitome of twentieth-century periodicals, the archetypal expression of Americana, and certainly it is the most well known today.[40] Its early history also typified shifts in American publishing around 1900. After Cyrus H. K. Curtis, the successful publisher of *The Ladies' Home Journal*, bought the *Post* for $1,000 (or about fifty cents per subscriber) in 1897, he oversaw a revitalization that sent circulation spiraling to 2 million by 1913.[41] The *Post*'s success derived from an editorial formula that emphasized business, public affairs, and romance, in that order.[42] Humor, variety (from sports to foreign affairs), and a focus on personalities made the *Post* immensely popular with American families.

The *Post*'s vision of America was socially conservative—no cigarette ads appeared in the *Post* until 1931, for example, and no liquor ads until after World War II—yet it held up scientific progress as an attractive and acceptable ideal, a glorious expression of national diversity and ingenuity.[43] And, from the 1910s through the 1950s, the *Post*'s editorial interest in science never wavered.[44] In the 1930s, accounts of expeditions and descriptions of field experimentation stations often centered on the rigors and inconvenience of scientific work; moreover, such articles assessed research quality in terms of its practical value and potential for technological exploitation, reflecting the magazine's "wholehearted devotion to material prosperity."[45] After World War II, articles continued this preoccupation with the practical, but focused less on individual researchers and more on the ramifications of their work and the potential of new industrial research facilities. Articles on research laboratories then reassured readers that, despite the Communist threat, the nation's intellectual resources were undiminished, and science still possessed the potential for victory.[46] For the *Post*, however, the 1960s harbored other enemies within its balance sheets. The publication held on longer than most of its competitors, but it too eventually folded in 1969.[47]

Another characteristic of the family magazines was their tendency to write about science in general terms, rather than to focus on a single research program or even a single field. This overview approach typified *Everybody's Magazine,* a monthly that flourished from the 1890s through the 1910s and fell victim to circulation shakeouts and editorial reorganization in the 1920s.[48] Emphasis on science was never a prominent part of *Everybody's* formula for success, although the quality of the science articles published was high. A random sample of half of the *Everybody's* issues published between 1910 and 1921 revealed just ten science articles (or about one in every seven issues). Most of these articles were general, issue-oriented features (only one was written by a scientist). The magazine's coverage of science declined to a negligible amount in the postwar period, however. Eventually, *Everybody's* began to publish only fiction, a policy change that culminated in an ignominious death—*Everybody's* 1929 merger with a magazine called *Romance.*

In contrast, *The American Magazine* remained consistently successful until the publishing industry shakeouts of the 1950s. Founded in the 1870s by the great magazinist Frank Leslie, *American* began its real rise to success in 1906, when it was purchased by a group of leading muckraking journalists led by John S. Phillips.[49] The owners, well known for their work with *McClure's Magazine,* included Ida Tarbell, Lincoln Steffens, Ray Stannard Baker, Finley Peter Dunne, and William Allen White. In the years preceding World War I, *American* became therefore a showcase of the muckraking movement; but that glory was short-lived, as loose editorial control and dissent among the partners led to a dissolution of their relationship.[50] By 1910, only Baker and Tarbell remained, and in 1915, the group sold *American* to the Crowell Company (publishers of *Woman's Home Companion*), which put John M. Siddall in charge.

Perhaps because of the editors' intense interest in other national issues, *American* published few science articles from 1910 to 1915. Siddall, however, shifted the editorial emphasis "to certain strong interests that exist in all families," and included science among those topics.[51] Another of his changes was to inject more human interest, which resulted in an increased number of biographies, including those of scientists. From 1910 to 1955, in fact, *American* ran more biographies of scientists per issue than any of the other magazines studied.[52]

Self-boosterism characterized many of the articles in *American* and the other family magazines after World War I, and this mood extended to science, as authors admonished young men to emulate various self-made scientists and inventors. During the 1930s, the content became more somber and sophisticated and began to emphasize politics rather than other national topics; but under the editorship of Sumner Blossom (former editor of *Popular Science Monthly*), the science content again slowly increased.[53] Following 1945, *American* concentrated more on rebuilding, rearmament, and the peaceful uses of the atom than on the ongoing debate over civilian control or over the terrible consequences of the bomb's use, and there was no evidence of significant criticism or negative coverage of science. Instead, science was continually presented as a routine part of both the entertainment and information function of the magazine.

A similar transformation from muckraking periodical to family entertainment took place in *American*'s sister publication, *Collier's, The National Weekly*.[54] *Collier's* participation in muckraking journalism extended from the turn of the century to about 1919. Especially under the editorship of Norman Hapgood (1902–12), *Collier's* exercised considerable influence in national affairs, criticizing government and industrial policies alike. In 1913, however, the publisher reduced the weekly's price to a nickel and reshaped its content to imitate the by then successful *The Saturday Evening Post*. By 1917, circulation reached one million; but those numbers were not enough. *Collier's* poor financial condition continued, and in 1919 the Collier family sold the publication to the Crowell Publishing Company, which had purchased *American Magazine* only three years before.[55]

During *Collier's* muckraking era, its science articles rarely described discoveries or results in any detail; instead, they addressed such subjects as the return of Halley's Comet or how psychologists had debunked a famous spiritualist.[56] By the time of the 1919 sale, however, *Collier's* articles had begun to stress the importance of research and the relationship between science and the national interest, and as the 1920s enthusiasm for science peaked, more scientists began to contribute to the weekly.

After trying three different editors in four years, the Crowell group finally settled in 1925 on William Chennery, and a revitalized *Collier's* began its second great era. Chennery believed that fiction constituted "the backbone of mass circulation," so each issue followed a strict formula that included at least seven pieces of fiction, four to six feature articles, and three to four departments (regular sections or columns).[57] Up through the mid-1930s, Chennery included few science articles among the features, but those he did choose were neither negative nor critical, and the overall image of science presented was positive. In the 1920s, *Collier's* in fact ran a popular science page, "Catching Up with the World," started by E. E. Slosson.[58]

Mott has made some useful comparisons between *Collier's* and its rival *The Saturday Evening Post* during this period.[59] Together, these magazines reached a significant proportion of the American public. In 1942, when both raised their cover price to a dime, they had combined circulations of well over six million, with the *Post* usually about half million ahead of *Collier's* in any one year. The *Post* had more than twice the advertising revenue (and thus twice the pages) but the competition remained fierce. Often, the magazines fought over the same authors as well as over the same potential subscribers.[60]

In the 1950s, as *Collier's* influence waned, its contents became, Mott observes, "a little more sensational, a little sexier, a little more violent," and there "seemed to be a desperate effort for circulation."[61] Eventually, the mid-1950s collapse of the Crowell-Collier publishing group brought *Collier's* long and varied life to a close, along with those of its sister publications, *American* and *Woman's Home Companion*.

One of the magazines that did survive the publishing upheavals of the 1950s and 1960s was *Cosmopolitan Magazine*—albeit in a greatly altered state.[62] *Cosmopolitan* first became a serious competitor in the market for general, illustrated, literary monthlies between 1889 and 1905, under editor John Brisbane Walker, who is credited with introducing "the newspaper ideas of timeliness and dignified sensationalism into periodical literature."[63]

In 1905, Walker sold *Cosmopolitan* to publishing magnate William Randolph Hearst, and the magazine's pages embraced new topics and new ideas, including a less dignified sensationalism. Under Hearst, *Cosmopolitan* participated actively in muckraking journalism, but Hearst wanted increased circulation, not social reform. By 1912, he had reduced the feature articles from an average of seven per issue in 1910 to three per issue in 1920, and begun to emphasize fiction. Circulation soared; from 1915–1925, *Cosmopolitan* outdistanced competitors by about 1 million subscribers per year.

Perhaps in consequence of the Hearst influence, *Cosmopolitan* articles on science published during this era often had the ring of fiction, even when their text discussed serious research. Articles on medicine stressed sensational cures, for example, "Smiling Surgery" and "The Conquest of Cancer."[64] Researchers in archaeology and paleontology were apt to be "Probing Pompeii" or "Solving the Riddle of the Sphinx."[65] There was concern with science's role in hastening death ("The Madness of Vivisection") and in prolonging life ("Why Not Live Forever?").[66] Sandwiched between romantic fiction and articles about movie stars, even well-written and apparently accurate science articles took on the color of their environment.

In 1925, when the Hearst company merged *Cosmopolitan* with *Hearst's International* (which had been its public affairs magazine), the resulting magazine once again emphasized nonfiction feature articles. During the 1930s, *Cosmopolitan* science also took on a more personal, friendly tone; the publication included more biographies of scientists, more articles written by scientists, and more articles on how science was affecting society.[67] The magazine seemed determined to "humanize" science, to make it appear more compatible with characteristic American manners and mores. Even the formidable psychoanalyst Carl Jung was named a "Cosmopolite of the Month" in 1939.[68]

By the 1940s, *Cosmopolitan* approached a circulation of two million but had again changed format to emphasize fiction, including entire short novels in a single issue. Fewer science articles were published during the early 1940s—especially as compared to the magazine's competitors—and none at all in the issues sampled for 1947–55. Attempts to attract readers with more fiction and better illustration raised the cost of production, however. In 1953, the Hearst group attempted to deal with spiraling production costs by cutting circulation to one million; but this effort only temporarily stalled the large losses and the other economic forces of the 1950s hammered away. In the 1960s, the publishers took a dramatic step and completely redirected the content toward a specialized audience: *Cosmopolitan* espoused the "Cosmo Girl," a new woman who juggled career and family with style.

Informing Individuals—Literary and Public-Affairs Magazines

Another group of successful magazines of the first part of the century aimed their content at Americans with interests in public affairs and literature.[69] One of the liveliest of the public-affairs monthlies that flourished until the 1930s was *The World's Work, A History of Our Time*.[70] Founded in 1900 by Walter Hines Page, *World's Work* offered a window on contemporary accomplishments and activities, especially those involving science and technology. Men "who feel the thrill of our expanding life" fascinated Page, and he included scientists in this group to such an extent that *World's Work* carried far more science articles per total pages published annually than any of the other periodicals studied.[71]

In the beginning, the Page formula proved quite successful. By the 1910s, *World's Work's* circulation topped 100,000 (slightly less than *Harper's* but four times the circulation of *Atlantic*) and it carried a well-regarded public-affairs content emphasizing business, industry, and finance. The science articles in the 1910s reflected Page's unswerving faith in progress and American industry. They discussed agriculture, basic research, and the great fairs and expositions, and they reflected continuing interest in research fields still open to amateurs, such as archaeology, anthropology, and astronomy. During World War I, the magazine "was filled with war material," but science coverage continued to grow steadily.[72]

In the 1920s, articles openly linked science to national economic progress. Floyd W. Parsons's "Looking Ahead in Industry" series, for example, told readers how "science and careful thought make possible increased output with decreased expense, and increased productivity."[73] Themes of unqualified prosperity ended for *World's Work* during the great depression, however. After 1930, the proportion of editorial space allocated to science (and to other serious topics) dropped markedly, and the publication struggled to attract new subscribers with a revised editorial formula. Nevertheless, circulation and advertising continued to decline, and in 1932 *World's Work* was sold to its closest competitor and effectively ceased publication.[74]

Two other high-quality public-affairs monthlies of the first quarter-century, *Scribner's Magazine* and *The Century,* had life histories that ended in similar financial collapse but were unusually entwined during their successful periods.[75] The original *Scribner's* was founded in 1879 by physician Josiah Gilbert Holland, lawyer Roswell Smith, and publisher Charles Scribner, who took over the subscription lists of the latter's religious and literary monthly, *Hours at Home.* The early *Scribner's* prospered by concentrating on essays, fiction, poetry, and light features, with splendid illustrations. By 1880, circulation topped 100,000. In 1881, however, the magazine's management fell out with the management of the publishing house; as a consequence, *Scribner's* was sold to Roswell Smith, under the conditions that he change the title and that Charles Scribner's Sons not start another magazine called *Scribner's* for five years.[76]

When the requisite period expired in 1886, the publishing firm promptly created a new *Scribner's* and entered it into a lively market dominated by *Harper's Monthly, Atlantic Monthly,* and Roswell Smith's *The Century Illustrated Monthly Magazine.* The new *Scribner's* successfully weathered the economic pressures of the 1890s and the advent of the ten-cent magazines, and by 1911, it had attained its highest circulation (215,000).

During World War I, such scientists as George Ellery Hale used *Scribner's* pages to argue for science's link to the pragmatic activities of everyday life, an editorial approach that characterized all the public-affairs magazines. The percentage of science articles increased in the 1920s, as did the presence of scientists as authors.[77] Moreover, these scientists represented a particular influential group within the research community: those involved in the budding national politics of science. In *Scribner's* issues published between 1920 and 1926, about one-third of the science articles were written by George Ellery Hale, one-quarter by Michael Pupin, and one-sixth by Robert Millikan.

Despite a lively content, *Scribner's* circulation and advertising declined. By 1930, the magazine was at 70,000, compared to the 100,000 + circulations of its competitors, *Harper's Monthly* and *Atlantic Monthly.* Successive new editors remodeled the content, but none attracted sufficient subscribers to replace the alienated devotees of the old format. By 1939, the publisher's working capital had been depleted, so the magazine was suspended, and the subscription list was sold to *Esquire.*[78]

The Century Illustrated Monthly Magazine, the magazine founded from the original *Scribner's,* had a similar history but an even swifter demise.[79] Although it initially prospered—circulation peaked at 200,000 in the 1880s—by 1910, while *Scribner's* readership was climbing, *Century's* had dropped to 125,000. So, in 1913, in an effort to woo subscribers, *Century's* editors began to emphasize liberal discussion of politics, modernism, and progressivism. Articles on the practical results or social impacts of science fit this formula.

Change occurred again in the 1920s, when a new editor gave *Century* "a distinctively literary tone," with essays, criticism, reviews, and social commentary.[80] The effect of this shift on science coverage was most apparent in the addition of analytical pieces such as biologist Julian S. Huxley's "Searching for the Elixir of Life."[81] In 1922 the magazine, like its competitor, *World's Work,* ran regular contributions from E. E. Slosson and the newly formed Science Service.[82] Within three years, the editorship had changed again, but this time science played less of a role in editorial strategy; the few articles that did discuss science took a retrospective or philosophical look.[83] The last three issues of *Century,* issued as *The Century Quarterly,* maintained high standards for printing and design, but the *Century* era clearly had passed.[84]

It was not unusual, therefore, for even the most successful magazines to undergo several editorial "facelifts" during their lifetimes. Few of the most popular changed as dramatically, however, as *The American Mercury.*[85] With crisp editing, exciting criticism, and some editorial daring, founding editors H. L. Mencken and George Jean Nathan achieved quick success with the *Mercury;* the science content during the Mencken years (1924–33) was timely and lively, for example.

Despite its early zeal in exposing what Mencken regarded as

"frauds" in society (a form of literary muckraking), the *Mercury*'s circulation, like that of many magazines, began to decline in the 1930s.[86] Changes in the editorship failed to revive circulation, so the magazine was sold to Peter Palmer and Lawrence Spivak, who promptly denounced the "left-wing tendencies" of the former owners and turned the publication's content toward "anti-New Deal, pro-capitalism" conservatism.[87]

Mercury issues of the late 1930s exhibited not just a hardening of the political line but also an overall weakening of the content. Production was less sophisticated. Arguments screeched and screamed, seemingly colored more by raw emotion than deeply held beliefs. This new *Mercury* doubled in circulation but lost advertising, perhaps because articles, although readable, were noticeably biased toward one political perspective. Accumulating financial deficits finally overwhelmed Spivak, and in 1950 he sold the magazine for about $50,000.[88]

Again, change in ownership affected the content dramatically, this time less in format than in tone. Diatribes against Communists, homosexuals, and intellectuals (including scientists) became common. In 1951, for example, editor William Bradford Huie published an article ("Who Gave Russia the A-Bomb?") that accused several scientists of "treachery and intrigue" and of having betrayed the nation's trust.[89] Part 2 of the series, in the following issue, contained similar content but focused on a new target, someone accused of (but not charged with) espionage.[90] Included in the same issue was such sensationalistic content as a column on "Sex among the Porcupines," and an editorial called "Draughts of Old Bourbon: A Distaff Judgment on Sonsabitches." By the next issue, the A-bomb series was retitled "Soviet Espionage: Part III, The Case of the Nervous Spy" and transformed into a thriller account of espionage with no discussion of atomic weapons and no mention of specific scientists. Similar unevenness of content and selection marked the magazine until early 1953, when anti-Communist and other political themes dominated completely, and the emphasis on sex and violence faded.

In contrast to the *Mercury*'s stormy editorial cycles, staid literary magazines, such as *The Atlantic Monthly,* consistently expressed a reserved, elite promotion of the scholarly and the academic.[91] Early in its history, *Atlantic* regarded Boston as the hub of all universes, intellectual and literary; but by the 1870s, as editor William Dean Howells explained, "Without ceasing to be New England, without ceasing to be Bostonian, at heart, we had become southern, mid-western, and far-western in our sympathies."[92] The addition of "science" to *Atlantic*'s subtitle gave further evidence of expanded editorial horizons, and reflected the growing national character of many popular magazines.

In 1909 Ellery Sedgwick ascended to the editorial chair, having in the previous year organized the Atlantic Monthly Company and severed *Atlantic*'s special ties to book publishers. At that point, according to Mott, the magazine began to take "increased interest in contemporary science," but it actually published about 20% fewer science articles than its major competitor, *Harper's Monthly.*[93]

Most of these articles were on general science topics, rather than on specific research programs or fields, for *Atlantic* authors seemed always to be searching for some way to accept science as part of their philosophical and intellectual schemes. Science bothered them. They wanted very much to understand it; but the harder they tried, the more questions they seemed to raise. Such ambiguous attitudes toward science were rarely prominent in the large family-oriented weeklies during this period. In the pages of *Atlantic,* where the critical tradition had been flourishing for over fifty years, one could almost see the editors and authors wiggle in discomfort, however, and the types of articles published there reflected this uneasiness. The monthly published considerable criticism that indicated deep mistrust of scientists and their troubling new ideas; yet it also included many articles promising great benefits and glorifying the scientific ethic. And in the 1920s, *Atlantic* published several notable discussions of science's effect on human values, for example, philosopher Alfred North Whitehead's observations on religion and science, and Joseph Wood Krutch's splendid essays.[94]

Other subtle shifts took place over the next few decades. Social criticism of science diminished in *Atlantic* during the 1930s; instead, most articles took a more literary or historical approach to science.[95] In the mid-1940s, articles again began to integrate discussion of science with social issues, especially as authors debated the new atomic politics.[96] By the mid-1950s, there was once again less emphasis on science and politics, and more articles focused on research. These changes may, in fact, simply indicate normal shifts in audience interests rather than a deliberate editorial message. Although *Atlantic Monthly* never achieved in this period the multimillion circulation of such magazines as *Post* or *American,* its core readership remained steady. In *Atlantic,* science, like philosophy, was always regarded as part of the mark of educated people.

The other "grand dame" of monthly magazines founded in the 1850s and still surviving is *Harper's Monthly Magazine.*[97] Throughout its life, historian Theodore Peterson has written, *Harper's* has been a "magazine for well-to-do readers of catholic tastes," its content not perhaps always of interest to *Saturday Evening Post* readers, but commanding a loyal following nonetheless.[98] It is useful in fact to compare an article on agricultural research published in *Harper's Monthly* with one on a similar topic published in the same year in the *Post,* for the differences in these articles illustrate well the subtle differences between the two general types of magazines.[99] The *Harper's* article ("The Soil as a Battleground," written by a British scientist), although detailing a research project similar to the one described in the *Post*, emphasized the undirected nature of the research. The *Harper's* article praised science because it added to the greater knowledge of the culture. The *Post* article ("Dethroning King Cotton," written by a journalist) glorified the project's practical side. In general, *Harper's* articles attended more to scientists' influence upon ideas than to their ability to remedy bad social conditions, whereas publications like the *Post* emphasized the reverse.

The background of the authors who published in these magazines may have influenced this bias. From 1910 to 1925, scientists wrote approximately 66% to 100% of the science articles published in *Harper's*. Although the proportion declined to under one-third in the 1930s, scientists still wrote well over half of the science articles in all *Harper's* issues sampled from 1910 to 1955, compared to about 8% in *Post* issues from the same period. Moreover, over 70% of the *Harper's* authors were discussing a topic within their field of expertise (e.g., they were biologists writing on biology), and this connection gave those articles a ring of special authority.

There was also a difference in how each publication assessed the value of science. Over half the *Harper's* articles (and in some years as high as 80%) analyzed some aspect of science's direct impact on society, usually in regard to abstract or long-term effects, rather than practical or short-term effects. These analyses frequently took the form of "what's the matter with science?" As they delved into the ethos of science (methods, philosophy, and equipment), they adopted tone and language spurned by the general weeklies. Early twentieth-century articles in *Harper's* assessed science's potential; later articles spelled out what science *should* be.

Although not as important a forum for criticism or for the discussion of science and religion as *Atlantic Monthly, Harper's* did publish some important critiques in the 1920s and 1930s, and scientists often shared the editorial platform with theologians.[100] In 1925, the abandonment of illustration (other than in a frontispiece) and the inclusion of "provocative, distinctively liberal articles" signaled *Harper's* revival as "a journal of diversified opinion, written by the leading thinkers of the new day."[101] The publication continued to print good-quality fiction but in lesser amounts.

From 1934 through 1941, the proportion of articles written by science journalists increased from 33% to 80%. Science writer George W. Gray, characterized by his editors as "one of the ablest expounders and interpreters of the scientific research of our day," wrote more than half the science articles published in the issues sampled for 1934–40.[102] His topics ranged across the breadth of modern science, from atomic physics to cosmology to influenza, and included analyses of research politics.[103] Such articles were meant to appeal beyond academic audiences; indeed, after the 1920s, *Harper's* editors no longer directed the magazine at "a distinct social class" but "to intellectually curious readers of any income."[104]

Following World War II, many scientists used *Harper's* and the other public-affairs magazines as forums from which to address their own colleagues as well as the public.[105] Journalists and scientists alike continued to regard science as more benefit than bane, however. Although a few articles, such as those on the Bikini Atoll bomb tests or "The Decision to Use the Atomic Bomb," reflected negatively on science, other articles placed atomic physics research in a more positive light.[106] During the 1950s, many *Harper's* authors debated the use of atomic energy, but they tended to emphasize society's responsibility for managing scientific research rather than to blame scientists for its misuse. *Harper's* settled into a balanced presentation of politics, social issues, literature, the arts, business, and satire which continues in the magazine today; science fit in smoothly as part of a well-regulated constellation of topics about which every educated American should know.

Conclusion

Like specialists in other fields, those who study science communication must always guard against viewing their subject in false isolation. The production of scientific information in twentieth-century America represents just one part of a national life that includes agriculture, medicine, the law, politics and government, social relations, the arts, and so forth. Just as we would reject the biography of a scientist that described only her research and neglected her employers, her family, the communities in which she lived and worked, and the events of the time in which she lived, so must we account for the characteristics of the media in which messages about science were displayed. When we discuss mass-media presentation of science, therefore, we must allow for editorial biases and changes mandated by forces unrelated to any positive or negative assessment of science's worth, such as the economics of publishing or the rise of competitive sources of information. In choosing magazines for the statistical study, I attempted to include publications that underwent the normal upheavals and alterations of periodical publishing, and the data show that, at points of radical reformatting or editorial reorganization, science underwent the same reevaluation as other topics. It was never dismissed altogether, however. Editors at all types of publications and in all circumstances continually selected science as a topic appropriately included in general content.

When the data for all the magazines are combined, they show that the intensity of editorial attention to science (as measured by the proportion of articles published in all the issues sampled for a given year) did vary. Although science articles represented about 4% of the total nonfiction articles in these magazines in the period 1910–1955, the magazines paid much more attention to science in some decades than in others, increasing coverage in the 1920s, reducing it in the 1930s, and increasing it after 1945 (Figure 2.1). In the 1910s, science was not perceived as the paramount solution to social ills; but as the perception of importance grew, so did the media coverage. *American, American Mercury,* and *Atlantic* all published many more science articles per issue after World War II, for example, than earlier in the century. That such an increase occurred in three magazines of such different types indicates that there was increased attention to science throughout the mass media. A similar rise in the number of articles in *Collier's,* which had given relatively little attention to science up through the 1940s, further supports this conclusion. The following chapter proposes some other explanations for these shifts, related

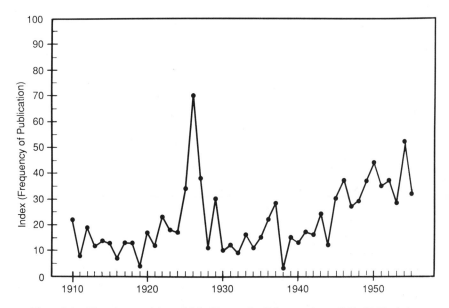

Figure 2.1. The science articles published by popular U.S. magazines, 1910–55. The index is the ratio, for each year, of the number of science articles published to the number of issues sampled (*n* = 687). A score of 100 indicates that, on average, every issue of all magazines sampled during that period contained an article on science; a score of 50, that half the issues contained science articles.

to who was actually participating in the popularization process during these times.

Although the most crucial measure of the editorial assessment of a topic was whether (and perhaps when) an article was published, *where* editors placed an article indicated the priority or importance that they ascribed to its topic or author. Editors used placement both to attract readers and to emphasize articles warranting special attention. As shown in Figures 2.2, 2.3, and 2.4, lead stories were usually publicized on an issue's cover. Considerations internal to each publication, such as format, tradition, and advertiser or publisher influence, as well as the editor's judgment of importance and reader interest, governed the choice of a lead. Therefore, lead stories provided an even better retrospective measure of editorial interest than the number of articles throughout an issue, which could have been influenced by outside factors. Variations in the percentage of science articles that were lead articles therefore further demonstrated how interest in science changed across the decades. In a few years, almost one-quarter of the science articles were lead stories (Figure 2.5), but usually the percentage fluctuated from under 5% to slightly over 10%. The 1920s saw more leads than did the 1930s, and after 1948 the proportion of leads grew steadily, possibly indicating increased audience interest in science.[107]

Although editors varied their emphasis on science, they also appeared to regard science as a monolith. In some editorial formulas, an article on physics may have been perceived as roughly equivalent to one on biology, either story sufficient to fill the "slot" (or "newshole") for science. Editors apparently paid "selective attention" to science; they were more apt to choose one science story over another than to increase attention to science overall. Comparing the proportion of lead articles that discussed biology with those that discussed physics, for example, (Figures 2.6 and 2.7) indicates that the magazines assigned special importance to biology in the period around 1925 and to physics in the mid-1930s and 1940s, even though the total number of popular articles in biology rose during the 1940s.[108] As one field grabbed the headlines, other science stories were pushed to the back of an issue or held for the next one. This choice reflected, I believe, how magazine editors ranked the importance of science overall. Most regarded it as just one of many topics suitable for literate conversation, but not necessarily deserving of special attention in every issue.

Study of the correspondence and records of the editors of these magazines might, of course, reveal particular biases and attitudes toward science not measurable in content analysis, and confirm how editors assessed the importance of science. More important for understanding the popular images of science in American national culture, however, is the consist-

THE LIFE STORY OF MADAME CURIE

Figure 2.2.   Covers of the family-oriented magazines, such as *Collier's* and *The Saturday Evening Post*, tended to stress patriotic or traditional themes. Note how this 1937 *Post* cover emphasizes a biography of physicist Marie Curie. Reprinted with permission from *The Saturday Evening Post*, © 1937 by Curtis Publishing Company.

THE SATURDAY EVENING POST

Founded A°D¹ 1728 by Benj. Franklin

Volume 210   5c. THE COPY   PHILADELPHIA, PA., SEPTEMBER 4, 1937 $2.00 By Subscription (52 issues)   Number 10

MARIE CURIE, MY MOTHER

THE ROMANTIC LIFE STORY OF THE DISCOVERER OF RADIUM

By EVE CURIE

Translated by
VINCENT SHEEAN

THE life of Marie Curie contains prodigies in such number that one would like to tell her story like a legend. She was a woman; she belonged to an oppressed nation; she was poor; she was beautiful. A powerful vocation summoned her from her motherland, Poland, to study in Paris, where she lived through years of poverty and solitude. There she met a man whose genius was akin to hers. She married him; their happiness was unique. By the most desperate effort they discovered a magic element, radium. This discovery not only gave birth to a new science and a new philosophy; it provided mankind with the means of treating a dreadful disease.

At the moment when the fame of the two scientists and benefactors was spreading through the world, grief overtook Marie. Her husband, her wonderful companion, was taken from her by death in an instant. But, in spite of distress and physical illness, she continued alone the work that had been begun with him, and brilliantly developed the science they had created together.

The rest of her life resolves itself into a perpetual giving. To the war wounded she gave her devotion and her health. Later on she gave her advice, her wisdom and all the hours of her time to her pupils, to future scientists who came to her from all parts of the world. When her mission was accomplished she died, exhausted, having refused wealth and endured honors with indifference.

It would have been a crime to add the slightest ornament to this story, so like a myth. I have not related a single anecdote of which I am not sure. I have not distorted a single essential phrase or so much as invented the color of a dress. The facts are as stated. The quoted words were actually pronounced.

I hope that the reader may constantly feel, across the ephemeral movement of one existence, what in Marie Curie was even more rare than her work or her life; the immovable structure of a character, the stubborn effort of an intelligence, the free immolation of a being that could give all and take nothing, could even receive nothing: and above all, the quality of a soul in which neither fame nor adversity could change the exceptional purity.

Because she had that soul, without the slightest sacrifice Marie Curie rejected money, comfort and the thousand advantages that great men may obtain from immense fame. She suffered from the part the world wished her to play. Her nature was so susceptible and exacting that among all the attitudes suggested by fame she could choose none, neither familiarity nor mechanical friendliness, deliberate austerity nor showy modesty. She did not know how to be famous.

My mother was thirty-seven years old when I was born. When I was big enough to know her well, she was already an aging woman who had reached the summit of renown. And yet it is the "celebrated scientist" who is strangest to me—probably because the idea that she was a "celebrated scientist" did not occupy the mind of Marie Curie. It seems to me, rather, that I have always lived near the poor student, haunted by dreams, who was Marya Sklodovska long before I came into the world.

I should have liked the gifts of a writer to tell of this eternal student—of whom Einstein said: "Marie Curie is, of all celebrated beings, the only one whom fame has not corrupted"—passing like a stranger across her own life, intact, natural, and very nearly unaware of her astonishing destiny.

—EVE CURIE.

Deep silence invaded the school building in Novolipki Street on Sundays. Beneath the stone pediment, carved in Russian letters

5

February

Harpers
M A G A Z I N E

IS SCIENCE A BLIND ALLEY?
By JAMES TRUSLOW ADAMS

HARPER & BROTHERS, PUBLISHERS
Price 35 Cents

Figure 2.4.   In the literary and public affairs magazines, the form of visual presentation was more restrained. The covers of some magazines simply listed the contents, as in this February 1928 *Harper's*. © 1928 by Harper's Magazine. All rights reserved. Reprinted from the February issue by special permission.

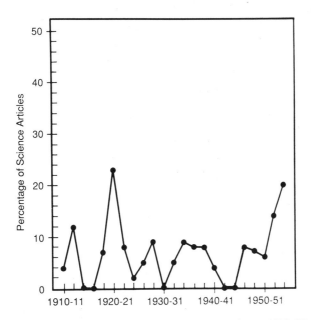

Figure 2.5. Lead articles, as a percentage of all articles on science, 1910–55. Data are taken from a sample of eleven U.S. mass-circulation magazines and are given as a percentage of all science articles published in those magazines during each two-year period ($n = 671$, 46 of which were lead articles).

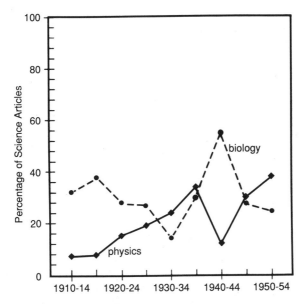

Figure 2.6. Popular articles on physics and biology, as a percentage of all science articles, 1910–54. (Physics, solid line, $n = 156$; biology, dotted line, $n = 204$.) Data are taken from a sample of eleven U.S. mass-circulation magazines and are given as a percentage of all science articles published in those magazines during each five-year period.

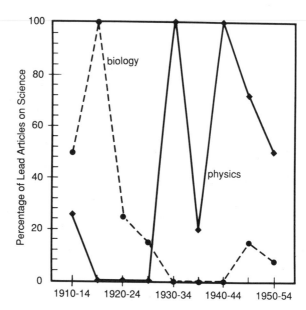

Figure 2.7.   Lead articles on physics and biology, as a percentage of all science articles that were leads, 1910–54. (Physics, solid line, $n = 15$; biology, dotted line, $n = 8$.) Data are taken from a sample of eleven U.S. mass-circulation magazines and are given as a percentage of all science articles published in those magazines during each five-year period.

ency of outlook and coverage represented by the content of these eleven periodicals. None of these publications presented an unqualified negative image of science. Even the most sensationalistic issues of *American Mercury,* which accused some scientists of espionage, did not dismiss scientific research altogether as worthless or as automatically harmful. Even when editors assigned greater priority to other topics, they did not ignore science. Instead, the popular magazines consistently approached science as a pragmatic and progressive national force, held up scientists as reliable authorities, and pointed to scientific knowledge as useful even when it seemed incomprehensible. The stylized images I shall describe in the following chapters serve as useful barometers of the images present elsewhere in the mass media of this century. The consistency in these ideas across seemingly different publications owned by different publishers lend them credibility as being representative not only of what was offered to the audience, but also of what millions of Americans agreed with, approved of, and found appropriate and correct.

3

Who Supplied the Images?
Authors and Sources

The line between beneficial and harmful publicity is exceedingly thin.

Roy Chapman Andrews, 1931[1]

American scientists participated actively and enthusiastically in telling the public about science in the twentieth century. In general-circulation magazine articles, for example, they described their own research, analyzed the work of colleagues, and gave free-wheeling interviews to journalists. Moreover, they knew exactly what they were doing. As *The World's Work* observed in 1910, "The leaders of human progress in the sciences . . . are discovering that the magazines are the most direct and effective instruments for reaching that most elusive and inaccessible of all things, the human mind."[2] When scientists wrote articles or served as journalists' sources, they were not just relating scientific facts; they were also attempting to advance the cause of science and to mold the public's images of science. In addition, many of the most eminent American scientists of this century have skillfully used the mass media in their efforts to influence national policymaking and attract funding for basic research.

Especially early in the century, the cooperation of these scientists spelled the difference in magazine coverage of science. In the 1910s and 1920s, American magazines paid extra attention to science, and scientists wrote more than 40% of the articles; in the 1930s, the number of articles declined and the proportion written by scientists dropped. Up through the late 1940s, as this chapter will show, American scientists were apparently able to influence, through their willingness to write articles and grant interviews, the attention that mass magazines paid to science.

The Specialized Communicators

Even when scientists actively participated in popularization, much of the general writing about science in magazines and newspapers was done by professional journalists who had no special expertise in science writing. A journalist who wrote celebrity biographies in the 1930s, for example, was as likely to choose a new Nobel laureate as his subject as to choose a Supreme Court Justice or Pulitzer-prize-winning novelist. Journalists who wrote about public affairs often focused on government-sponsored science projects (see Figure 3.1).

Another group of writers grew in size and importance through the century, however: journalists who specialized in reporting on science, some of whom had had formal training in science or had even worked as scientists. When and to what extent these specialists dominated magazine science writing, in fact, also tells us a great deal about the popularization efforts of scientists. Many scholars have asserted that science journalism did not become a regular, professionalized specialty, with a "critical mass" of practitioners, until after World War II, the most common explanation

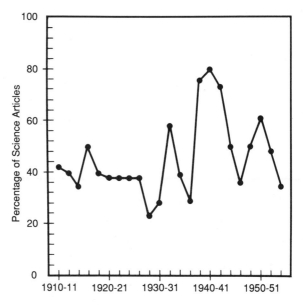

Figure 3.1. Articles by professional journalists, as a percentage of all science articles, 1910–55 (*n* = 298). Data are taken from a sample of eleven U.S. mass-circulation magazines and are given as a percentage of all science articles published in those magazines during each two-year period.

for this phenomenon being the growth of science itself (that is, more science required more reporters on science).[3] This interpretation may be true in the sense of the journalism profession's recognition of such a category; but we should not assume that these journalists lacked the skill or desire to cover science, for, as Michael Schudson has pointed out, many journalists at the turn of the century were "either trained in a scientific discipline or shared in the popular admiration of science."[4] Perhaps such interpretations have been proposed because the general reporters writing about science early in the century did not always fit modern assumptions about a science journalist's enthusiasm for his or her topic. These early writers rarely appeared to be overly sympathetic to science and neither boosted nor promoted science as did some of their modern counterparts. Their objectivity in writing about science reflected the news journalist's traditional attachment to facts and realism, not some special approach to science.

Modern classifications of who was or was not a science journalist early in the century also may be influenced by the scientific community's own myth that "only a scientist can understand science" and that therefore a real science journalist must have scientific training or, at least, sympathy for the scientific way of life. In fact, in 1940, journalist Hillier Kreighbaum noted, in his survey of science writers, that over one-quarter lacked any academic degree in science.[5] Given the relatively high quality of magazine science reporting throughout this century, the credentials of a scientific degree or scientific training obviously were not necessary for success in science journalism.

The development of a group of specialized science journalists, in fact, fit the trend toward specialization in all of American journalism; as the media grew larger (and the issues seemed more complex), practitioners naturally specialized. Certainly, the proportion of science articles written for magazines by all journalists (both general writers and science specialists) increased steadily over the decades, from under half in the 1920s to almost three-quarters in the 1940s. When we look at only those writers who specialized in science, however, the data show pronounced shifts (see Figure 3.2). The proportion began in the 1920s to grow steadily and reached a high in the 1940s, when during some years science journalists wrote half or more of all the science articles in the magazines.

The science journalists' increased participation matched declining participation by scientists, who by the mid-1930s were writing only one-fifth or less of the science articles published in these magazines, compared to almost three-fifths in the early 1920s (see Figure 3.2). Scientists represented under one-tenth of the authors during the early 1940s. The unevenness of scientists' participation as authors matched similar changes in the

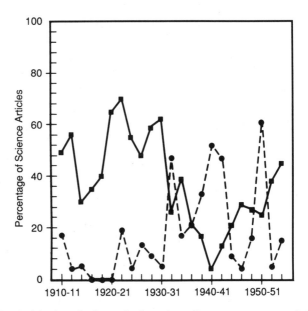

Figure 3.2. Articles by scientists and science journalists, as a percentage of all science articles, 1910–55. The category of scientist (solid line; $n = 256$) includes all authors with training in science or engineering; the science journalist category (dotted line; $n = 88$) includes journalists who specialized in writing about science. Data are taken from a sample of eleven U.S. mass-circulation magazines and are given as a percentage of all science articles published in those magazines during each two-year period.

number of magazine biographies of scientists published in those years. General magazines traditionally paid a lot of attention to personalities—movie stars, baseball players, and novelists—the more glamorous and exotic the better. In all the magazines, the proportion of science articles that were biographies of scientists (see Figure 3.3) ranged between one-tenth and one-half. The proportion of biographies climbed steadily from 1910 to 1935 but then, like authorship by scientists, dropped in the mid-1930s and stayed relatively low until the end of the war.[6] Similar patterns show up in the proportion of articles that were first-person commentaries written by scientists (see Figure 3.4).

Clearly something was going on, for the changes in both authorship (presumably under the control of the scientist) and biographies (for which a magazine usually initiated the request or idea) seem more than coincidental. In fact, comparing the data in Figures 2.1 and 3.2 shows that magazine coverage of science overall varied at similar turning points, increasing sharply in the 1920s, declining and then leveling off in the 1930s and 1940s, and increasing again in the late 1940s and 1950s.

The intensity and extent of scientists' participation therefore appears to have influenced the *amount* of science published in the magazines. Scientists have always stood at a key node in the communication process, for they represent the most authoritative sources for interviews and information. Mass-magazine interest in science apparently remained consistent during the early twentieth century, but the active involvement of scientists in the popularization process influenced how much attention they paid to science. When fewer scientists wrote articles (or granted interviews or cooperated in biographies), then the magazines gave less space to science overall. Similar changes occur in the proportion of biographies, thus supporting the conclusion that scientists' involvement in the popularization process affected coverage more than did the magazines' overall interest in scientists.

Other measures add further substantiation. The number of science articles in magazines declined during World War II, for example. During this period, when scientists assigned to various war projects were prohibited (or voluntarily refrained) from speaking to journalists, none of the magazines published first-person narratives by scientists, yet the proportion of articles written by journalists specializing in science increased.

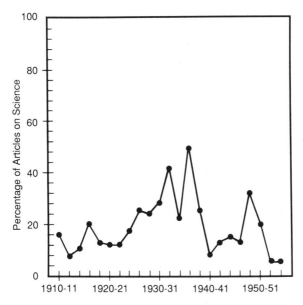

Figure 3.3. Popular biographies of scientists, as a percentage of all science articles, 1910–55 (*n* = 128). Data are taken from a sample of eleven U.S. mass-circulation magazines and are given as a percentage of all science articles published in those magazines during each two-year period.

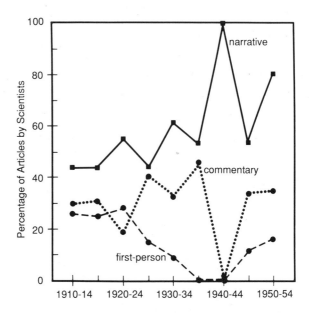

Figure 3.4. Styles of popular articles written by scientists, 1910–54. The proportion of articles written by scientists which were commentaries (*n* = 90), first-person articles (*n* = 46), or narratives (*n* = 148). Data are taken from a sample of eleven U.S. mass-circulation magazines and are given as a percentage of all science articles published in those magazines during each five-year period.

After 1945, when scientists could again grant interviews and were free to publish, magazine science articles increased and, through 1955 at least, the proportion of articles written by science journalists declined.

Who Spoke for Science?

Certain scientists appeared repeatedly in the magazines studied as authors and interview subjects. Ranking them according to the number of articles they wrote in the issues sampled, in fact, gives a rough guide to their public prominence as celebrities in the period 1910–1955 (see Table 3.1). Unless you are a historian of American science, however, you may not recognize all these names. Some, such as Margaret Mead, stayed celebrities well into the 1970s; a few, such as Robert Millikan, appear in standard histories of science as major figures. The prominence of others, however, came not from their position or scientific accomplishments but because of their articulateness and their desire or reasons to communicate. They could describe even arcane topics in terms that laypersons could understand, and they dearly wanted to speak out.

Sometimes their communication efforts related more to a specific public issue than to any apparent long-term commitment to public education; following World War II, for example, many physicists attempted to influence government policy on atomic energy through public statements and writings in popular magazines and newspapers. Other scientists and naturalists, such as John Burroughs and Loren Eiseley, were prolific and skilled translators of science in general, not just of their own field of expertise; their publishing careers spanned decades, and their prose sparkles as brightly today as it did then.

Some of these scientists, notably Robert Millikan, Michael Pupin, and Harlow Shapley, represented the counterparts of such modern scientist-celebrities as Carl Sagan; they exhibited many of the characteristics of what journalism researcher Rae Goodell classified as "visible

Table 3.1   Scientists Prominent in Popular American Magazines, 1910–1955

Rank	Author/Subject
1	Thomas A. Edison (scientist-inventor)
2	George Ellery Hale (astronomer)
3	Roy Chapman Andrews (zoologist)
4	Michael Pupin (physicist)
	Robert A. Millikan (physicist)
5	Charles F. Kettering (scientist-engineer)
	Charles P. Steinmetz (physicist)
6	Luther Burbank (botanist)
	Julian S. Huxley (biologist)
	Vernon Kellogg (entomologist)
7	Loren Eiseley (anthropologist)
	E. E. Free (chemist)
	Harlow Shapley (astronomer)
8	John Burroughs (naturalist)
	Vannevar Bush (physicist)
	Ellwood Hendrick (chemist)
	Ralph E. Lapp (physicist)
9	Leo H. Baekeland (chemistry)
	Woods Hutchinson (physician)
	Alexander McAdie (astronomer)
	Margaret Mead (anthropologist)
	John C. Merriam (paleontologist)
	J. B. Rhine (psychologist)
	Wernher von Braun (rocket scientist)
	Joseph D. Wassersug (physician)
	Henry S. Williams (physician)
	Robert Williams Wood (physicist)

Note: Individuals are ranked by frequency of appearance as author or subject of a biography in the statistical sample. More than one name indicates a tie.

scientists," because they were newsworthy subjects as well as skillful communicators.[7] The public reputations of such men as Hale and Millikan derived not only from their scientific abilities but also from their skill in interacting with journalists and their frequent appearances in the mass media.[8] How well they articulated technical explanations, their knowledge of journalistic techniques and traditions, and their sensitivity to editorial agendas probably contributed as much to their attractiveness to the magazines as what they said or advocated. They represented congenial and cooperative sources of information; however, as Chapters 4, 5, and 6 will show, the magazinists may have also favored these scientists because they fit a characteristic *image* of some ideal scientist.

Motives

The idea that there is a direct relationship between scientists' involvement in public communication and popular magazines' attention to science contradicts the conventional notion that scientists were uninterested in their public image. There are several reasons such ideas permeated discussions of science early in the century. Both scientists and communicators asserted that most scientists were not publicity-hounds, but were instead shy and modest and that they avoided the limelight in order to devote themselves to their research. In addition, throughout this century there have been substantial, effective barriers to easy relations between scientists and journalists.

Early in this century, many scientists regarded popularization with only qualified approval.[9] They did not necessarily regard speaking out as bad, but they refrained from making public statements unless they could control the communication's content, structure, and tone, and urged colleagues to be similarly cautious. They justified this control in terms of the public interest. Irresponsible popularization, they argued, could harm the public if it included misleading or even dangerous information disguised as fact. Only *scientists* could assure the quality and accuracy of scientific information because they alone were the technical experts. As one writer argued in the 1920s,

> The great scientist is not misled. He is usually the humblest of men, acutely conscious of the little he knows. It is the lesser mind that is misled and in turn misleads and, particularly, that most dangerous of modern preachers, the popularizer of science, who builds up his eloquence about the scantiest frame of first-hand knowledge.[10]

In some cases, extensive, favorable media attention became ammunition for jealous colleagues. Contemporaries of physicist Robert Millikan, belittling the attention he drew from journalists, defined the *milli-kan* as "one-thousandth of a unit of publicity,"[11] despite the fact that many of Millikan's public writings were directed at securing government funding for *all* basic research, not just his own work. Because disapproval by peers could be so strong, and because popular magazine writing brought few professional rewards, a scientist needed powerful motives in order to participate in popularization.

For centuries, money, power, and fame have justified all sorts of public communications, from Brutus' "defense" of Caesar to television interviews of newly published authors. Poets, lawyers, college professors, all types of people who seemingly eschew publicity-seeking may, at some time in their careers, give newspaper or television interviews in order to publicize an institution or activity, or to advance a political cause. Scientists, too, used the media in this way, for publicizing their activities, for gathering support from colleagues, and for seeking funding for research. Many scientists who wrote for general magazines had recently published books, or were also active on the lecture circuit; magazines provided coordinating publicity for authorship and aided the pseudoevents, such as the media interview or news conference, that accompanied image-shaping.[12] Biologist Henri Bergson's 1913 tour of the United States, for example, and concurrent coverage in popular magazines were linked directly to U.S. publication of his book *Creative Evolution*.[13]

Especially in the early part of the century, scientists from every discipline used popular magazines for a different type of reputation building, as public forums from which to answer critics of their work. Researchers in a new discipline or proponents of a new theory, discouraged by criticism or rejection by colleagues, sometimes felt compelled to circumvent traditional channels for scientific communication; when that occurred, they often used popular magazines as pulpits from which to evangelize back to the scientific community while simultaneously arguing for public acceptance (and possibly funding) of their work. When attacks on psychology's legitimacy as a scientific discipline increased in the 1920s and 1930s, both from within science and in the public press, psychologists, for example, used popular magazines in just such a way to confront their critics (see Figures 3.5 and 3.6).[14]

Some more entrepreneurial scientists courted public support for their theories in an effort to see them applied in social or political contexts; Frederick W. Taylor, for example, wrote many articles promoting his notion of *scientific management*. All sorts of researchers tried this route to acceptance: Eugenicists under attack in scientific journals frequently sought access to the public through the popular press, as they promoted social policy based on their "New Science."[15]

On occasion, scientists also were pushed into the limelight to fulfill

54 / *Chapter Three*

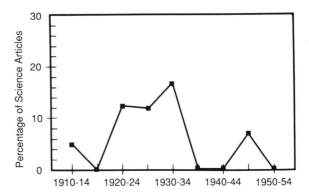

Figure 3.5. Articles written by psychologists, as a percentage of all science articles, 1910–54. The proportion of articles written by authors identified as trained in psychology or working as psychologists ($n = 18$). Data are taken from a sample of eleven U.S. mass-circulation magazines and are given as a percentage of all science articles published in those magazines during each five-year period.

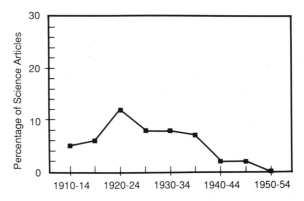

Figure 3.6. Articles on psychology, as a percentage of all science articles, 1910–54. The proportion of articles on psychology ($n = 36$). Data are taken from a sample of eleven U.S. mass-circulation magazines and are given as a percentage of all science articles published in those magazines during each five-year period.

the motives of others; the General Electric Company campaign to promote physicist Charles Proteus Steinmetz exemplifies such efforts. Sometime in the 1920s, General Electric is said to have realized "the value of impressing the personality of some important figure in their organization on the reading public."[16] Steinmetz proved to be an excellent subject for such promotion; he was eccentric, brilliant, accomplished, and willing. Moreover, his research seemed comprehensible to laypersons, and it had a distinct air of usefulness. "The public thought of him as an inventor," a contemporary biographer wrote, "but he had invented nothing of importance and never did. The man on the street could tell you that he was an electrician, but not what part of electricity was his province."[17] "Steinmetz, like Einstein," the biographer continued, "stood in the public mind for the kind of science not far removed from magic or religion."[18]

General Electric's publicity department marketed Steinmetz relentlessly. Writer John Dos Passos, in his evocative prose poem, "Proteus," accused General Electric of having "poured oily stories" about Steinmetz "into the ears of the American public every Sunday" and of using Steinmetz for publicity as if he were "a piece of apparatus."[19] Journalistic exaggeration helped to accomplish some image shaping (e.g., "The mild mathematician whose only weapon was a pencil changed into a human Jove hurling artificial thunderbolts"[20]); other writers chose to associate Steinmetz with evocative cultural symbols (e.g., "The simple little man . . . became overnight an infallible wizard, capable of judging all matters human, scientific, and divine"[21]). Figure 3.7 (a, b, and c) shows some of the consistent Steinmetz images—cigar, crowded desk, and brooding stare. Eventually, the company's artful use of publicity, in effect, fictionalized Steinmetz, as his reputation "outgrew the actual man to such an extent that it lost even a family resemblance to him."[22] "Such publicity-built characters are not human," his biographer wrote; "they have printers' ink in their arteries instead of blood."[23]

Some scientists flourished in the public arena because they fit general cultural symbols. The immigrant Steinmetz provided a quintessential example for articles on the self-made man, and he was mentioned often. Another scientist of the 1920s, physicist Michael I. Pupin, served a similar use. An eleven-part autobiography published in *Scribner's* described the hardships Pupin encountered when he immigrated to the United States.[24] Both the Steinmetz and Pupin series exemplified how magazines linked scientists to national myths or ideals—in their cases, to the American dream of "rags to riches."

Other powerful motives for publicity related to personal or professional gain, as scientists sought support for specific laboratories or projects (e.g., funding for a research expedition). Early in the century, inventors, explorers, and expedition leaders who needed investors wrote popular magazine articles to draw attention to the importance as well as the adventure and mystery of their work. One of the most colorful of these was zoologist and explorer Roy Chapman Andrews (Figure 3.8). With exceptional skill, Andrews glamorized his long treks through Asia by weaving tales of dramatic encounters with "vipers" and blinding sandstorms into serious technical descriptions of the flora and fauna he had observed.

Andrews recognized the magazines' potential as effective publicity

Figure 3.7. Three representations of Charles P. Steinmetz, showing the consistency of his public persona, especially the cigar and slightly eccentric appearance. (a) A full-page photo accompanying an article by Steinmetz in the May 1918 *American Magazine*. Photo by Blank and Stoller, New York City. (b) News photo of Steinmetz "speaking by radio for the first time," 27 March 1922. The accompanying news text read: "DR. STEINMETZ EXPLAINS LIGHTNING BY RADIO . . . From the General Electric Company broadcasting station, W.G.Y. in Schenectady, Dr. Steinmetz gave a popular talk, telling all about lightning . . ." Photograph by Underwood & Underwood, New York, courtesy of the Prints and Photographs Division, Library of Congress. (c, p. 58) Illustration for Jonathan Norton Leonard's biography of Steinmetz in the February 1929 *World's Work*. "At the Ordinary Routine Job He Was a Brilliant Failure, But as a Research Worker [He] Had No Equal." Drawing by Loren F. Wilford.

devices. In a candid *Post* article in the 1930s, he even advised scientific novices that the "ability to lecture or to write entertainingly" was an invaluable professional asset, because then "you do not have to depend upon a second person to state your thesis, and the public learns to know you at first hand."[25] In an interview, a scientist should phrase technical information correctly and appealingly, Andrews advised, because "a newspaper reporter must have some peg upon which to hang the serious account of

what you intend to do or have done. He wants something with a popular appeal . . ."[26] If the scientist's words do not match the journalist's needs, then what the scientist really wants communicated can be "distorted or lost entirely."[27] Andrews appears to have recognized a central truth of public relations: in the game of image shaping, scientists could never be all-powerful and could not construct the final product, only the degree to which they cooperated with the journalist who wrote it. He warned that interaction with the press carries certain risks to the subject: "the line between beneficial and harmful publicity is exceedingly thin." "Overpublicity is a danger," he wrote; "people become bored if too much is written about an expedition . . ."[28]

Articles about L. O. Howard, Chief of the U.S. Department of Agriculture, Bureau of Entomology, in the 1910s, illustrated yet another motive for seeking publicity: to attract funding for a particular research field or facility. To solidify political support for more funding of entomology, Howard needed to have farmers use the work of his bureau. So, to get the message out, he wrote popular magazine articles and granted interviews. Reporters aware of these motives apparently did not disapprove and may even have aided Howard's search for publicity because they judged his motives to be professional not personal. His efforts were directed at convincing the public of the connection between research in entomology and

Figure 3.8.   The most active science popularizers not only wrote books and articles but also gave lectures and, later, radio talks. This 1926 news photo shows explorer Roy C. Andrews aboard the liner Aquitania, "enroute to London to lecture." Photograph by Underwood & Underwood, New York, courtesy of the Prints and Photographs Division, Library of Congress.

"the practical affairs of everyday life," not at self-promotion. "Notoriety, or even notice for himself he has never sought," Samuel Hopkins Adams observed in a contemporary magazine biography of the entomologist.[29]

Howard also possessed the skills with which to craft a successful media relationship, especially in knowing how to make esoteric research seem attractive to the press. As biographer Adams observed, "shrewd newspaper men in Washington began to perceive, as they came in casual contact with him, that there was 'special' news of interest to be obtained from the obscure bureau devoted to the study of insect life."[30]

Undoubtedly the most well-known and probably the most artful of these publicists was Thomas Alva Edison.[31] While the modern history of science and technology classifies Edison as an inventor, not a "scientist," the popular magazines of his time considered him to be a member of the community of scientists, and referred to his work as "scientific research" not invention. (The same was true for other prominent research entrepreneurs, such as Charles F. Kettering.) The magazines published more biographies, articles, and interviews of Edison than of any other person classified as a scientist.[32] His face was said to be "as familiar as that of any American of his generation,"[33] not the least because his imposing physical appearance and eccentric personality invited lavish description, and his philosophy fit the times.[34] He also courted publicity with enthusiasm, believing it essential to the successful marketing of his ideas; his showmanship in theater demonstrations, for example, was said to be extraordinary.[35]

Edison's enduring popularity as a public figure can be traced also to his skill in using the media and his usefulness as a cultural symbol (see Figure 3.9). He possessed a keen sense of how to court journalists. Although generally cooperative with the press, he nevertheless cultivated a reputation of semireclusiveness, which enabled him to manipulate reporters by scheduling or terminating interviews at will. Perhaps because of his reputation for gruff resentment of interruptions, many journalists approached Edison with awe rather than skepticism or inquisitiveness. This 1916 report from *Collier's,* for example, revealed a reporter shaking in his boots:

> I talked with Mr. Edison for nearly half an hour, and I asked nearly all my questions, but as I sit down to write I don't feel that what I have to say will much enlighten the scientific world as to the coming age of electrical marvels. I felt like the provincial who went to see Paris, saw Napoleon ride by on a horse, and returned home unable to talk about anything else but the great general.[36]

Edison's personal and business philosophy also fit well with the political spirit of the times and the 1920s emphasis on self-sufficiency. Magazines called him such things as "A Great National Asset,"[37] "An American Symbol,"[38] and "The Greatest American of the Century."[39] To these writers, Edison epitomized the hardworking, determined, creative scientist, as well as the successful businessman (Figure 3.10).

For a few other scientists, the political motives driving popularization extended beyond the advancement of their own careers and beyond specific projects or business activities to the promotion of the general idea that the nation should support and fund scientific research. These motives spurred the efforts of two other loosely organized groups of prominent American scientists, the first of which, led by George Ellery Hale and Robert A. Millikan, operated during the 1920s and 1930s. The quantity and type of the scientists' participation in magazine popularization shows

THOMAS
ALVA
EDISON

HIS FAITH unconquerable, his passion for work irresistible, his accomplishment not surpassed in the annals of invention, Thomas Alva Edison has achieved far more than mankind can ever appreciate. February eleventh is the eightieth anniversary of his birth.

Wherever electricity is used—in homes, in business, in industry—there are hearts that are consciously grateful, that humbly pay him homage.

GENERAL ELECTRIC

Mention of Harper's Magazine is the best introduction to our advertisers

Figure 3.9.   The most popular scientific figures were also exploited in magazine advertising. In this ad from a 1927 *Harper's*, General Electric used Edison's face and references to his doggedness and record of accomplishment to sell a corporate image. Courtesy of General Electric Company, Hall of History.

Figure 3.10. Three public communicators of science and technology from the early twentieth century, representing the combination of inventive genius, naturalism, and business acumen. *Left to right:* Thomas A. Edison, John Burroughs, and Henry Ford, shown on the grounds of Edison's home, c. 1914. Photo by Hunt, courtesy of the Prints and Photographs Division, Library of Congress.

the extent of their influence, for Hale and Millikan together figured prominently in over 3% of the *entire* sample of 687 articles, either as authors or as subjects of biographies or interviews.

Many of Hale's articles, especially in the 1920s, concentrated on his own field of astronomy, for example, "The New Heavens" (1920), "Great Stars" (1921), and "Cosmic Crucibles" (1921); but he also wrote about other fields; he described, for example, archaeological discoveries in Egypt (1923) and the career of orientalist James Henry Breasted (1923).[40] Constructed with considerable literary skill, the articles integrated precise technical terms and scientific language with clear definitions.

Millikan was also a skilled and innovative magazine writer, contributing often to *Scribner's* in the 1920s.[41] In 1923, *Scribner's* published Millikan's "Cook's tour" of recent advances in astronomy and physics, and in 1925 the magazine reprinted his Nobel prize acceptance speech.[42] Historians today generally regard him as "one of the most avid publicists in the scientific community" and, as both a potential source of news and a reasonably good writer, he stayed in the good graces of magazine editors for some time.[43]

Many historians link the Hale and Millikan publicity efforts in the 1920s directly to their lobbying for the establishment of a National Research Endowment and to Hale's involvement in the founding of the National Research Council.[44] The increased numbers of science articles that were published in popular magazines during this period certainly provide support for that interpretation. In 1925, *Scribner's* and other literary magazines began to devote increasingly greater amounts of space to the discussion of all types of public affairs, and Hale and Millikan were among those contributing articles on science policy.[45] Other scientists active in national policymaking during that time, such as John C. Merriam (president of the Carnegie Institution), Vernon Kellogg (permanent secretary of the National Research Council), and Nobel laureate Arthur Holly Compton, could be found in the magazines as either authors or interview subjects. Historian David Rhees sees a less tangible but more insidious goal for these popularization efforts, identifying a "disturbing element of elitism" in the scientists' concerns. Popularizers who spoke for the scientific establishment, such as E. E. Slosson, "clearly viewed themselves as the advance guard of civilization, whose moral obligation was to lead the inferior 'multitudes' down the 'safe blazed paths' of science . . . [and] any movement that threatened to impede the march of scientific progress . . . was labeled as antiscientific, irrational, and hence immoral."[46] Such elitism may have contributed to the inability of even the successful news operation, Science Service, to breach the ever wider gulf between the interests of the scientists and those of the public.

By the late 1930s and early 1940s, military security restrictions prohibited many researchers—especially in physics and chemistry—from talking to journalists, but after the war another group of prominent scientists, concerned with postwar science planning, wrote articles and granted interviews in substantial numbers. Harlow Shapley and Vannevar Bush, both of whom sought to create a federal science agency, could be found frequently in the pages of the magazines then, as could also physicist Ralph E. Lapp, who was engaged in the debates on civilian control of atomic energy research. Magazine issues from the 1940s and 1950s included articles by many scientists eager to comment on political debates over atomic energy policy and weapons-design strategy.

Whether intended to publicize industrial research activities, to attract backers for a scientific expedition, to sustain funding for existing research projects, or to create new funding opportunities, scientists thus employed the same methods for seeking and shaping publicity as did other professional groups. By influencing the media presentation, scientists hoped to affect public beliefs and public opinion. Analysis of the institutions that promoted science communication in the decades after 1945—publishers, scientists, journalists, government—shows in fact that these groups tended to perceive public understanding of science not as "comprehension of concepts" but as "appreciation" of the benefits science provided to society.[47] That is, they assumed that when the audience's information needs (as defined by the scientists) were met, the result would be positive support for science, especially political support for its funding. The role of the scientific associations and of prominent scientists in this effort, as documented by Bruce Lewenstein, bespeak a deliberate, orchestrated attempt to influence public opinion. Science journalists in the postwar period, as earlier in the century, imitated these attitudes because they shared a common view of science with the scientists.[48]

The actions of the publicity-seeking scientists simply represented new versions of an old practice. The utopists of previous centuries were often "creative, albeit literary, scientists . . . powerful publicists in extending the scientific doctrine and in gaining its acceptance."[49] The history of nineteenth-century science shows many prominent scientists routinely playing an active part in public communication, through public lectures and occasional articles in literary magazines. The difference between these gentle promoters and the more aggressive entrepreneurs of the 1930s was affected most by changes in the mass media, with which scientists could attempt to manipulate audiences throughout the nation, not just the educated few in the urban areas.

The scientists became one of many professional groups using the mass media for promotion or sales. People who had something to sell needed publicity for their products. It made little difference whether they were promoting a new toy, a new soap, a moral theory, or political support for the federal financing of scientific research; the procedures were the same. Edison had inventions to market; Hale and Millikan solicited funds for research. To define or articulate such motives is not to judge them *ab initio* as unethical or improper, but it can help to explain the types of images present in these scientists' popular communications.

At some times in this century, however, even powerful personal or political motives could not overcome the scientific community's rejection of publicity and the researchers' natural tendency to talk only to each other. Motives for communication had to be accompanied by colleagues' approval of popularization as a worthwhile activity. When the reasons for communicating coincided with such a climate of approval within science, then mass-media coverage of science increased. When popularization was discouraged and not perceived to be in the scientists' best interests, then interaction declined, and coverage decreased. As I will describe in the next chapter, this influence of the research community frequently extended far beyond *whether* magazines published articles on science to *what* image the popularizers chose.

4

Characteristics of "The Men of Science"

I've yet to meet that "coldly calculating man of science" whom the novelists extol. . . . I doubt that he exists; and if he did exist I greatly fear that he would never make a startling discovery or invention.
C. G. Suits, 1945[1]

Many of our strongest beliefs about science come from what we think scientists are like, principally because those beliefs include assumptions about how the appearance, personality, and intellect of scientists relate to the importance and consequences of their work. Several landmark attitude surveys have documented this linkage. From Harry S. Hall's 1956 study of politicians' images of scientists, to the 1958 analysis by Margaret Mead and Rhoda Métraux of essays written by high-school students, to the National Science Foundation surveys of the 1980s, psychologists, sociologists, and pollsters have shown that what people believe scientists are like can powerfully affect their assessment of the scientists' moral intentions, and influence whether they regard science in general as morally "good" or "bad."[2] Popular magazine descriptions of scientists demonstrated this same linkage: scientists came to be described in terms related to their work, and through the use of anthropomorphic language to describe research, science acquired characteristics of morality and ability more appropriately ascribed to people.

Even though they often confused the researchers with the research, the magazine writers viewed scientists as unique and as set apart from society. Although the British science writer J. W. N. Sullivan observed in 1923 that "outside their views on purely scientific matters there is nothing *characteristic* of men of science,"[3] the American popular magazines invariably treated scientists as if there were. When they were not in their laboratories, these scientists in fact looked, dressed, and acted like other members of their local communities or socioeconomic class. No special physical or mental trait automatically or uniformly distinguished a physicist from a physician, a cosmologist from a cosmetologist, a lepidopterist from a lawyer. Nevertheless, writers for popular magazines constantly celebrated a myth of scientific differentness. They implied, through both text and illustration, that it was somehow possible to distinguish scientists from ordinary people other than by the occupational label, and thus implied that some discernible difference existed between "the ordinary mortal and the man of genius."[4]

Moreover, this distinction went beyond mere "brainpower." These were not just people who were supposedly smarter than people in other professions, but people set apart in many ways—primarily because of an unusual combination of both insightful genius and physical stamina. Popularizers preferred to emphasize the former; scientists, the latter.[5] Elmer A. Sperry explained to one reporter: "I don't think there's much in this thing called genius . . . except the capacity for work. If you have persistence and patience with a problem it's bound to yield . . ."[6] These characteristics—brains and stamina—were almost always presented together (Figure 4.1).

The Scientific Mind

First and foremost, the magazines praised scientists for having extraordinary mental abilities. Their intelligence and rationality, coupled with their curiosity and creativity, distinguished scientists from other highly-trained professionals. The capacity to think—that is, "brainpower"—could, of course, be measured by the amount of education or by childhood prodigiousness (e.g., "he was computing the timetables of favorite [celestial] stars at [age] six."[7]). More often, however, writers used the range of a researcher's knowledge, what they called the extent of an *encyclopedic memory,* as a social yardstick. The ideal scientist was both an "encyclopedia of his own branch of science, and a living directory of every other branch."[8]

These capabilities encompassed all types of intellectual skills. Portrayed simultaneously as an analyst and a synthesizer, the typical scientist made "highly specialized and minutely accurate observations" that in turn led to dynamic worldviews and broad-based theories.[9] When describing how scientists made decisions, however, writers consistently chose such terms as "cold," "calculating," and "impartial," thereby evoking comparison to dispassionate, mechanical operation. Scientific thinking, more than one author observed, resembled a mechanical procedure.

This linking of scientists to machine appeared often when writers wished to excuse a researcher's seeming lack of humanity—the scientist's

Figure 4.1. Not just brains but brawn. This March 1947 *American* profile of chemist Jack DeMent implied that not only could the ideal scientist make "pretzels out of crowbars," but he could also twist molecules into practical products for postwar reconstruction. Photograph by Bradley Smith for *American Magazine*. Reproduction from the collection of the Library of Congress.

passion was of a different sort, the image proclaimed. The image portrayed emotional rigidity as normal and therefore excusable. Mathematicians—described as the most remote of all scientific minds—appeared to be "only slightly human, having, in fact, like their subject, no souls."[10] Writers even excused animalistic attitudes toward research, as in one scientist's habit of "ripping into the heart of things with the sharp fury of a predatory and scientific hawk."[11] They never condemned researchers for being "detached" or for having "coldly scientific" minds.[12] Some articles rebuked emotionalism of any sort. In a description of research on Rocky Mountain spotted fever, for example, the author criticized a scientist for being angry at contracting the same disease he had been studying—such anger was "not the perfect embodiment of scientific detachment," the author arrogantly declared.[13] Writers appear to have expected scientists to have "minds set apart," and bodies detached from their hearts.

Although the ideal scientist might be dispassionate, he was neither shallow nor lethargic, however. Scientists rejected superficial explanations and left no questions unanswered. Everything in life lay open and vulnerable to scientific examination. No idea, however traditional or plausible, could be exempt from scrutiny: "[T]he genius is at home to new ideas. . . . He's not held down by the dead weight of tradition."[14] Scientific minds "must be brilliant, curious, skeptical and roving. They do not take things for granted."[15]

Curiosity—the desire "to get to the bottom of things"[16]—was good in appropriate doses. Writers played with the notion of intellectual impatience, sometimes setting it forth as the appropriate rationale for research. Thomas Edison advised magazine readers "to always be on the lookout for surprises." "If a man is a good observer," Edison believed, then "he will find plenty of these, and they will lead him on to more."[17] Many writers held up Edison as a model of scientific practice. He was said to scrutinize every idea and fact for its potential use, to seine "every little creek and inlet that empties into the streams of knowledge." When he "exhausted the resources" of one stream of knowledge, he lowered "his nets" into the next.[18] In a 1917 *Scribner's* article, George Ellery Hale praised similar traits in French scientist Louis Pasteur:

> [He] was impelled by that ungovernable instinct to extend the boundaries of knowledge, to reach out into the vast unknown, which every true investigator feels so keenly. He must know more, no matter where his discoveries might lead.[19]

Such scientists enjoyed "the feel of progressing work. . . . A biologist gets real fun from seeing the queer forms squirming under his microscope, a chemist from watching the explosions in his test tube."[20] Restlessness served as an acceptable motive for gratifying this delight.

Some scientists admitted that curiosity was "habit-forming." "In research," one observed, "once you start, you can't stop."[21] No matter what the consequences of the action, the scientist always attempted to climb the next mountain peak, or to open the next door in an effort to bring the light of knowledge to the "tantalizing never-to-be-accepted darkness" of ignorance.[22] Once resident in a new intellectual environment, a scientist could employ "tremendous feats of imagination"[23] and thereby progress even farther. The metaphors employed in such descriptions could be wideranging and fantastic:

> To every investigator there come moments when his thought is baffled, when the limits of experimental possibility seem to have been reached and when he faces a barrier which defies his curiosity. Then it is that imagination, like a glorious greyhound, comes bounding along, leaps the barrier, and a vision is flashed before the mind.[24]

Whatever the language, such descriptions shared a common assumption: that restless curiosity was both a natural and a necessary trait among researchers.

This proclivity to flaunt custom and to ignore the inhibitions of tradition enhanced the ease with which scientists supposedly made leaps of faith. Writers constantly dismissed cultural traditions and customs as "purely human"—that is, unscientific—factors.[25] To be successful, scientists had to reject tradition, to be openminded, to be ready "to change plans as circumstances required,"[26] and to be "willing to change them quickly and painlessly."[27]

> No truth is sacrosanct. No belief is too generally accepted, too well established by experiment, to escape the challenge of doubt. And no doubt is too radical to receive a hearing if it is seriously proposed.[28]

The scientific imagination thus epitomized "the latest phase of the evolution of the human mind."[29] As naturalist John Burroughs wrote:

> This power of interpretation of concrete facts, this Miltonic flight into time and space, into the heavens above, and into the bowels of earth beneath . . . a warring of the powers of light and darkness, with the triumph of the angels of light and life . . . makes Milton's picture seem hollow and unreal.[30]

Mentally, socially, and emotionally detached from the majority of human beings, the scientist in popular magazines "peered out at the world" from within a culturally narrow mind. Even the most sympathetic commentator might admit, as this writer did, that

> the mind that has been trained simply or predominantly in Science is an unconsciously meager and ill-furnished mind. The range of its interests is mainly technical and specialized. To look into a mind of this type is like looking into a laboratory. It is excellent as a workshop, but there are no pictures on the walls, no books, no flowers. . . . What are the resources of such a mind, its points of contact with human-kind?[31]

Extreme as this particular description was, it exemplified the conventional explanations in that it did acknowledge but did not condemn such intellectual detachment outright. From the 1910s on, writers justified the scientists' seeming remoteness by explaining that difficult mental tasks required isolation. Moreover, the images projected a strong sense of inevitability and implied that scientists, in their research, routinely violated not only intellectual but also social conventions.

Burning the "Midnight Oil"

Popular descriptions, such as the one from which the heading for this section was taken,[32] also extolled scientists' extraordinary physical strength and stamina—not necessarily as expressed in unusual athletic ability but rather as reflected in their persistence, diligence, willingness to work, and positive mental attitude. Writers frequently chose such *active* metaphors as "coiled springs" or "gas under pressure" to describe scientists, rather than metaphors that suggested *passive* reservoirs of knowledge. Researchers therefore were dynamic; their potential was high, and their "natural state" one of productive inner turmoil and intellectual motion. To observers outside of science, researchers seemed "full of wire springs that constantly coil and uncoil," their faces "alive with insistency and driving force."[33]

Whether engaged in a "personal sacrifice" or in a "long, painstaking" group effort, researchers worked "day and night." This image of twenty-four-hour dedication to one's profession also appeared continually throughout the magazines. One biographer of Robert Millikan told how the physicist, still dressed in formal "evening clothes," returned to his laboratory to work late at night.[34] This description of the scientist as someone who burns the midnight oil showed him as serious, not frivolous. The scientist came to work, not to play. Moreover, such "unflagging, unwearying, patient industry" demonstrated a scientist's diligence as well as his ability. Adjectives that implied perseverance and persistence abounded.

The ideal scientist—"Mr. Persistence"—represented "a marvel of concentration, energy, and endurance," and this image did not change.[35] For example, a 1916 profile of a chemist listed "days and nights of tireless experiment and patient research"; a 1950 article about a physicist described how he had "been known to forget the outside world completely," working "forty-eight hours and longer without sleep and with very little food."[36]

Sleep was dismissed as an activity in which only "ordinary" people indulged. Edison was "almost literally sleepless," his biographer wrote; "it is his custom to take only a few hours' rest at night."[37] The descriptions implied that all scientists worked very long days and that they frequently stayed overnight in their laboratories. As geniuses "in constant conflict with the slow tempo of the rest of the world,"[38] their efforts were never-ending. Even when they left their laboratories, their minds never rested. One chemist, said to sleep only a few hours each night anyway, kept "a thick, black 'Idea Book' by his bedside" for recording any middle-of-the-night inspirations.[39]

There were special images of dedication for each field. Stories about astronomers, for example, emphasized their nighttime work in unheated observatories, where—bundled in heavy coats, hats, and gloves—they changed photographic plates for large telescopes and kept "vigil" over their research. Writers reinforced such theological images of monastic devotion by praising the "concentration—almost consecration—with which astronomers pursue their work."[40]

Journalists who wanted to illustrate how hard scientists worked would often turn to Edison as a model. They stressed that his success came not just from chance or coincidence; rather, if he "had what seems suspiciously like a magic touch, it was because he was markedly in harmony with his environment" and he worked hard.[41] Edison's "genius" was "not in the sense that his inventions and discoveries have been revealed to him in sudden flashes."[42] "Popular fancy pictures him as a lightning-rod delegated by providence to catch dazzling inspirations," a *Cosmopolitan* writer observed, but he actually "arrives at results as a coral reef pushes to the surface—by infinite painstaking, microscopic construction."[43] In another *Cosmopolitan* article on Edison, industrialist Henry Ford wrote that the inventor "never wastes time" and "rides no hobbies."[44]

These descriptions painted scientists as patient and purposeful, but driven. Although the "seemingly toilsome road" of science may have been "adventure's path," the work nonetheless extracted "whole-souled devotion and unremitting toil" from a researcher.[45] Laboratory achievements resulted from "years of patient, tireless effort directed toward the solution of a specific, practical problem."[46] Endurance and a willingness to work hard were, of course, just as necessary for success in other professions, yet writers implied that there was something special about scientists. Millikan's greatest strength, for example, lay in his exceptional work habits. He was simply "ten men in one":

> Millikan is just—well, just the average man. Except that he does about ten times as much work, ten times as well. You might call him the superaverage man.[47]

These descriptions never explored the neurotic aspects of scientists' behavior. Writers dismissed overwork, intensity, even neglect of family, in a flurry of praise, as if it was understood that to be a scientist was to be compulsive by nature.

Emphasis on self-assured strength and admirable work habits fit well with the popular images of all types of successful people in the 1920s and 1930s. Especially in those decades, American magazines preached that, with sufficient intelligence and hard work, any problem would yield. Scientists, however, were unerringly presented to readers as members of some superclass of success, for they could do anything. One journalist held out as typical this poetic motto observed in chemist Irving Langmuir's office:

> Got any rivers they say are uncrossable?
> Got any mountains you can't tunnel through?
> We specialize in the wholly impossible;
> Doing the thing that no one can do.[48]

When combined with the attributes described above, the writers' emphasis on the power of persistence had complex implications for the public image of science. Such beliefs all too often fueled unfulfillable expectations of research—that with just a little persistence, every one of society's most difficult problems could be solved.

Appearance and Personality

More writers early in the century emphasized the physical appearance of scientists than did writers in the 1940s and 1950s; but most writers, from 1910 through 1955, assumed that some definable scientific type existed, and most compared a scientist's appearance to some supposedly typical scientist. Profiles of Robert Millikan emphasized his middle-class persona: "at first sight he looks more like the business man than the scientist."[49] Another Millikan biographer could see "Little suggestion of the scientist . . . in this clean-shaven, business-like man of the kindly blue-gray eye, ready smile, and gentle humor, whose hair, touched by the first frost, is smoothly brushed, and whose face has the ruddy tint of health."[50] The writer thought him more like a "banker than . . . any of the scientists one commonly meets, though now and then there creeps into his conversation that air of precision so characteristic of men in his profession."[51] Chemist Willis R. Whitney possessed similar attributes: he was "rugged, forceful, thoroughly human, and approachable" and "really three men in one—an executive who might hold his own in any high-geared business office, a trained scientist . . . and a man of vision. . . ."[52]

As reflected in which scientists wrote for the magazines and which were the subjects of magazine biographies and interviews, the "typical" American scientist was a white male. Most scientists who wrote for popular magazines were male physicists or biologists who worked in universities or industry. Of the scientists who were the subjects of biographies, again, most were male, most were physicists or biologists, engaged in university or industrial research, rather than in teaching or management.[53] Only two biographies (1.6% of all the biographies of scientists) specifically identified a scientist as African-American; both of these articles appeared in the 1940s.[54] There was only one biography in the issues sampled of an American scientist with an Asian surname.[55]

This image mirrored the white male scientists' domination of mainstream science in the United States during this time; few members of minority groups earned doctorates in science and engineering, and even fewer held offices in scientific societies or were elected to scientific academies. It could, of course, be sheer statistical coincidence that none of the over three thousand issues sampled contained biographies of well-known black scientists, for we know that other general magazines did publish articles on these people; but it is far more likely that the data simply reflect the covert racism of the time, in and out of science. Editors chose scientists who fit the conventional and acceptable image.

Time and time again, biographers characterized their subjects as either looking or not looking, dressing or not dressing like scientists in such comparisons as "looks like the young, earnest scientist that he is" or "is a scientist, and looks the part."[56]

> To look at [him] you would not take him for the eminent, Grade-A scientist that he is. You would know right away that he is somebody in particular . . . even if he did not happen to be wearing his black-rimmed spectacles.[57]

The most extreme stereotype created a scientist with "whiskers, stringy hair, total absence of paunch, . . . a shape somewhat like violin cases, dandruff on the coat collar, and a black string tie."[58] Later, the type was more apt to be cleanshaven and wearing a neatly-pressed white lab coat, but always the scientist seemed indifferent to fashion. In fact, writers often cited athletic build and good taste in clothes as proof that a subject did not look like a typical scientist, because those particular attributes deviated from the accepted stereotype ("his winged collar and carefully selected tie and his suede spats hardly suggested the traditional scientist").[59]

Mechanical aids to eyesight served as evidence of extraordinary mental ability. "Spectacled professors" were said to look "wondrous wise" because behind their thick lenses lay the windows to special intelligence.[60] In psychologist Carl Jung's "deep brown and searching" eyes, the biographer caught "a hint of his sixth sense."[61] Other researchers' eyes appeared "serene and searching" or "brooding" or "piercingly brilliant."

Journalistic biographies may, as a matter of expository convention, always refer to the subject's eyes; but writers of popular science appear to have been especially intrigued by scientists' "clear", "steady", "penetrating", "keen", and "serious" eyes. They chose vision as a metaphor for intellectual ability or character. The article "Pioneers of Invention," for example, portrayed a group of six famous inventors at the turn of the century as "keen-eyed children exploring the shores of a new-found sea"; before them, "the vistas of electrical science . . . unrolled." The eyes of one of these inventors emitted "a dark, limpid gaze, vividly acute." "They are the eyes," the writer continued, of one who "continually retires to the hinterland of science and returns invigorated by new discoveries."[62]

The scientist did not just look to the future, however, but was also a prophet, a fantastic Tiresias whose eyes were said to "see much more than you or I" and who could thereby identify discoveries not yet made.[63] In the 1930s, writers began increasingly to imply that this gift of distant vision might allow scientists to recognize research potential far in advance of application—although some sadness was associated with the foresight. Journalist Waldemar Kaempffert described one biologist as if he were dressed for some medieval tournament: "There, in a windowless laboratory, so completely robed in a sterile costume that only his eyes can be seen through slits in a hood, he stands face to face with immortality every day."[64] In another article, the same scientist was called a "good genius" attempting to rescue "forlorn humanity" from sickness and death.[65]

These portrayals of scientists as reluctant prophets continued through the 1950s, but then the images changed. Researchers seemed to withdraw from what they saw. An engineer who had worked on the atomic bomb was described as having "heavily lidded" eyes, "half closed in solemn contemplation of some dusty problem of thermal coefficients."[66] His work was "hidden behind [a] shield of secrecy"; his thoughts and personality shielded behind half-closed eyes. As he talked about his work, this engineer's eyes, unlike those of the stereotypical scientists of the 1920s, did not "sparkle with geniality."[67]

Perhaps journalists chose to emphasize scientists' eyes because their real attributes sometimes seemed less attractive. A scientist was "a thinker and a worker, not a talker," his speech tightly controlled.[68] Although he relied on "a rare vocabulary," his conversation was spiced with a special type of intellectual humor, with "a biting wit, a satire that could burn."[69] Yet the typical scientist was also solitary, aloof, and independent. He preferred activities that did not require the participation of others; he "would rather bake a cake in the kitchen, tootle a hymn on his French horn, or read up on some abstruse subject than entertain guests or go out to shows."[70]

Journalists sometimes rationalized such preference for solitary recreation as a natural shyness and related it to scientists' general reluctance to speak to the public.[71] Scientists supposedly did not boast about their accomplishments. Always "modest about their work," they let others praise them[72] They were "so modest in manner and scientific in spirit that they deprecate their valuable achievements and putter behind shabby scenery without fuss or flourishes . . ."[73] Even a Nobel laureate biologist was said to have "fled in panic from notoriety, fame, money."[74] The "true" scientist, journalists implied, did not push his own interests; he might "talk for hours about his work—not at all about himself."[75] As a fictional chemistry professor explained in a 1935 *Post* short story, "Why is a college professor essentially a comic figure, even to racing touts and chorus girls? Because even though our brains bulge to the point of malformation, we are the most timid people in the world."[76]

An Image of Difference

Because every article contained multiple expressions of these attributes, the coupling of various traits—extraordinary intelligence, persistence, foresight, modesty—created a powerful, overarching image. One aspect of this image (reinforced by descriptions of scientists' mental and physical strength) combined respect with fear. The nonscientist could only stand and stare and admire the scientist's strength. The other aspect reflected the audience's speculative expectations. They waited to see what this Goliath, science, would do for (or to) society, and thus their attitude combined confidence in the scientists' abilities with the hope that the scientists' actions would be beneficial for society.

Viewed from the perspective of the scientist, the attributes that contributed to the image of "differentness" undoubtedly seemed positive. Strength, intelligence, patience, and endurance all seemed admirable traits. Such characteristics also enhanced the scientists' attractiveness to journalists as news subjects, making them appear colorful, interesting, and important. The consequences of a "myth of differentness"—promoting awe, respect, confidence, even a little fear, in public attitudes to science—may have been unconsciously encouraged by scientists eager to maintain a special social status above criticism and aloof from social responsibility. It was certainly in science's best interest to encourage (or, at least, not to discourage) the development of this image. R. G. A. Dolby, in comparing how scientists communicate to colleagues with how they speak to popular audiences, identifies certain artificial barriers that experts, past and present, have constructed in order to maintain "intellectual distance" between their expertise and any encroaching public questioning.[77] The scientific expert, Dolby maintains, usually attempts to sustain this distance by demonstrating how the two spheres of activity are different, and differentiating between forms of expertise.

Not all aspects of the image of difference were positive. In a time that glorified the individual but promoted conformity to current fashion, to be perceived as "set apart" did not necessarily increase popularity. Moreover, the perception of differentness extended beyond the physical or psychological traits of scientists and may have influenced what people believed researchers could accomplish, as well as their motives for action. When writers succumbed to the temptation to promote as special not just scientists but also the scientific process, then science as a whole appeared "different" from other intellectual or professional pursuits. As later chapters will discuss, this image has had important consequences in the debates over national science policy.

5

Women in the Laboratories

Statistical reality, compiled in dozens of government reports, in lists of doctoral candidates, in the photos of Nobel prize winners, tells us, unsurprisingly, that men dominated American science in the early twentieth century. Far more men than women trained or worked as scientists.[1] As sociologist Jonathan Cole bluntly phrases it, "science was populated almost exclusively by men, and thus the phrase 'men of science' was almost equivalent to the non-sex-linked tag 'scientist'."[2] The study of cultural images of scientists reveals an even more troubling reality, however—that there also existed a deep-seated cultural bias against science as an activity appropriate for women. It was not just that science was regarded as a masculine occupation, but that the mass media also routinely placed women scientists in a negative light when they depicted them as both atypical scientists and atypical women.

These images were constructed through journalistic practices and through repetition of certain messages. First, the type of person who interpreted science (e.g., who wrote a magazine article or was interviewed by a reporter) gave an unmistakable message to the audience about who spoke for science, that is, about what type of person best understood science or had power to represent the views of the research community. If in the magazines fewer women than men acted as the communicators of science, then readers were exposed to subtle messages about women's abilities to comprehend science. Second, popular biographies and other de-

78

scriptions (or illustrations) of women scientists contributed to beliefs about what typical women scientists were like, in personality and character. If there were few such descriptions (as was true in the magazines), then the message given was that, aside from a few superstars described as possessing unusual abilities, women played an insignificant role in the scientific research process.

Most magazine descriptions of scientists implied that success in scientific research required certain "masculine" attributes such as intellectual objectivity, physical strength, and emotional detachment.[3] They thereby defined research as an activity not only socially inappropriate for women but probably impossible for them to accomplish as well. The magazines ran fewer biographies of female scientists than of male scientists, and until the late 1930s, women (either journalists or scientists) rarely wrote popular magazine articles on science.[4] Although the percentage of women biography subjects and women authors rose slightly during the 1930s and 1940s, the tone of presentation remained unchanged and sent an unattractive message to the magazines' female readers, especially to schoolgirls: If you choose a career in science, you will be one among few, the work will be hard and lonely, and popular opinion will most likely regard you as an abnormal woman.

Who Spoke for Science?—Women as Authors of Popular Science Articles

Men have dominated mass-magazine presentation of science in the twentieth century. We can observe the imbalance in three aspects of the content: first, to what extent women wrote popular science articles; second, how often those women were scientists (compared to the proportion of articles written by male scientists); and third, how often women scientists were subjects of magazine biographies or interviews.

In the sample of magazines, only 6.4% of all articles on science were written by women, including both journalists and scientists. As Figure 5.1 shows, before the 1930s, the proportion of such articles written by women was even smaller. From 1910–1914, women wrote only about one-fifth of the science articles in the issues sampled; from 1915–1919, none of the science articles were written by women. In the 1920s, the percentage of female authors increased, but the proportion still averaged only about one-tenth of all authors. There are several reasons for both the relatively small numbers and the variation.

Female authors could, of course, be found during these decades discussing science and medicine in such traditional women's magazines as *Ladies' Home Journal*, and the circulation of some of these magazines

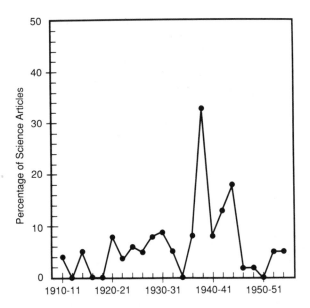

Figure 5.1.   Science articles written by women, 1910–55. The percentage of popular science articles written by women (*n* = 44), including both scientists and professional journalists. Data are taken from a sample of eleven U.S. mass-circulation magazines and are given as a percentage of all science articles published in those magazines during each two-year period. Data are adjusted to account for articles on which no author was listed (under 5% of all articles).

was considerable; but in periodicals directed at general audiences and containing public affairs and literary content, such as *Collier's* or *Harper's*, few science articles before the 1930s had female authors. During the 1930s and 1940s, this situation changed: Women wrote far more science articles than in the previous decades.

This shift was influenced by changes taking place everywhere in journalism. Women journalists—editors as well as reporters—began to achieve key positions throughout American publishing, and more newspapers were allowing female reporters to tackle so-called serious subjects like science.[5] Dorothy Thompson and her colleagues gave women a new visibility on the front page; Sylvia Porter translated high finance for *The New York Times;* Margaret Bourke-White and Dorothea Lange advanced the aesthetic and social content of American photojournalism. Women journalists fought typecasting that had previously assigned most of them only to what were considered "women's topics" (primarily food and fashion), and they moved aggressively into reporting on subjects they found interesting—including medicine and science. *Cosmopolitan* writer Maxine Davis, for example, is said to have wanted to "put politics rather than beauty hints on the women's page" and to have preferred writing about Einstein to "writing about good recipes."[6]

Following World War II, the percentage of science articles written by women returned to the pre-1930s levels, probably reflecting prevailing social conditions rather than changes in science. In the budding field of science journalism, as in many other occupations, women had been regarded as substitutes for male employees. As men returned from the front, they reclaimed their positions as the real interpreters of serious topics. By the mid-1950s, this situation had not altered; less than one-tenth of the articles were written by women, a trend sustained for decades in all types of U.S. science journalism.[7]

When we look not just at whether women wrote science articles but also at what they wrote about, we can see further indications of how popular science reflected attitudes about which careers were best for women. Women wrote more about some fields of science than about others. In the eleven magazines sampled, no woman, either scientist or journalist, was listed as author of an article on mathematics, astronomy, archaeology, or paleontology, despite the fact that some women were actively engaged in research in those fields. Women authors were more active in writing about the social and biological sciences, perhaps because those fields were widely perceived as having more "immediate human applications" than other parts of science.[8] Women wrote one-fifth of the articles on the social sciences (including anthropology), and almost one-seventh of the articles on psychology, but were much less visible as authors of articles on physics and chemistry.[9]

The small number of women *scientists* writing for popular magazines gave an unmistakable message about the importance of women in the public activities of American science (Table 5.1). In the thousands of issues analyzed, male scientists wrote 255 articles on science and women scientists wrote only 5 (under 2% of all articles by scientists and less than 1% of all science articles published in those magazines). All 5 articles appeared in issues published between 1924 and 1934, and 2 of them were written by the same woman, anthropologist Margaret Mead.[10] In the years following World War II, the proportion of women scientists visible in the magazines declined even more.

Even if we combine the data on articles written by women scientists with data on biographies of women scientists to construct a measure of media visibility, the total still represents only about 3% of all the articles.[11] To quantify the magnitude of the imbalance, we can calculate that, in this study at least, male scientists were fifteen times more visible—either as authors or biography subjects—than were women scientists.[12]

The relative invisibility of female scientists in the mass media was undoubtedly affected by their numbers within science; the pool of potential female authors and biography subjects was small. Although the women's suffrage movement and employment shifts during World War I had attracted more women to the laboratories, neither the general status nor the power of women in science had changed.[13] Increased numbers of women in the scientific workforce were not matched by comparable improvements in the representation of women on science faculties or as graduate students. The absolute numbers of Ph.D.'s in science awarded to women did increase during the late 1920s and 1930s; but so did the numbers of all science doctorates awarded to both men and women[14] (see Table 5.2). In fact, the proportion of degrees awarded to women decreased during the 1930s and, although there was some improvement in the early 1940s, the proportion dropped again in the mid-1940s, "as the [predominantly male] veterans returned home and the G.I. Bill filled the nation's colleges to overflowing."[15] Even in the mid-1950s, the proportion of all science and engineering doctorate degrees awarded to women remained under 10%. Moreover, women played minor roles in the governing hierarchy of science, either as members of the National Academy of Sciences, as officers in the professional societies, or as winners of the prestigious prizes in science.[16] Of the 430 scientists nominated for the Nobel prize between 1901 and 1937, for example, only 2 were women (Marie Curie and Lise Meitner, both physicists), and only Curie won the prize; in that same period, such scientists as George Ellery Hale were nominated dozens of times.[17]

Scientists' beliefs about the importance of popularization also undoubtedly influenced the extent of participation by women scientists in the

Table 5.1   The Visibility of Women Scientists in Popular Magazines,
             as Authors of Articles, 1910–1954

	% Science articles[a] written by female scientists[b]	% All articles[c] by scientists written by female scientists[d]
1910–14	0	0
1915–19	0	0
1920–24	1.4	2.3
1925–29	.8	1.5
1930–34	6.0	14.3
1935–39	0	0
1940–44	0	0
1945–49	0	0
1950–54	0	0

[a]Articles in sampled issues of eleven U.S. mass-circulation magazines ($n = 687$).
[b]$n = 5$
[c]Articles in sampled issues of eleven U.S. mass-circulation magazines ($n = 256$).
[d]$n = 5$

Table 5.2   The percentage of science and engineering doctorate degrees
awarded to women in the United States, 1920–1959

Field	1920–29	1930–39	1940–49	1950–59
Mathematics and physical sciences	7.6	6.6	5.0	3.7
Life sciences	15.9	15.1	12.7	9.1
Social and behavioral sciences	17.1	15.8	14.5	11.0
Engineering	0.9	0.7	0.5	0.3
All science and engineering fields	12.3	11.3	8.9	6.7

Source: Data are taken from Betty M. Vetter, "Women's Progress," *Mosaic* 18 (Spring 1987): 2.

public communication of science. At many times during this century, the scientific community has considered popularization to be an activity of low prestige.[18] A female scientist, whose position as a minority member of a male-dominated community was tenuous at best, had few incentives (and probably little encouragement) to write articles for the popular press. To popularize was to risk censure from her colleagues.

Biographies of Women Scientists: Domesticity or Denial

If the low visibility of female science writers of all types reinforced the myth that women were less able to comprehend science and hence less capable of doing scientific research than were men, then the lack of attention to women scientists via biographies or interviews further implied that they were outside the mainstream of science. The magazines clearly did not seek out women scientists as subjects for biographies or interviews. Of all biographies of scientists published in the issues examined across the entire forty-five-year period, slightly over 14% were biographies of women; but for the years 1910–15 and 1927–34, none of the sampled issues contained biographies of women scientists (Figures 5.2 and 5.3).[19] During 1925 and 1926, over one-fifth of the biographies published were about female scientists. Only in the 1930s, when the absolute number of all types of biographies rose, did the proportion of biographies of women scientists increase. When magazines published fewer biographies of scientists, then the proportion of them that were about women again declined.

Magazines tended to select biography subjects from certain research fields, and here, too, the choices reflected attitudes toward careers for women. Although the absolute numbers were small, women constituted a significant proportion of the social scientists and geologists discussed by

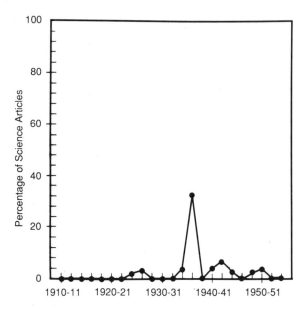

Figure 5.2.   Popular biographies of women scientists, as a percentage of all science articles, 1910–55 (*n* = 18). Data are taken from a sample of eleven U.S. mass-circulation magazines and are given as a percentage of all science articles published in those magazines during each two-year period.

magazines. About one-fifth of all the biographies of physicists and of astronomers were about women, but there were no biographies of female psychologists, archaeologists, paleontologists, or mathematicians.[20] Most of the women described were researchers associated with universities but not at professorial rank. Although some articles described women engaged in independent research (e.g., a biography of Catherine Macfarlane, cancer researcher and chief of Gynecology and Obstetrics at a Philadelphia hospital[21]), more articles featured women in subordinate staff positions than was true for all biographies of men.

The increased numbers of biographies of women scientists in the 1930s and in the late 1940s did not portend any appreciable change in the image conveyed in these articles. There were few positive aspects to the image, and its negative aspects—that to be a woman scientist required extraordinary hard work and sacrifices—altered little through the years. Thousands of women turned out to honor physicist Marie Curie when she visited the United States in 1921,[22] but admiration did not necessarily translate into imitation. The flapper Zelda Fitzgerald expressed typical feelings when she observed that scientific careers called for "hard work, intellectual pessimism, and loneliness," and said she would not want her

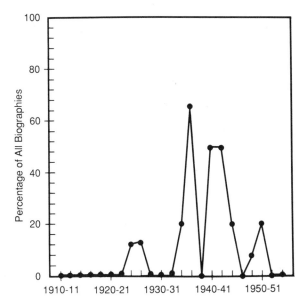

Figure 5.3.   Popular biographies of women scientists, as a percentage of all biographies of scientists, 1910–55. Data are taken from a sample of eleven U.S. mass-circulation magazines and are given as a percentage of all science articles published in those magazines during each two-year period.

daughter to choose such a life.[23] Through their language and ideas, magazine biographers echoed such attitudes by asserting that women—even women who were successful scientists—were invariably more fulfilled through marriage and motherhood than through research. The "intellectual" and "detached" aspects of a woman scientist appeared to be different from her "feminine" and "intuitive" side—and these sides were not reconcilable. Moreover, a research career demanded, as one biographer wrote, "absolute and narrow abnegation of human relationships."[24] Two biographies in particular show how these attitudes toward women scientists were expressed in popular biographies.

Eve Curie's biography of her mother Marie exemplified how negative images infused even intrinsically favorable descriptions.[25] First published in France, the best-selling book was translated for a *Saturday Evening Post* serialization in 1937.[26] The series drew a portrait of Marie Curie typical of descriptions of her found in other magazines (see Figure 2.3, for example). Although the articles explored the physicist's scientific accomplishments at length, they also relentlessly emphasized (in text and illustration) her devotion to her husband and children. She was praised for being "a friend and a wife, a lover and a scientist" to Pierre. In accounts of her struggles with chauvinism in the predominantly male scientific establishment of France, readers caught a glimpse of real barriers and biases that Curie had encountered, but the text hinted that such costs—and Curie's stoic acceptance of them—were merely part of the game. In its glorification of Curie's personal as well as scientific devotion, the biography unabashedly promoted an image of her as superhuman.

Similar presentation of the personal price of becoming a scientist marked a 1926 biography of public health specialist Alice Hamilton.[27] That article, written by a female journalist, paid considerable attention to Hamilton's support of Hull House in Chicago, praising her social commitment as much as her scientific reputation. The author also analyzed the tensions that arose between the demands of Hamilton's public health research and the supposed siren call of more traditional female activities. For women, the author implied, scientific ambition invariably required personal sacrifice. Hamilton—neither married nor a mother—was thus "compelled to abandon well-tried domestic paths."[28] Moreover, it was her "fate in her public, humane, and scientific role to live the very opposite of the secluded life which her personal atmosphere seems to demand."[29]

This and other popular biographies also painstakingly described differences in how women and men conducted scientific research. With remarkable consistency, the magazines asserted that scientific research required such "masculine" attributes as intellectual objectivity, physical strength, and emotional detachment. In science, professional women were said to be "borrowing . . . many hard and objective qualities from the other sex," yet nonetheless making "exquisite and easy adjustment of both sides of life—the tough and the tender, the hard work and the human relations—without sacrificing the virtues of either."[30] Hamilton, for example, was said to have neither renounced her feminine traits nor used them in her career; instead, "the intellectual and detached aspects of her mind [i.e., the so-called masculine traits] have increasingly served the more instinctive feminine side."[31]

Although the biography of Hamilton mentioned her substantial "sacrifice," the author did not dwell on either the social forces that discouraged her or the gender-linked bureaucratic and administrative barriers placed in her way. In her fifties, by then an acclaimed expert in her field, Hamilton accepted appointment as an assistant professor at Harvard University Medical School in a "specially created post." Although the article mentioned that Hamilton thereby became the first "and so far, the only, woman to be invited to that conservative medical faculty," it did not acknowledge the attitudes within science that had created that situation. The fault, such magazine treatments implied, lay in the accident of gender. A more recent biography by Barbara Sicherman shows that Hamilton herself may have shared this view with journalists at the time. Asked what she thought of her appointment at Harvard, Hamilton reportedly "attributed it to the new-ness of her field and to luck."[32] Yet, in private, Hamilton was said to have confided that she "found her position as Harvard's only woman often frus-trating and disappointing."[33]

In their tendency to hint at but not confront gender bias in science, these biographies exhibited an ambiguity present in other popular discus-sions of women scientists. If women wanted to pursue science as their life's work, these texts implied, then they must accept certain situations as unchangeable, such as that they must carry out their research in a predom-inantly male environment. At the same time, authors tended to gloss over the emotional and psychological pressures placed on women as a result of having to work in unfriendly and lonely circumstances.

The biographers also carefully cultivated an image of domesticity, often overemphasizing the researchers' femininity. Despite their presence in a male environment, these scientists were still "real" women, the mag-azines argued. Female scientists were portrayed as "devoted" to their fam-ilies and to their work in equal measure and (by implication) in that order. Journalists frequently listed "normal" activities, such as cooking or sew-ing, as proof that the women were not only productive researchers but also good wives and mothers. An *American* profile of University of Toronto astronomer Helen Sawyer Hogg (Figure 5.4), who was at the time the president of the American Association of Variable Star Observers, blithely referred to her as a "housewife" who was conscientiously attentive to her real responsibilities: ". . . Even if her mind is in the sky, Dr. Hogg keeps her feet on the ground. She runs the house for her husband and three kids, collects stamps, makes bedspreads."[34] The mahogany furniture of Florence Rena Sabin was said to be "gleaming," thereby presumably indicating her diligence in keeping house.[35] A profile of Margaret Mead described how she could make "corn fritters with crocodile eggs" while on an expedi-tion.[36] Even though she was pictured at her desk, Muriel Mathez, the chief of the mineralogical laboratory at the Atomic Energy Commission, was praised because she "designs and makes her own clothes."[37]

If we compare the image of the woman scientist to that of her male colleagues—for whom neglect of domestic duties, long hours in the lab-oratory, absentmindedness, and lack of social graces were cited as proof of devotion to science—then the disparity in the two images is even more apparent. Women scientists were expected not only to excel in their work but also, if possible, to be perfect wives and mothers.[38] The discussions presented no contradictory or alternative models; some even hinted that women scientists' contributions to scientific progress may have been largely accidental and certainly not as significant as those made by men. Other articles implied that women perhaps could make greater contribu-tions to science as the wives of scientists.

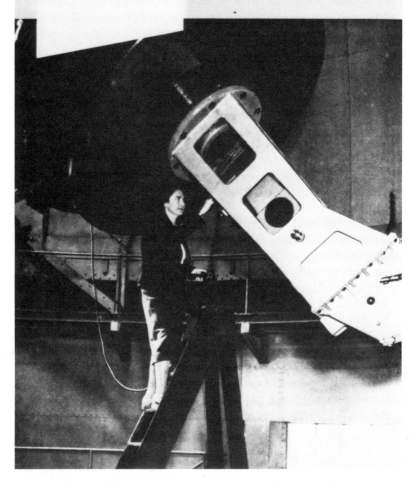

MOST housewives call it a day when they finish drying the dinner dishes, but not Dr. Helen Sawyer Hogg, of Toronto, Canada. America's busiest night watchman, she's kept a nightly vigil for 10 years, watching the behavior of variable stars—the ones that vary in brightness —and looking for new ones. Chalked up to her credit are 150 that no one ever knew existed before. Her expert stargazing won her a post as research astronomer at Toronto University and the presidency of the American Association of Variable Star Observers. That's an organization of 350 enthusiasts in 27 states and 11 countries who spend an hour or two every night with their eyes to their telescopes. Their findings help professional astronomers solve the mysteries of the universe. But, even if her mind is in the sky, Dr. Hogg keeps her feet on the ground. She runs the house for her husband and three kids, collects stamps, makes bedspreads.

Watchman

Figure 5.4. Astronomer Helen Sawyer Hogg. Billed as "America's busiest night watchman," Hogg is shown at her "nightly vigil" at the telescope in this *American* profile of March 1940. Reproduction from the collection of the Library of Congress.

For the male scientist shown in the magazines, family relationships supported his ego and daily comfort; they were essential to his success, and the family functioned as an adjunct to his research team. Its support helped him to concentrate on science night and day; in the name of science, the family tolerated a wide variety of faults. A male scientist could ignore the normal responsibilities of family partners; he need "never let his mind get cluttered with detail debris" and his spouse "learned not to ask him to pick up a quart of ice cream on the way home."[39] Thomas Edison may have been characterized as "The Most Difficult Husband in America,"[40] but his uncooperative nature was excused as simply another manifestation of his brilliance. Edison's wife described "What It Means to Be Married to a Genius": a woman had no greater mission than "ministering to her husband's well-being," she told the interviewer.[41] Society should not criticize Edison's apparent lack of regard for family "niceties" or his occasional inattention to family matters, the authors of another profile asserted, because his work was so important.

The familiar picture of the "absent-minded" scientist fit this lovable, laughable image well. In the laboratories, researchers used complex instruments, but "at home they [were] baffled by kitchen can openers and patented potato peelers . . ."[42] Moreover, the family tempered and balanced the male scientist's life, acting as a reality base:

> His laboratory tells him what a precarious and fragile thing life is, how material and condition-ruled and circumscribed a living creature is. But his wife and child and his own consciousness tell him how much more, how immeasurably more, there is in life than he learns in his laboratory.[43]

A male scientist stood in the center of attention, excused from the duties of normal fathers because of the importance of his work. In some cases, the mere existence of a family added to a scientist's social worth. One writer, speaking glowingly of the family of Alfred Kinsey, argued that even though some Americans found Kinsey's research on sexual behavior to be morally repulsive, his Hoosier family life was proof that he actually revered traditional American values.[44]

If a male scientist was obtuse and a little odd, his family supported him and forgave his little eccentricities. If he gave the impression of being cold and objective, his family was cited as evidence that, in his heart, he was warm and loving. No such excuses were available to female scientists. Instead, the image was reversed. They were required not only to prove their worth as scientists, but also to prove that they were still "real" women. The articles in American magazines surely left many readers doubting both these things.

Inappropriate Activities

These images of domesticity were accompanied by assertions that scientific research was an activity inappropriate for women. Although few magazine writers asserted that women were unfit for scientific work—an attitude that sociologists argue is quite common—many did imply that women could not conduct research as well as men and, even though women were admitted to laboratories and graduate training, they were not fully accepted as scientists.[45] When women became scientists, they violated the notion of research as a male activity; they acted contrary to nature.

Magazine discussions promoted such attitudes in a number of subtle ways. When authors consistently emphasized the inconveniences of research and listed sleepless nights as normal for scientists, for example, they implied that scientific research was invariably an uncomfortable and physically demanding activity. Women (defined by many of these commentators as the weaker sex) might not be strong enough to persevere. And, just as in modern debates about the role of women in the military, some commentators queried whether it was morally correct to expose women to the risks of certain types of laboratory or field work.

Those women scientists who did brave the physical dangers of field work were often portrayed in terms negating their femininity. Alice Hamilton was said to have "gone everywhere that a man could go—never considering herself a woman when it came to danger or fatigue . . ."[46]

The presence of a woman in the laboratory or on an expedition posed another potential danger—a danger to the success of the research itself. They might not be able to play a full role in the work:

> On an expedition, how can a woman be anything but a liability? There are few women who are able to do technical and scientific work better than a man. . . . undeniably women are not so strong as men, physically.[47]

Some experiences (such as sandstorms) "would have been ten times more difficult for a woman," the author added.[48] Women also posed a potential distraction to their male colleagues. The same author discreetly alluded to "the sex problem": "two or three women would simply invite trouble," he cautioned.

The continual use of discriminatory language reinforced such negative images of the appropriateness of a woman's presence in a scientific setting; adult female laboratory technicians were called *girls,* for example, but male technicians were referred to as *men.*[49] A 1951 article on the Massachusetts Institute of Technology included this comparison of students:

"To find a sprinkling of perhaps seventy-five girls among 5000 men invariably surprises visitors."[50] Illustrations for articles, too, depicted women as minority characters in the drama of science. In the drawings accompanying a 1953 article on space research, for example, all of the subordinate technicians and assistants were female; the supervisors and the test subjects (astronauts) were male.[51]

Some observers felt that women should support research projects, not run them. A profile of a female laboratory technician described her as "another pair of hands for the professional man" and included the following passage about her male lab chief:

> Dr. Koprowski insists that a scientist should look for the same qualities in his feminine assistant that he would in a wife. The doctor is quite ready to elaborate on this morale-building opinion. 'And why not? After all, a scientist spends as much time in his laboratory as he does in his home. Attractiveness, compatibility, and mutual respect—they are all important with people who have to work together as closely as you must do in research.'[52]

The actual status and numbers of women in science certainly influenced the amount of attention that magazines paid to female scientists, but the openly biased language is more problematic. One explanation is that the language simply reflected the male-dominated scientific community's image of itself. Evelyn Fox Keller, in her work on gender and science, asserts that most scientists see science as male, defining it as macho, virile, active, and energetic.[53] Certainly, the popular presentation of science tended to equate intellect, detachment, and objectivity with masculinity, and to equate instinct, intuition, and emotion with femininity. Professional women were said to "borrow" their objectivity from men: they imitated their male colleagues because they did not innately possess such necessary abilities. When scientists wrote about their female colleagues in the popular press, they simply employed the same images and language current within the scientific community.

When journalists wrote about women scientists, they perhaps also unconsciously repeated the biases prevalent in the scientific community; for even when there were more women working as scientists, their visibility in the popular magazines remained low. In the 1940s, as the image of science as a male activity persisted and was reinforced by the prominence of male scientists during the war, women scientists still appeared to be at odds with the convention. The writers and editors, again seeking consensus with prevailing notions, continued to choose male subjects for their biographies, to interview men rather than women, and thereby to perpetuate an image of science as a predominantly male domain.

Role Models

When women scientists did gain some visibility in the popular magazines, they were usually at one of two extreme positions: either subordinate assistants or "superscientists." Only males were the subjects of articles about "normal," "ordinary," or "everyday" scientists. Women scientists, most notably such women as Marie Curie or Margaret Mead, were depicted as something more than ordinary, as not only exceptional scientists but also exceptional women.

Mead, a major figure in twentieth-century anthropology, was one of the most visible scientists (male or female) in the magazines studied, either as an author or as a subject of biographies (Figure 5.5). She was tough and durable, not only a brilliant researcher but also a pioneer in her field.[54] In contrast to the descriptions of Marie Curie, who was drawn as cool, remote, and calm, as a pragmatic and methodical worker, a quiet mother, and dignified spouse, articles on Mead showed her as friendly and gregarious; they emphasized her bright and engaging personality. A profile in *American*'s "Interesting People" series depicted Mead as a daring but still feminine adventuress: "From [her] first expedition [she] brought back a husband, Dr. R. F. Fortune, famous anthropologist."[55]

Although courageous and daring, the female scientist shown in the magazines was protected from emotion, for she was above all a *scientist,* an objective, hard-working machine. Even if she appeared to have relinquished some of the conventional trappings of femininity, she seemed undeterred by discrimination. "Opportunities for women in the field are not really so abundant as for men," wrote the biographer of Florence Rena Sabin, "yet for those women who strive in deadly earnest openings may be had and a chance to rise."[56] Women who were not serious about science would, such assertions implied, have neither opportunity nor success. Because she challenged scientific orthodoxy by her very presence, the superwoman scientist was expected to be impervious to the stings of criticism. In reality, her exhaustion may have been boundless, but in the pages of the magazines she, like most scientists, never seemed to tire. The images were those of audacious explorers of new intellectual territories (Mead) or austere and dedicated saints (Curie) but rarely anything in between, and never ordinary.

By focusing on the exceptional woman, the magazines reinforced cultural stereotypes of women scientists as glamorous stars in the drama of science, but not as indispensable links in the process. To be a scientist was to be different. To be a woman scientist was not only to be different from other people and from other women—mentally, physically, perhaps even sexually—but also to be strong enough to perform like a star and to

HEADHUNTER

HERE'S the only white woman to live alone among cannibals. Ever since she was 21 Dr. Margaret Mead has been going into the bush—not for thrills, but to study family life in the raw. An international authority now at 33, she is one scientist whose books are best sellers (*Coming of Age in Samoa, Sex and Temperament in Three Primitive Societies*, etc.). First woman to tell the civilized world about sex life of head-hunters. Returns to the U. S. only to get rid of malaria, catch up on new slang. Makes friends of natives by kissing greasy babies, eating big hunks of taro, a potato tasting like soap. From first expedition (to Samoa) brought back a husband, Dr. R. F. Fortune, famous anthropologist. Returned from last trip (to New Guinea) with 19 heads, 3 new languages. In New York she's an Assistant Curator of the American Museum of Natural History. No swimmer, natives frequently fish her out of streams, because she's never learned how. Makes good corn fritters with crocodile eggs. You'd like them.

Figure 5.5.   The young Margaret Mead. This 1935 *American* profile attempted to make the controversial anthropologist seem more feminine and less formidable, even though she was "the only white woman to live alone among cannibals" and had returned from her last expedition to New Guinea "with 19 heads, 3 new languages." Photograph by Irving Browning for *American Magazine*. Reproduction from the collection of the Library of Congress.

do so alone. The male scientist's support structure—his wife, children, assistants, colleagues, neighbors—were ready at his side; the female scientist either had to be a Joan of Arc, alone at the top, or a dual-role housewife/scientist, one hand holding the mop (or child), the other steering the telescope toward the stars.

No matter which way you turned this image it remained unappealing. It presented research as an arduous and lonely enterprise requiring many personal sacrifices, yet successful women scientists reportedly engaged in all the activities of "real" (i.e., feminine) women as well. This was hardly a role model likely to attract young girls into scientific careers. By implying that the options of a regular family life, home, and possibly motherhood were closed for all but the superwomen, this public image may have dissuaded many students from choosing scientific careers. A female scientist seemed to compromise normality. For girls raised in conventional family environments, to enter science was to defy tradition, at least as defined by popular culture.[57] These images parallel those of career women in general, as portrayed in the mass-periodical fiction of the time. One study of fiction in the 1920s and 1930s, for example, showed such heroines as perhaps achieving great success in their careers, but "bearing extraordinary burdens" in order to do so; heroines who were career women had less security and love and fewer affectional relationships than heroines in traditional roles.[58]

In an age when racism as well as gender bias still percolates through all aspects of American academe and all professions and occupations, the narrowness of racial stereotypes expressed in these images should probably not be shocking, but it is no less reprehensible. Young women who were members of racial, ethnic, or religious minorities found few encouraging role models in the popular magazines. The only recognition of black women scientists in the issues sampled was a biography of anthropologist Katherine Dunham.[59] Titled "Anthropological Katie," the article gave much more attention to the entertainment aspects of her dance troupe than to her research and preservation of the dances of tribal cultures. In its closing paragraphs, the article described Dunham's problems with so-called Jim Crow laws and singled her out as "terribly conscious of her responsibility to her race." Although the article listed her successes and praised her credentials (which included a Ph.D. from the University of Chicago), this wrap-up paragraph, like so many other paragraphs in other articles on women scientists, subtly reminded readers that the road to success in science was roughest for those who did not fit the traditional image.[60]

Legacy

Throughout this century, whenever the mass media have not ignored female scientists altogether, they have treated them as unusual. The small numbers of women in science meant that they were less accessible for interviews with journalists. Their low status in the scientific community made them less appealing editorially. Each situation—unappealing image and invisibility—fed the other and reflected what Harriet Zuckerman and Jonathan Cole call the "triple penalty." Women are penalized before they even begin to compete, for three reasons: actual discriminatory practices and women's own self-doubts, reinforced by a culture that defines scientific careers as inappropriate for women.[61] In the early part of this century, the perpetuation of an unattractive, negative stereotype, combined with the mass media's lack of attention to "ordinary" women scientists and with the relatively small number of female authors writing about science, implied that women were of little consequence in science.

The circumstances cry out for change. In the 1970s and 1980s, several national commissions have examined U.S. science education and found it wanting. All have predicted dire consequences for the nation if no correction occurs in the quality of classroom instruction. To improve national strength in science, however, the scientific enterprise must also draw from the widest possible pool of bright young students, and the effort to attract and sustain women students must extend beyond the classroom. Even if young women begin to perceive science as an activity open equally to all, they must believe that for them such a career will be possible. The highest goals of affirmative action are doomed to failure if the image of women scientists in the popular culture remains bogged in "superscientist" or "domestic whiz" cliches. Educational programs must "change the perceptions of young girls about the barriers to scientific careers," even as the barriers themselves are lifted.[62]

Some recent research on what influences the decisions of women undergraduates to major in science found that new educational programs played less important roles than did "the set of conceptions, predispositions, and expectations" derived from each student's previous experience: "Women enter college with different notions, implicit if not explicit, of what science will be like and the role it will play in their lives."[63] One useful change, the study's authors argued, would be to help women "to feel that being a scientist is appropriate, normal, and not unfeminine . . ." As Jonathan Cole concludes in *Fair Science*, "in the final analysis, the real battle for improving the situation for women in science will be fought out before women ever reach the borders of the scientific community."[64] In the twentieth century, many battles have been lost in the popular press.

Negative stereotypes common in the mass magazines persist in popular culture today. Some images are, fortunately, slightly more positive, but media coverage as a whole has not been not radically reshaped by either feminist philosophy or affirmative action.[65] As a woman, I do not doubt the ability of any person to juggle two careers, to parcel her mind into two parts, and ultimately to emerge with the prize; but such requirements have not been routinely imposed on male scientists as part of our nation's cultural attitudes toward science. Like astronomer Helen Sawyer Hogg in the 1940s, modern women scientists still feel they must "run the house," even while their eyes are on the stars.

6

Scientific Stereotypes:
Point and Counterpoint

They made a myth of you, professor,
you of the gentle voice,
the books, the specs,
the furtive rabbit manner . . .
Carl Sandburg[1]

Biographies and other magazine descriptions of scientists contributed to the building of cultural stereotypes through a fluid and interactive process. No one article created a stereotype; no one article stood uninfluenced by other stereotypes existing at the time. Moreover, writers consciously exploited or rejected what they perceived as contemporary stereotypes. Consider this example from *American* in 1929:

'Most laymen,' laughed Doctor True, 'look upon the botanist as a queer, bespectacled chap who spends a great deal of his time hunting strange flowers with long names and pressing them in books.'[2]

This author then listed how Doctor True differed from the prevailing image of the botanist but, in the process, the author built up a new one. In similar fashion, in the 1946 *American Mercury,* a journalist asserted that the prewar stereotype of astronomers as impractical dreamers could no longer be considered accurate because astronomy itself had changed:

The astronomer can no longer be thought of simply as the tiny little professor peering through an outlandishly large telescope at comets and stars. He's a handy man to have around an atomic bomb laboratory, as the work of astronomers in the war demonstrates.[3]

Each writer thus tended to create a picture of an individual scientist and compare him or her to selected facts, stereotypes, and expectations.

In some cases, writers believed the scientist to be like the type; in other cases, they did not. Physical characteristics might be listed objectively, but even they could be exaggerated or distorted. By simply emphasizing some attributes and denigrating others, a writer could make powerful assertions about a scientist's motives for doing research, about the applications of research, or about its potential for harm or good.

In their descriptions of scientists, writers frequently combined groups of attributes or employed well-worn metaphors to evoke particular value-laden themes. Four themes appeared consistently, each emphasizing different social roles for scientists, each having positive and negative sides, and each having different implications for the image of research in general: the scientist as wizard, as expert, as creator/destroyer, and as hero.[4]

The Magician or Wizard

For centuries, the wizard metaphor has been a popular literary device for conveying excitement and beneficence, and this was no less true in twentieth-century magazines. A 1912 *Collier's* article repeatedly referred to one biologist as a "Wizard of Oz";[5] in 1927, *World's Work* readers were given "glimpses of the Wizardry in the General Electric Laboratories";[6] and in 1947, the *Post* praised a group of botanists for their "magic," their "horticultural wizardry," and their "laboratory wizardry."[7] By using such metaphors, writers implied that scientists employed potentially dangerous magic.

Some of the most exaggerated uses of this imagery peppered the articles on Thomas Edison, the "Wizard of Menlo Park." Assertions that Edison was *not* a wizard rang false when routinely followed, a few paragraphs later, by some description of his "miraculous power." A 1917 biography began thus:

> Mr. Edison is not a wizard. Like all people who have prodigiously assisted civilization, his processes are clear, logical and normal.
> Wizardry is the expression of superhuman gifts and, as such, is an impossible thing.
> Man cannot perform miracles, however cunningly he employs his miraculous powers.
> And yet, Mr. Edison can bid the voices of the dead to speak, and command men in their tombs to pass before our eyes.[8]

Biographers of Edison attempted to transform his "practical" skills into supernatural, almost mystical powers; they referred to his "magic touch."[9]

One writer even devised a special chant based on the "magic" in Edison's name:

> Behold! The cryptic secret is disclosed: E for energy, D for doggedness, I for imagination, S for sobriety, O for organization, and N for *nil desperandum*. He is energetic, determined, uses his imagination, avoids excesses, labors methodically, and never quits—therefore his success. Be likewise; and you may in like wise make a magic name.[10]

Edison's work with electrical devices contributed to his "wizard" status because electricity was a "field of invention which really caught the popular imagination" during that time.[11] The association of research engineers and physicists with magic was especially common in the 1920s.[12] *World's Work* articles on General Electric, such as "The Electrical Brains in the Telephone"[13] and "Makers of Lightning,"[14] described conventional engineering innovations as if they were the result not of applied physics research but of supernatural incantations.

Use of the wizard image and hints of magical discoveries reinforced a popular assumption that, despite what scientists said, scientific discoveries always contained an element of chance or serendipity. Writers frequently explained how "scientists who have thought they were discovering one thing, have discovered something else . . ."[15] The scientists' apparent intellectual flexibility contributed to this serendipity: they were not only receptive to inspiration, but also ready "to change plan as circumstances required."[16] Nine out of ten discoveries, Floyd W. Parsons wrote in the *Post*, "come by accident, and very often are put to uses that were not dreamed of in the beginning."[17]

The suggestion that chance played a significant role in research was at odds, however, with the image of rationality that most scientists probably preferred to have the public accept. Engineer Charles F. Kettering complained that the imagery of chance represented "the modern ballyhoo that has turned simple fixers and searchers into credible magicians," an assessment that other scientists echoed.[18] In interviews and in their own writings, researchers attempted to qualify and restructure this image, therefore. If discoveries were accidental, they argued, then they must have been "planned accidents," which never could have occurred if the scientist had not placed himself in position for the "lightning of discovery to strike."[19]

> 'Does accident often play a part in chemical discoveries?' I inquired. 'At times it does, but not as rule,' Dr. Stine replied. 'Even when it does, the circumstance is not, strictly speaking, accidental . . . the chemist invariably

has to put in some mighty hard work in order to bring about fortunate accidents.'[20]

By and large, attempts to "correct" the image failed. For every such qualification, there were dozens of articles in which other scientists, with appropriate modesty, characterized a discovery as "accidental" or assured reporters that practical applications simply represented the accidental byproduct of pure research.

Why was this image so popular, even though it contradicted what both professional journalists and scientists knew to be true? Popular writers may have clung to the image because it helped them conveniently to explain the unexplainable. Many people, including professional writers, believed that science was simply beyond understanding; the metaphor of magic enabled one to discuss the topic without really comprehending it.[21] Journalists also seem to have used the "accident" image as a way to avoid assigning complete control over nature to scientists. Some serendipity, some element of forces other than those of science, *must* exist, they may have believed. The idea of accidental discovery, although clearly false if the scientist had adopted a research plan, probably also fit the scientists' internal mythology of their modesty. Even when research was described as directed and planned for success, therefore, this older image of research as part wizardry, part chance, persisted.

The Expert

A second powerful type, that of the scientist as expert, further extended the wizard/magician image. The theme exploited the scientist as a practical polymath or problem solver, rather than as a Merlin who creates dreamcastles out of air or changes sticks into serpents. Using technical knowledge, the scientific expert analyzed and solved problems in a rational, deliberate, and efficient manner.

The development of the image of the scientist as technical expert appeared to be almost self-perpetuating. As popular culture increasingly linked social progress to science, scientists found their intelligence and knowledge to be unchallenged and their opinions in great demand. In the 1920s, "faith in experts, in research and scientific method for gaining social knowledge" was part of the middle-class spirit, as people turned to experts to "keep them informed" on everything from new techniques for child rearing (psychology) to new medical treatments (biology).[22] In such a climate, journalists touted scientists as the ultimate experts and pestered them for statements on every conceivable public issue, scientific and nonscientific alike. As humorist Stephen Leacock later observed, any scientist who was inclined to stop "recording phenomena" and to offer "a general statement of the nature of what is called 'reality', the ultimate nature of space, of time, of the beginning of things, of life, of a universe," found a forum in the mass media.[23] Those who wished to promote their social or political ideas found audiences willing to listen to just about anything.

More importantly, those scientists who entered the public arena received little criticism from outside the scientific community. Although a few writers complained about the over-reliance on experts and the tendency to drag in the expert "as a superior sort of magician who could whisk a complete scientific solution out of his hat," such criticism was in the minority.[24] Some critics berated technical experts for being "self-appointed priests," dispensing scientific theory like theological dogma, but the image of scientists as unassailable experts generally drew little questioning. Neither readers nor journalists insisted that scientists prove every statement, however outrageous. Especially during the early decades of this century, Leacock quipped, "To 'doubt science' was to be like the farmer at the circus who doubted the giraffe."[25]

This unquestioning acceptance extended to scientists even when they were speaking outside their field of expertise—a practice common in the popular magazines. One-third of the scientists writing in these magazines discussed topics outside their educational or professional experience.[26] In only one magazine, *Collier's,* were almost all of the articles written by scientists on topics within each author's field of expertise.

Apparently unable to resist the temptation, some scientists even phrased their religious or political beliefs in scientistic language, or otherwise used the authority of science to substantiate claims unrelated to technical issues. An interview with Robert Millikan titled "A Scientist's God" exemplified this practice.[27] Written as one long, continuous quotation, the article tendered the physicist's personal beliefs as proof that all of science was not "opposed" to religion. An interview with Thomas Edison published in *Cosmopolitan* similarly outlined the "sum of years of thought by America's great inventive genius" on the subject "What *Is* Life?"[28] These and other narratives were predicated on the idea that society should always attend to the scientific expert. In order to be accepted, scientists need neither to persuade nor to cajole their audiences. Even when a scientist was incorrect or illogical, he was heeded simply because he was a scientist.

Magazine treatments of Albert Einstein also show how this "expert" image served inadvertently to erect barriers of authority between readers and scientists. In the 1920s (by which time Einstein's name was well-known) journalists generally regarded his work as "quite incomprehensible" to the general public. Some writers reportedly regarded the physicist with "almost superstitious awe"; they fastened on him as the ultimate expert and clamored for his opinions on all sorts of topics.[29]

The complexity of Einstein's theories, as well as the scientific controversy surrounding them, enhanced his attractiveness to the journalists. Both journalists and scientists pronounced Einstein's theories to be so complicated that it was futile even to try to understand them. According to historian Daniel Kevles, Einstein never announced "that only twelve men in all the world could comprehend his general theory"; nevertheless, in the magazines, the myth of the twelve men, and of the incomprehensibility of Einstein's work, persisted.[30]

Talk about scientific controversy helped to solidify barriers between the "initiated expert" and the "uninitiated layman."[31] The laymen, one historian has argued, were thereby relegated to keeping score on the number of scientists who were for or against the theories and waiting for the experts to agree.[32] In 1930, although she complained that she was not "one of the reputed twenty who understand completely Einstein's theory of relativity," one journalist nevertheless accepted its accuracy: "enough of this theory has already touched and been assimilated by the thinking public to make us aware that the definitions . . . formerly laid down by Science, are now already discounted."[33]

This mixture of first awe and then resignation to ignorance continued through the 1950s. After the publication of Einstein's 1949 paper on unified field theory, Robert Yoder chastised "the old master" for having developed yet another body of work that would be exceedingly difficult, if not impossible, to understand. Using a baseball metaphor, the journalist accused Einstein of having pitched laymen "another cosmic bean ball."[34] The difference between a scientist's work and that of other intellectuals seemed to lie in an implicit expectation that laymen *must* try to understand the scientist. Yoder confessed that he was willing, almost eager, to be confused by physics. The difficulty of Einstein's work, in fact, gave it a certain air of mystery, like a maze in a fun-house. He wrote:

> As one of the thousands who tried to follow Professor Albert Einstein through curved space with ruts in it . . . , I welcome the news that the great thinker has done it again, if anybody knew what. The timing is nice. It's been about twenty years since all right-thinking citizens were struggling to understand Einstein's relativity, so that we should be rested and ready for another romp, and I, for one, am tired of being confused by trivialities; it will be a pleasure to be confused about something cosmic.[35]

Accounts like Yoder's were, in reality, thinly disguised criticism of the scientists' presumption that every well-educated citizen *must* understand even the most poorly-explained science. These commentators objected to the expectation that every literate person should be prepared to strive for such understanding. According to this view, the confused layperson should not protest but should instead try to puzzle through new theories, no matter how difficult they seemed. If the readers did not understand, then it was their fault, not that of the scientists.

The Creator/Destroyer

> The present direction of economic and political forces holds out no hope that physical science can . . . escape from being used for the destruction of the world that it has helped to create.[36]

Twentieth-century advances in medicine restored health to millions, but they also disrupted natural cycles of aging and death. Advances in botany and chemistry increased crop yields, but many were later discovered to have altered the natural ecology. Even the most seemingly benign scientific knowledge, therefore, could bring unpredicted side effects or create new problems. As a consequence, the theme of science as both creator and destroyer played often in the writings of critics, and was the basis of a third general stereotype.[37]

This stereotype contains special ambiguity. In creating scientific knowledge, a scientist initiated some action or provoked some reaction, usually positive; however, unlike other creative people in society (such as artists, musicians, or architects), some scientists worked on ideas intended to destroy (e.g., on chemical weapons). Moreover, research could lead to products initially regarded as helpful but later found to have negative side effects (e.g., DDT). Science also enabled people to think in new ways that altered the political and social status quo; to see, for example, animal species as evolutionary rather than discrete, or to regard mental illness as related to some environmental, physical, or genetic cause rather than to the impurity of a patient's soul. Writers linked experimentation on nitrogen fixation for fertilizers to the use of the same ideas in World War I explosives, for example.[38] Charles F. Kettering observed in 1933 that each laboratory discovery seemed to have double potential:

> So that we might kill one another more expertly, science found wonderful ways to live more comfortably, richly, to communicate more rapidly. So that we might exterminate one another more successfully, science showed us how we might all live longer and stronger . . . [39]

In the popular magazines, this image appeared to be peculiarly personal; that is, it regarded the individual scientist as creator or destroyer. It was the image of an actor, not an action. Some of this emphasis resulted from standard editorial practices that, in mass-circulation magazines, searched for the human element. Science writers hoped to animate, not just illuminate, science by focusing on one person rather than on a laboratory or project. During the late 1940s, stories about atomic-bomb research, for example, would often center on anecdotes about the physicists who worked at Los Alamos, rather than on explanations of the principles of atomic physics or organization of the project.

The journalistic practice of linking scientists directly to their scientific accomplishments represented more than a convenient rhetorical device; it was derived from the social structure of science itself. Although scientific norms emphasize coordinated effort and shared knowledge, they also require careful assignment of reward and credit. Scientists' names appear on all their published works. Moreover, the scientific practice of eponymy—that is, affixing the name of the scientist to all or part of what he or she has found (for example, the Salk polio vaccine)—further assures that an individual's accomplishment will be credited outside some immediate circle of knowledgeable colleagues.[40] When discoveries proved beneficial, this connection of worker to work had pleasant ramifications for the scientists' public image. When the same notion linked creators to harmful effects, then the practice backfired. The research and theories of Charles Darwin, for example, made possible an extraordinary new understanding of the natural world, but many religious people regarded those concepts (and, by implication, the very name of Darwin) as inimical to the most sacred assumptions of their faith. Similarly, as Sigmund Freud's ideas gained popularity in the United States, as scientific support for a biological concept of human nature grew, and as many scientists proposed startling theories of sociological and psychological deviance, Freud's name became a term synonymous, for some people, with amorality, liberal sexuality, and a general decline in social values.[41] Magazine writers frequently used the names of Darwin and Freud as examples of "disruptive" scientists who had "deliberately" attempted to destroy social and moral ideals. Such use of scientists' names thus helped to reward individuals with perpetual credit, but it also assigned blame.

The image of the scientist as a Janus-like creator/destroyer occurred most often in conjunction with descriptions of physicists. In the 1930s, astronomers and physicists proposed views of the universe that some people found alien and disconcerting—for example, the idea that the universe was expanding or that all physical reality is composed of particles too small to be seen with existing measuring devices. Astronomy showed the universe as "a bubble," "a mirage."[42] Many articles implied that physicists were directly responsible for unsettling the foundations of some of humanity's most cherished philosophical and religious beliefs.

After Hiroshima, physics had an even more tangible product that journalists could use as evidence of science's dangers. Immediately after the war, a few scientists even enthusiastically claimed credit for winning the conflict. The realization of what the Manhattan Project had done, however, forced most physicists to contemplate their social and professional responsibility in a new light. As the physicists' internal debates spilled into the pages of popular magazines, the discussions reinforced the implication that scientists could rationally decide between creation and destruction, an unflattering image at best. Articles described the struggles of conscience among Manhattan Project researchers and pointed to their "anachronistic American attachment to fair play even in warfare."[43] Readers were told how scientists worried about employing "the bomb with fullest effect without being accused by the world and ourselves of surpassing the Nazis and the Japs in barbarism."[44] When nuclear weapons testing continued in the 1950s against a background of increasingly hostile U.S.–Soviet relations, expressions of fear increased in the magazines. The magazines reported that no practical countermeasures or defense existed against the bomb, but that a few scientists still had "an odd proprietary pride in the monstrous weapon they helped create."[45] They characterized the new bomb, an "apocalyptic mushroom-topped mountain of nuclear fire," as "the greatest threat to the survival of the human race since the Black Death."[46] As the tone of fear increased, journalists pointed toward the scientists, the designers of destruction.

Such linkage probably contributed to a shift in the images of all sciences which took place in the early 1950s, as the locus of responsibility was extended beyond the act of creation to how knowledge is used. Commentators implied that scientists had some new obligation to construct a technical fix for any problem they identified or created. Once biologists identified a disease agent, the logic ran, they had a social responsibility to develop a vaccine. Likewise, new weapons must be deployed once they were designed, but the scientists who developed more efficient means of warfare were also expected to create technical defensive countermeasures. Knowledge carried with it a mandate for action. It was the scientists' responsibility to provide the defense against any potential destructive impact of science, and they should want to do so. After all, one article pointed out, scientists "do not like the idea of going down in history as merchants of death on a colossal scale."[47]

To the mathematician or astronomer working in scholastic isolation, these discussions perhaps seemed irrelevant. Their work only rarely produced any dramatic results worthy of public attention; the problem appeared to be one for other scientists, not for them. In fact, because popular accounts frequently obscured the distinctions between the disciplines, the audiences most likely applied such responsibility to all researchers. It mattered little whether the adverse consequences were those of a persistent pesticide, a wayward microbe, or an apocalyptic weapon. Scientists were all part of a unified community of responsibility, this image declared.

The development after World War II of powerful electronic computers further complicated these attitudes, for computers posed a threat heretofore discussed only in science fiction. When writers asked "Can a Mechanical Brain Replace *You?*," they described machines perceived as similar to the human processes they modeled.[48] Stories about computers also directed attention to the dual nature of intellectual discovery. A *Post* article called computers "wonder-working robots whose power for good or evil, for creativeness in peace or destruction in war, exceeds that of supersonic flight and nuclear fission."[49] The new machines threatened "human security and welfare," the author declared. Even cyberneticist Norbert Wiener was quoted as being afraid that "if the robots could be used as tools to manipulate a national economy wisely, they could also, in the hands of greedy individuals or totalitarian governments, be used as deadly weapons."[50] These and other articles portrayed computers as "monsters" that worked through the "apparently heartless mechanics of numbers"; many writers referred, in conjunction with articles on computers, to the classic "mad scientist" legend of Frankenstein.[51] *Collier's* editor John Lear asked, "Isn't this a fulfillment of Frankenstein—that man would someday build a thinking machine which would plot his own subjugation?"[52] Although in the next passage Lear answered no, the overall tone of the article left the question open.

It would be easy to assume that the creator/destroyer image was wholly negative. Some modern critics in fact assert that references to the "mad doctor" image indicate "a legitimate public fear of the scientist's stripped-down, depersonalized conception of knowledge—a fear that our scientists . . . will go on being titans who create monsters."[53] However, when popular magazine writers used this creator/destroyer image, they usually did not assess scientists' intentions; instead, the image reflected a more matter-of-fact, neutral assigning of responsibility. The image did not, of itself, portray scientists as bad. It assumed a simple form of public equity: those who sought credit or reward for their actions or ideas were expected to accept blame if science went awry.

America's New Heroes

Drawing on many positive attributes, such as diligence, intelligence, creativity, and luck, the image of the scientist as hero combined several types widely represented in popular culture: an athletic or outdoors type who was self-reliant and strong, competitive but fair; a self-made man, exemplified by an attractive, well-dressed, successful inventor; and a "Lucky Lindy" or "Boy Scout" hero, who resembled the traditional American frontiersman but who advocated good citizenship, was confident and courageous, yet shy and unassuming, even unsophisticated.[54] Components of each type existed in the images of scientists as new national heroes.

"Boosterism" attitudes of the 1920s played a significant role in the magazines' hero-worship of scientists. After World War I, America underwent "a notable quickening of the pace of change, a period when things began to move so fast that the past, from then on, looked static."[55] Picking up on this theme, magazines encouraged readers to strive harder to improve themselves in all sorts of ways, intellectually as well as physically. A plethora of self-help publications and courses instructed novices in "self-boosting." In *American* articles then, young people were admonished to emulate this or that "self-made" scientist. Alexander Graham Bell advised young Americans to "Get an Idea of Your Own."[56] Intuition was "merely another name for mental laziness."[57] To Charles Steinmetz, "The World Belongs to the Dissatisfied"; the best scientist was never content with traditional explanations and methods.[58] Inventors and scientists, Steinmetz said, must always be willing to work hard to achieve their goals. The personal philosophy of an industrial chemist similarly held that "The World's Most Tragic Man Is One Who Never Starts."[59]

Magazine coverage of Charles F. Kettering epitomized the use of this hero theme.[60] A six-part biography in the *Post* emphasized Kettering's practical philosophy and intense drive, calling him a "monkey-wrench scientist," a practical man who "detests . . . modern ballyhoo."[61] In another article, Kettering himself asserted that "imagination and faith backed up by determination and hard work" would get America out of the Depression.[62] Especially during the 1930s, articles in the *Post* and similar magazines admonished readers to become "self-starters" in order to pull themselves out of the current economic crisis. In these stories, writers held up science as a primary means of achieving fame and fortune. In a 1937 article, Kettering directed readers down "Ten Paths to Fame and Fortune," all of which went by way of the scientific laboratory.[63]

This theme evolved from descriptions of accomplishment as well as from promises. The scientist as hero "delivered" consistently and constantly; moreover, he was never content to rest on his laurels. Creative, inspired, dedicated, and self-reliant, the scientist forged ahead, always seeking new territories to explore. The public must not question if the scientist would succeed, this image declared; readers should only wonder when. Public beliefs that allowed writers to ask such questions as "Can the scientists get there in time with new sources of food?" excluded the possibility of failure or defeat.[64] They relied on a determined social optimism and a near-spiritual faith in science's heroic spirit. Historian Charles Rosenberg believes that the research scientist of the 1920s in fact represented the availability to American writers of a new heroic type, exemplified by Sinclair Lewis's choice of a scientist as protagonist for his heroic novel *Arrowsmith* (1925).[65] This fictional researcher was a "hero not of deeds, but of the spirit," one who overcame material values through a near-spiritualistic calling to science.[66] To Lewis, the scientific hero possessed integrity and dignity as well as the restlessness of the pioneering spirit. As the magazines of the time show, this image was widely accepted.

Summary

Each of these stereotypes characterized scientists as somehow distinguishable from ordinary people. The themes stressed differences rather than similarities. When the scientists were described as wizards, they seemed mysteriously clever, possessing secret knowledge and holding considerable power over nature. As experts, they knew all and could be asked to share their knowledge with society. As creators and destroyers, they bore responsibility, both positive and negative, for the end results of that knowledge. As heroes, they combined an optimistic belief in a better future with insatiable curiosity, restlessness, a drive to explore, and the ability to explore new paths.

Hard work was an important aspect of each type. At the laboratory bench, scientists exhibited strength, endurance, and a willingness to make personal sacrifices; they gained sympathy and respect, even if the knowledge created also had negative effects. The belief that scientists "embody the ideal of selfless devotion to truth," coupled with the conclusion that "what they discover also contributes to practical improvement," thus helped to support contemporary faith in science.[67] Higher goals kept scientists in science, lest "the strenuous, strength-consuming, self-dominating practice of science" seem, by comparison to other professions, "not worth the unceasing, nerve-racking exertion . . ." [68] In descriptions of scientific work, writers frequently threw out some anchorline to usefulness. Even the most glamorous research, they implied, required drudgery if it was to be real science.

In 1918, the typical physical stereotype (e.g., "whiskers, stringy hair, total absence of paunch . . ."[69]) suggested a person who was out of touch with fashion and therefore out of touch with reality—that is, an impractical theorist. By 1926, many U.S. scientists promoted science's value to industry and proposed plans for national support of research. Popular descriptions praised scientists who combined dedication to work and unlimited scientific vision with a practical business sense. This emphasis also reflected the growth of industry funding for research. By the 1950s, the mention of such intimate personal details as dandruff or untidy clothing had disappeared from even articles critical of science. Writers were far more likely to paint a scientist in realistic but pragmatic, impersonal strokes. Articles focused less on the individual, on the "human" side of science; instead, they included nonevaluative recitals of a scientist's education or experience.

Some of these shifts in images reflected changing journalistic or editorial styles; but it is also likely that, by the 1950s, events had proved that science was not automatically innocuous. Chemistry in World War I, pharmaceutical side effects, the atomic bomb, and many other scientific creations demonstrated once and for all that the stereotype of a personable but ineffectual scientist was simply wrong; neither writers nor readers found it credible any longer.

7

Defining Science: How Scientists Work

I can hear my good friend, the Professor of Biology, rather
impatiently reporting that his science asks assent only to what it can
demonstrate. "Come with me to my laboratory, and I will give you
proofs. . . ." But how am I, quite untrained in his science, to weigh
his arguments or interpret what his microscope may show?

R. K. Root, 1912[1]

Every basic journalism course begins with the five W's: who, what, when,
where, and why. In teaching about science journalism, we usually add
"how," for the methods far more than the facts provide the authority that
underpins scientific proofs. Trust in science, faith in science, fear of science, all are influenced by beliefs, correct or incorrect, about the accuracy,
reliability, and certainty of researchers' methods. Nonscientists cannot independently verify scientists' conclusions; they cannot repeat the experiments; they may not even know how to focus a microscope—they must
trust the researchers' account of what appears in the lens. When they are
couched in authoritative scientific language, all arguments can seem
equally legitimate to the person who is not a scientist; only the scientists'
endorsement promotes one and dismisses the other. Moreover, the methods
empower the scientists' promises. Even if we do not really understand the
methods, we must take the proofs of the promises on faith because the
methods cannot be doubted.

Despite their importance to the ultimate message about science, descriptions of research methods in twentieth-century popular magazines
were uniformly inaccurate, and this failing was not apparently connected
to the author's background or training. Both scientists and journalists
wrote a lot about what took place in the laboratory but explained little.
And both engaged in oversimplification and exaggeration. Such inaccurate
descriptions of research methods encouraged a false idea of what science
could do.

110

One common writing practice served to widen the gulf of misunderstanding further: popularizers tended to describe not just scientists but scientific work as "different" and failed to define that distinction precisely. Although some authors declared that "the method of science is only the ordinary method of men, more carefully and critically worked," others implied that scientific work differed mysteriously from ordinary work.[2] Neither the underlying cognitive processes, the administrative organization, nor the methods of analysis were perceived as the same as those used by other professionals who accomplished complex tasks.

To demonstrate one aspect of this difference, some authors dwelled on the extraordinary objectivity and neutrality of scientists' methods. They called scientific research free from the prejudices and biases normally inhibiting human judgments and actions. "Science is but a method," Hans Zinsser wrote; "Whatever its material, an observation accurately made and free of compromise to bias and desire, and undeterred by consequence, is science."[3]

Some magazine descriptions concentrated wholly on specific techniques or equipment; some ignored technique and concentrated on theory. Whatever the chosen focus, however, writers almost always evaluated research by comparing it to some hypothetical set of typical methods. They used this comparison as the yardstick for assessing legitimacy, for determining what was science, and for determining who was a legitimate scientist. Ultimately, those biases constructed an image of irresponsibility, for the criteria they emphasized were those acceptable to mainstream scientists, not necessarily those desired by society.

Emphasizing the Concrete

Science is in fact ready-made for presentation as drama; it has suspense, action, and resolution, and early popularizers enthusiastically exploited these characteristics. "Heartbreaking failures, death, apparently insurmountable obstacles" all resolved once a project was completed—researchers then "breathed a collective sigh of relief."[4] Science epitomized America's greatest adventure, and scientists, its most altruistic heroes.

A tendency to personify research aided this dramatization. In all types of writings about science, the "worker" sometimes became synonymous with the "work," particularly in the characterization of intellectual or moral attributes.[5] Journalists rather naturally sought to personalize descriptions of research, for that helped to make abstract ideas seem comprehensible. Moreover, long explanations of rational decision processes were dull fodder for some magazine writers; the temptation to insert an unrelated anecdote or to romanticize a description must have been very strong. Writers also often lacked the skills required to describe research completely and accurately; personal anecdotes thus could substitute for more thorough explanations of research projects.[6]

Another popular method for "humanizing" descriptions of science was to glamorize the equipment and laboratories. Flames in Bunsen burners, rows of glistening glassware, crackling electronic equipment, and cluttered lab benches were popular subjects for science writers. Although a few journalists attempted to describe laboratories seriously and accurately, many more built up fantastic settings for high drama. They told of "fancy" laboratories with "batteries of microscopes, fuming retorts, mathematical formulas a mile long."[7] "Dedicated scientists," readers were advised, could be found "happily lost in their maze of pipettes, smells, and gas flames . . ."[8] One interviewer said that Charles Steinmetz had "a manner of moving about which resembled countless little sparks that flashed from the electrodes of an experimental apparatus which formed a background for him while he talked,"[9] although other writers stated just as clearly that Steinmetz needed only "pencil, paper, cigars, and a five-place table of logarithms"[10] to do his work.

For many writers, the chemistry lab represented the archetype of the scientific environment (see Figures 7.1 and 7.2). A magazine laboratory was incomplete without "orderly racks of test tubes lining the black, unpolished work tables, the many-sized chemical bottles crowding the shelves."[11] This attitude spilled into evaluations of the legitimacy of other fields. An *American* article described a parapsychology laboratory as "unlike any other scientific workshop in the world," primarily because it had "no Bunsen burners or smelly retorts, no shelves of many-colored chemicals in jars"; nevertheless, the author asserted, the findings of parapsychology "are as real as chemicals in a test tube."[12]

Writers sometimes used equipment as a metaphor for scientists' attributes and motives, referring, for example, to "the quiet, workmanlike dignity" of a laboratory and its contents.[13] This practice was common in articles on astronomy, where mechanical aids to vision took on almost metaphysical importance, helping astronomers peer into the future, just as microscopes helped biologists see beneath "the surface of things."

The instruments most frequently described were those that extended a researcher's vision: microscopes and telescopes. Despite authoritative assertions in the 1910s that a modern astronomer "does not rely on his telescope for measurements" and instead "uses the spectroscope and the interferometer,"[14] journalists writing about astronomy in the 1950s still emphasized descriptions of telescopes, probably because such instruments were familiar in design and impressive in size. Historian Nathan Reingold has observed that large-scale scientific instruments, such as the Mt. Palomar telescope and the cyclotron, were popular because they "reflected the

IT'S THE LITTLE THINGS THAT COUNT

By LOGAN CLENDENING

CARTOONS BY WYNCIE KING

internal structures, close you up and put you back to bed without doing you any real harm at all, and yet he doesn't know how to cure a fever blister.

This is especially true if he is a younger man in medicine. His time has been too much taken up tending to the big subjects—operations and queer complicated deviations from the smooth curve of the normal. As time goes on, he finds, too, that it's the little things that count—more people have them, and they are more anxious to get rid of them. Not long ago, in conversation with one of the most distinguished surgeons of the United States, I asked what was the subject of his paper before the surgical congress, with delegates from all over the world. His answer was "Corns." All of which forcibly reminds me of my first patient. Every doctor, I suppose, has a story about his first patient—we should get up a collection of them sometime.

She came in the office, that first patient of mine, I remember, with a troubled countenance, and began with great volubility to explain exactly why she had chosen me for consultation. She had heard that I had just completed a course of hospital residence in the East, and she felt certain that I must have the very latest ideas on medical science.

What, I kept asking myself—what wild and exotic derangement of function could be going on inside that superficially very healthy-looking exterior? I was fully prepared for something extremely choice, when finally I ventured to ask her what was her trouble, and she answered, "Sweating feet."

I must have looked abashed. I had never heard of a remedy for sweating feet, nor even that one had ever been suggested. If my patient had had some fancy and involved ailment, such as myelogenous leukemia, or subphrenic abscess, I would have been perfectly capable of attending her with every display of that very latest lore for which she yearned. We had plenty of those cases in the hospital. But sweating feet had never been mentioned by any of my instructors or chiefs.

Ignominiously I excused myself and rushed down the hall to the office of an older practitioner, who chuckled at my story and whispered the magic words, "Formaldehyde, teaspoonful to a pint of cold water; soak 'em night and morning."

There seems, however, to have been a change in the attitude of the faculty minds in this respect lately. A few years ago the least thing that any research worker would stoop to consider as a research subject was the cause of cancer. Propaganda in the form of the formation of societies for the control and prevention of were formed for heart disease and cancer. We were treated to hair-raising discourses on Sunday evenings on the increasing mortality of heart disease. The lecturer, selected from the less-busy group in the local medical society, had, in most instances, apparently been spending a good part of his time in the deadhouse, and he brought an unetuous enthusiasm to the description of the situation, which caused many of his auditors to stagger out into the night for a gulp of air. The death rate from heart disease is increasing—that was the burden of the song.

Symptoms and remedies were described most graphically. The lecturers were like the fat boy in Pickwick, "I wants to make your flesh creep."

SCIENTIFIC LABORATORIES ARE EXTERMINATING THE LITTLE FLEAS OF PATHOLOGY

What difference is all this to a person who hasn't got—and probably never will have—heart disease or cancer, but whose whole career is soured by warts, and superfluous hair, and sweating under the armpits, and white spots on the skin, and monthly attacks of migraine? There is something heroic about heart disease. You die a martyr's death, leaving pathetic little notes around, about what you want sung at your funeral. Or if you don't die, you are the center of every solicitude, surrounded by handsome nurses day and night, assisted in every move, and visited by friends who blink to keep back the tears, thinking of what a loss you will be to the community.

But, to repeat, things are changing. The gleaming armamentarium of the laboratory is turned on many of the annoying little fleas (Continued on Page 89)

ot a matter of life and death," bout her ailments, "but it's so metimes I wish it were."
e first English dermatologist, same strain: Speaking of bald-disease is not much of Danger, rpitude or Disgrace, insomuch g the Romans, labouring under dervalued and sold at a much

of a good many letters from iesses and bodily troubles, and s are of that minor kind. And the medical profession doesn't most cases, about how to help h things.
question that the medical man . And if you want to witness try it on some distinguished to meet in a social gathering. t noble and shining figure, al-surance and ability. Stroll up ctor, what's good for a fever

anybody, at least any doctor, ut he can't. He doesn't know n you do. He smiles and says,
   if the
torts,
ack,"
d; has

, that
on. It
ad of
" ad-
ce, in
were
uldn't
And it
tating
man
rrange
cious-
aping
rough
ne of
rtant

WYNCIE   KING

Figure 7.1.   Instruments such as microscopes were the frequent subjects of cartoons or drawings used to illustrate articles on science. These whimsical cartoons by Wyncie King nevertheless made subtle statements about the scientists' willingness and ability to solve "real-life" problems like baldness and the common cold. From Logan Clendening, "It's the Little Things that Count," *The Saturday Evening Post,* 7 March 1936, 27. Reprinted with permission from *The Saturday Evening Post,* © 1936 by Curtis Publishing Company.

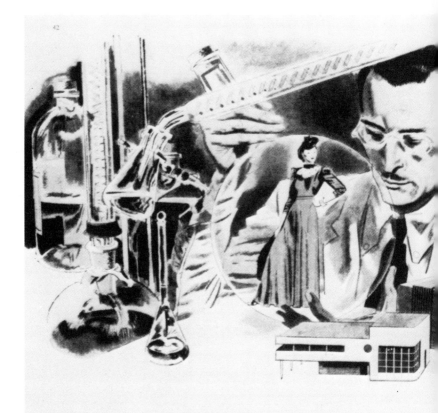

Out of the test tube comes a thrilling age of magic, in which you will melt your un—
dishes down the drain, buy 50 new suits of clothes and throw them away unlaundered
Today your toothbrush handle is a laboratory product; tomorrow your whole home s

THE alarm clock rings. Seven o'clock. You yawn, stretch, roll out of bed, and make your way to the shower. The curtains that you throw back and forth are—what? Waterproof synthetic fabrics. You step out and sit down to dry yourself—on what? A stool enameled with a synthetic lacquer.

The shaving brush and toothbrush that you manipulate a few minutes later have gaudy handles. Bone? No. Synthetic resin. Maybe you use an old-fashioned glass for your mouthwash, but if you don't—and the chances are twenty to one that you don't—the tumbler is sure to be a synthetic plastic.

At breakfast you dig into a grapefruit. What chilled it? Ice, of course, but ice made by a synthetic in the coils of the kitchen electric refrigerator. Glance

around and take stock of the dining-room. Those curtains at the windows—? They look like silk, and maybe they are. Yet, if your home is furnished more or less like millions of others, they are fashioned of one of a half-dozen types of rayon.

You climb into your car to catch the 8:15 for town and your office. The steering wheel that you clutch is a synthetic cousin of the shaving-brush and tooth-brush handles and of the tumbler that you grasped an hour ago. The shatter-proof windshield through which you keep an eye on the road is a sandwich consisting of two sheets of glass and a transparent synthetic "ham" that prevents splinters from flying if there should be a crash. Even the spectacle frame that encloses the lenses on your nose is

a synthetic product of the la

In this sense women are e "synthetic" than men. The coating of their heels, the trim their hats, the lipstick with w improve on nature, the holder i they thrust a cigarette, the ha which the usual odds and end ried, the jewelry that matc rayon gowns or their eyes, the teners that take the place of t much of what they hang upe selves has no counterpart in tl or vegetable world.

To John Doe "synthetic" tricky substitute for something tic—a meaning which is an un relic of prohibition, when raw alcohol was inexpertly flavore duce a potent but unconvin

Figure 7.2.   The opening to "The World Has Just Begun," Waldemar Kaempffert's predictive article in the January 1940 *American*, shows many of the common visual images of scientific

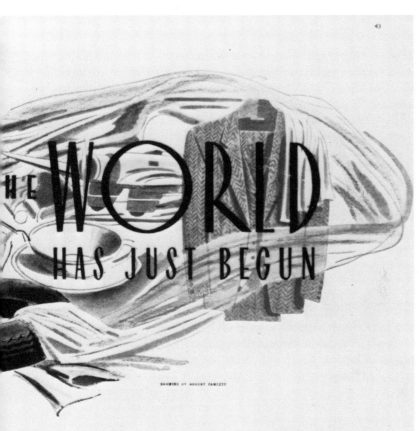

43

THE WORLD HAS JUST BEGUN

DRAWING BY ROBERT FAWCETT

derstanding makes chemists
py To them synthesis means
ways meant—a putting to-
ynthetic is one of the noblest
an, because it is a deliberate
very difficult assemblage of
nto a compound which may
new and which always has
and sometimes commer-
ble properties.
tic vanilla that cannot be dis-
from the natural extract, a
ndigo that is a duplicate of
e extracted from a plant, a
amphor that has broken the
ests for purity, a synthetic
ich a screen play is photo-
delight and thrill millions, is
deception. Nor is a synthetic
or sulfapyridine, which is
dreds stricken with pneu-
r are the scores of artificial
ries, horns, and tortoise shells
pose half the gadgets in a
ne
s books are full of fairies who
wands and change pumpkins

into glass coaches and hovels into pal-
aces. The chemist does not work on a
scale quite so grand. Yet his feats in
synthesis startle even him. Synthetic
stones still called "precious"; exquisite
fabrics on which ink can be poured without leaving a spot; camphor made in a
factory at 48 cents a pound against the
$3.75 once charged for the pure, natural
product; synthetic musk, base of all per-
fumes, at $7 a pound against $300 for
the very impure secretion obtained from
a Tibetan deer; cement which does away
with the necessity of stitching the uppers
and soles of women's shoes together;
fiber that looks and feels like silk but is
worked up from acetylene gas; explosives and fertilizers plucked out of the
air—he and we survey his accomplishments and ask: What next? The answer is never long in coming.

Hardly a month passes but a new compound turns up with amazing properties.

One of the latest is a plastic as clear as
glass but only half as heavy. It leaves
you wondering if you have not been the
victim of a trick, even after you have ex-
perimented with it yourself. Throw it
against a wall. It bounces back un-
broken. Airplane and bus windows are
being made of it.

At night on a dark road the beams of
your headlights fall on little jewels of it
which stud road signs and gleam like
rows of cats' eyes. Take a thick cork-
screw of it ten feet long and hold a light
at one end. The rays follow the coils and
come out at the other end—cold. Already physicians and dentists are beginning to use this lucite, as it is called.

An up-to-date specialist, for example,
will thrust a rod of it back of your palate
and illuminate your larynx with a bright,
cold light. The latest illuminated tongue
depressors are made of it, so that they
glow like (Continued on page 129)

by Waldemar Kaempffert

research: test tubes and beakers, a scientist in white coat and glasses, and a cornucopia of
new products emerging from the research lab. Drawing by Robert Fawcett.

115

nation's natural endowment; great instrumentation reflected the supposed American propensity for 'practical' devices rather than the abstruse theorizing of true savants."[15] This preoccupation was borne out in the magazine articles. "Big Eye," a 1935 article in *American,* outlined the construction of the new 200-inch telescope at Mt. Palomar;[16] "Peephole on the Universe," published in the same magazine in 1947, related the problems that had plagued the project when construction was halted by the war;[17] a *Collier's* article in that same year, "The Big Eye," described the installation of a new mirror.[18] Palomar was especially popular with journalists because it fed neatly into an attractive metaphor: it represented a "Window to the Universe."[19]

Journalists' inclinations to write about equipment and instruments varied of course with editorial styles and requirements, and with changing fashions in research (reflecting what scientists themselves said in their interviews), but scientific instrumentation remained a consistently popular topic. There were identifiable shifts in how writers described the research process, however. In the 1910s and 1920s, writers presented research more as a set of measurable activities (e.g., "observing, charting, and cataloging the world"[20]) than as a cognitive process. Writers chose active verbs to present science as a series of precise steps, definable and replicable. They simplified the scientific method into "mainly a matter of knowing a certain number of facts, putting them together in many different ways, and adding up the results correctly."[21] "The modern chemical method" of synthesis, Samuel Crowther wrote, "is first to find out what is needed, then to study the property of various substances until all the factors needed are present and then combine these elements into a whole in much the same way that a mason builds a house."[22] Such action, he summarized, "is the scientific way as opposed to the unscientific . . ."[23]

Although these and similar descriptions proclaimed that "the scientist's method of doing things isn't nearly so mysterious as people think,"[24] they may have inadvertently increased the sense of mystery. Because nothing was ever actually explained in such articles, they created an atmosphere of scientific unintelligibility. For example, the phrase "putting them together in many different ways" gave a superficial impression of precision, yet actually obscured the details of the methods. In the magazines, simplistic descriptions of research—where data collection or meaningless measurement was used to imply precision—may have fooled some readers into believing that they had been told how science really works.

The image of research also underwent a crucial shift in emphasis somewhere between the world wars, a shift away from research as a physical activity and toward research as primarily intellectual and passive. Here are some typical pre-1930 descriptions of what scientists supposedly do:

'A little bit of this, a little more of that, a pinch of something else, boil blank minutes, and set aside in the same vessel'—thus might read the biologists' formula for creating life . . . [25]

[A scientist's] real work is done in the silent hours of thought, the apparently aimless days of puttering around in the laboratory, and the mighty searching through reference books.[26]

Each of these methods involved specific, familiar actions, such as "pinch" and "boil" or "searching through reference books." The tone appeared to be one of admiration, even if tinged with amusement and tolerance. The scientists in the 1920s may have been odd, but they were nevertheless likable and their research methods benign.

Then, in the 1930s and 1940s, the tone of the descriptions of methods began to change:

[Research] may use a laboratory or it may not. It is purely a principle, and everybody can apply it in his own life. It is simply a way of trying to find new knowledge and ways of improving things which you are not satisfied with.[27]

Today, just about anything we can figure out on paper can be done in the laboratory, and eventually in the factory. Our technology has reached the stage where the scientist can safely say: 'If we can write it down, we can do it.'[28]

Scientific work, in the magazines of the 1930s and 1940s, appeared more as "a principle," an approach to action rather than action itself. Instead of measuring chemicals or creating electrical sparks, the scientist engaged in quieter, intellectual activities. He wrote; he theorized; he shuffled papers. The "big machines" of physics in the 1940s and 1950s also projected an unemotional, quiet image (see Figure 7.3). As the individual faded from the foreground in the articles, research seemed more an abstraction than an activity performed by a person. Research became an end to itself. The sense of human engagement faded.

Comparing hundreds of popular descriptions published before World War I with those from after World War II showed that the image of scientific methods shifted from an active, physical endeavor to one that was more reflective and cerebral. In the late 1940s, articles placed less emphasis on researchers' daily routines or laboratories and instead stressed empirical reasoning and the theory behind (or implications of) new data. As scientific methods and equipment increased in complexity, few writers attempted comprehensive explanations of what was happening in the laboratories, perhaps because of lack of expertise, perhaps because of chang-

Figure 7.3. By the 1940s, the *Post* tended to favor photographic illustrations for articles rather than line drawings. Here, in characteristic shots, physicists work on the "Big Berthas" of science: "atom smashers" at the University of California and a cyclotron at Columbia University. The article, William L. Laurence's "The Atom Gives Up" (*The Saturday Evening Post*, 7 September 1940, 12–13), was also notable for its extensive discussion of U-235 before the curtain of secrecy rang down. Reprinted with permission from *The Saturday Evening Post*, © 1940 by Curtis Publishing Company.

118

aviest found in nature, elements beyond uranium, heavyweight of the natural components of the special universe.

Meitner and Hahn devised a highly delicate atomic microscope" that enabled them to "see" what was happening chemically on the "atomic" scale of course" more clearly than could be done before, then proceeded to fire slow-speed neutrons à la carte at the uranium nucleus. And the result surprised and startled them so much that they believed some serious error had been made. They repeated the experiment, only to observe once again what they had seen in the first place—an "atomic ghost" that had no business being there. Instead of an element resembling uranium they observed an element totally different, having an atomic weight slightly little more than half the weight of uranium. The "atomic ghost" was seen to materialize itself, and lo, here, out of nowhere, appeared the element said in the taking of X-ray pictures of internal organs—barium.

A Deep Mystery of the Laboratory

BARIUM! How the deuce did it get there? Where could it have come from? There definitely was a trace of barium present when the experiment started, and yet here it was. It was like placing a duck's egg in an incubator and suddenly seeing it hatch out into a chicken.

Before a solution could be found to this scientific mystery of the first magnitude, Hitler's racial decree brought Doctor Meitner's career in Germany to an end. It had been discovered that Doctor Meitner, a scion of a family that had lived in Germany for many generations, was not "Aryan." She was forced to leave her native land to seek a haven where she could resume her life's work. Lise Meitner was on the train bound for Stockholm, sadly looking out of the window at the Berlin where she had spent her life devotedly in the pursuit of knowledge. That was a closed chapter. She was sixty years old, unmarried, and a woman without a country. She was going to a strange land, where she would try to resume her work, her unfinished strange experiment, barium.

She could not get barium out of her mind. Could it have been an impurity? Doctor Hahn was the most careful of chemists. He had been meticulously careful to exclude any possibility of the uranium being contaminated with barium, and yet, in spite of the most careful precautions, the barium appeared, like Hamlet's ghost on the ramparts. Where could the barium have come from? Nothing ever comes from nothing, and there had been no barium there to start with.

Lise Meitner's thoughts wandered far afield and kept coming back to barium. Suddenly, what seemed at first an idle thought, to be dismissed as daydreaming, flashed into her mind. Barium has about half the atomic weight of uranium. Could it be possible that the bombardment of the uranium with the slow-speed neutron bullets split the uranium atoms in two nearly equal halves, one of which was the mysterious ghost of barium that appeared in the experiments?

She attributed the thought as most likely being due to the strain she had been under during the past few days. It was too fantastic to be true. For nothing like it had ever happened before in the hundreds of thousands, if not millions, of atom-smashing experiments in leading scientific institutions all over the world, during the past twenty years. Not even the most powerful atom-smashing machines in America, largest of their kind anywhere in the world, had ever succeeded in chipping off more than a small bit of an atom. Even an elementary student of physics knew that there was not enough power available anywhere on earth to split an atom in halves, particularly the heaviest of all the elements.

She began jotting down figures on paper. Every well-informed layman knows by this time that the material universe is made up of ninety-two fundamental elements, beginning with hydrogen, the lightest, at No. 1, and ending with uranium at ninety-two. What makes the elements differ from one another is the number of positively charged electrical particles, known as protons, in their nucleus, or core. Thus hydrogen has only one positive electrical particle in its nucleus. Helium has two. Carbon has six, nitrogen seven, oxygen eight,

and so forth. If helium were to be split in halves, each half would be not helium but hydrogen. If oxygen were to lose one positive particle (proton) it would no longer be oxygen but nitrogen. Mercury contains eighty positive particles in its nucleus and gold has seventy-nine; hence if one of these could be knocked out of the mercury nucleus it would be transmuted into gold. Similarly, uranium contains ninety-two, barium fifty-six, and krypton thirty-six positive particles respectively, in their central core. Hence, if uranium could be split by some process into two uneven pieces, of fifty-six and thirty-six units each, the broken parts would be, respectively, barium and krypton.

56 and 36 and Energy Undreamed Of

HAVING scribbled the figures 56 and 36 on her notebook, Lise Meitner began doing a little more involved calculation. It takes tremendous energy to hold the unit particles in the central core of the atoms together. This is known as the "binding energy" of the atom. If an atom were to be broken in halves a certain portion of this binding energy would be released, and, in the case of a heavy atom, the amount of such binding energy that would be released should be of tremendous proportions. How much? she wondered. With expert mathematics she quickly arrived at the result and then went over her figures to make sure. . . . Yes, she was right. If a uranium atom of ninety-two positive particles were to be split into two parts, one of which consisted of 56 (barium) and the other of 36 (krypton) particles, the amount of atomic binding energy released would be the hitherto-undreamed-of figure of the order of 200,000,000 electron volts per atom, an energy 5,000,000 times greater than that released in the burning of coal.

The figures before her overwhelmed her. She was experiencing sensations that must have been akin to those of Columbus when he first sighted land, without knowing exactly what the land was. Was it the East Indies? A mirage? A new continent of untold wealth? If her figures were right, and they could well be checked, she and Doctor Hahn had accidentally stumbled upon Continued on Page 60

Dr. Winfield W. Salisbury, busy on the ions of the University of California's 225-ton atom smasher, world's largest.

Today Germany is neck-and-neck with this country in the race to develop the full powers of U-235. At left, Berlin's atom-smashing plant, which German press agents claim is the largest in the world.

ing public beliefs. By the 1950s, descriptions across the board were more likely to emphasize the cognitive processes than the physical activities of scientists.

Who's On the Team?

Similar changes occurred in images of who conducted research, especially in the idea of research as a collective activity, involving many scientists working in cooperation, and as an activity linked to credentialed professionals. Although the real rise of team science occurred after World War II, subtle shifts in the public image of science as more the product of an intellectual team than the domain of a solitary individual had in fact begun to occur earlier.[29] In popular magazines in the 1910s, individual scientists were portrayed as the center of activity; by the 1940s, however, a scientist could confidently assert that "no important scientific device in modern times has been invented by one man—no matter what the novels and movies may sometimes . . . say."[30] By that time, "the notion of the lonely genius puttering in his basement with an invention that will set the world afire" was considered to be "out of date."[31]

The shift in image coincided with science's increasing entanglement with government and politics. During World War I, magazine writers mentioned the interconnectedness of research activity, but glorified the contributions of individuals. By the time the United States entered World War II, they placed more emphasis on science as a collective activity. Waldemar Kaempffert's account of the development of the vacuum tube epitomized this approach:

> No one genius deserves all the credit. Fully a hundred first-class physicists and engineers contributed some discovery, some observation, though most of them were utterly unaware of what would flow out of their work.[32]

Following the war, emphasis on the power of teamwork continued.

Concurrent with this changing image of research as a collective activity was a persistent assertion that science should be open to amateurs. From its beginnings, American science was described as democratic, and especially early in the century, mass magazines vigorously endorsed science's egalitarianism and celebrated a stereotype of a scientific amateur. The democratic populists of the nineteenth century had asserted that scientific expression was part of the "natural disposition" of every American, was some inherent talent that anyone could cultivate if he or she only possessed sufficient intelligence and a capacity for hard work. The magazines adopted this position in the twentieth century as well.

The magazines heaped praise on obscure amateurs, especially on those who maintained some connection to the official scientific community. *American Magazine,* in particular, loved to publish profiles of such people as the California citrus farmer who did "his comet- and star-gazing in his chickenyard with a telescope he fashioned and bolted together himself."[33] This farmer was "no ivory-tower savant," however, for he routinely telegraphed his astronomical data to the Harvard observatory in Massachusetts.

Such promotion of amateur scientists fit neatly with traditional American values of entrepreneurship and enterprise. To succeed, one needed only to try, this image proclaimed. Success was possible, even in science, without such artificial aids as inherited wealth or expensive education. In fact, the magazines often implied that, next to the simpler traits of optimism and ingenuity, education and technical experience were much less significant as indicators of potential success in science. Curiosity, engineer Floyd W. Parsons summarized, was indispensable:

> The greatest discovery of this generation may be made by someone who can lay no claim to an intimate knowledge of science. The nation that will rule the earth tomorrow will likely be the one whose people have the most curiosity.[34]

The realistic potential of any amateur's contribution, of course, contradicted traditional ideas of how scientists should act; but independence, even in limited amounts, attracted journalists. *American*'s "Interesting People" section often praised those amateur scientists and inventors considered to have "bested" the establishment scientists in some way. Inventors, in particular, were regarded as acceptable rebels. Profiles of inventors frequently emphasized the victories of unconventional practitioners: "by ignoring scientific taboos and daring to be unorthodox," they created "a surprising array of new ideas."[35]

Images of amateur accomplishment in science and the potential for "chance" discovery by creative renegades could be found in magazines from the 1910s through the 1950s. In 1915, *Collier's,* for example, praised the "Pioneers of Invention."[36] In 1951, a *Post* article ("Are We Stifling the Inventors?") took a similar approach, touting innovative research as the key to maintaining the nation's "technical superiority" in military technology.[37]

This popular celebration of the amateur actually reflects somewhat the history of the scientific disciplines themselves. In their intellectual youth, chemistry and physics were indeed the domain of "amateurs," in that few scientists derived their living from their science. There was little uniformity in education and training, and relatively few scientific journals existed. Professional associations for the natural and physical sciences were founded in the nineteenth century; post-baccalaureate training in science improved with the strengthening of American graduate schools in the twentieth century. As each field became more professionalized, the role and status of amateur scientists in it diminished. In some fields, however, such as astronomy and ornithology, the amateur still plays a significant role in data gathering, if only a peripheral role in status and reward.[38]

Although the popular image, then, tended to reflect an exaggerated role for the amateur scientist, it was not altogether incorrect in allocating major importance to their contributions.

Legitimate Science

Because of confusion over who should be labeled as professional scientists, popular magazines tended to use the methods and processes of science, much more than the formal credentials of the persons employing them, as touchstones for scientific legitimacy. *Proper* science and *proper* scientists used scientific methods in appropriate ways, according to certain conventions and rules. Moreover, hard work (usually defined as long hours spent in laboratories or observatories) lent credence and authority to a field.

One indicator of legitimacy commonly used by popular writers was technical language. Harold Goddard, writing in *Atlantic* in 1918, explained that the "genius scientist" may be distinguished from the charlatan by examining how each used scientific terms.[39] The unreliability of such a criterion became evident, of course, whenever writers labeled something as scientific simply because it "sounded like" science.

Most often, the magazine's labels reflected the mainstream scientists' own assessment of what was appropriate science. In the 1920s, for example, many natural and physical scientists did not regard psychology as a legitimate, mature scientific discipline, and magazine articles from this period attended to the debate.[40] The new field of psychology had "captured the public imagination" quickly, and people wanted to know more about the psychoanalytic techniques of such people as Freud, Adler, and Jung: "The psychologist's word, from industrial management to child-rearing, held new authority."[41] But the rest of science did not share this enthusiasm. Physicists and biologists, believing that psychology studied factors that were intrinsically unmeasurable (in particular, such intangibles as emotion), argued that psychologists were not legitimate scientists. They considered psychologists' research methods less rigorous than those used by other sciences, and expressed those opinions strongly in interviews and articles.

Debate quickly spilled from the scientific meetings into the pages of the popular magazines. Sensitive to the criticism, many psychologists countered these attacks by publishing articles in popular magazines which described their methods at length and emphasized the applicability of their work. Other scientists responded with even more stinging criticisms of psychology. Zoologist Julian Huxley, writing in *Harper's* in 1926, asserted that psychology "is still in her first period. She teems with violent and mutually contradictory theories . . ."[42] But he then defended the legitimacy of its results, acknowledging that psychological data "have as complete validity on their own level as do biological data on the biological level . . ."[43] In the next issue of *Harper's,* psychologist John B. Watson set down the criteria necessary for psychology to achieve validity: some common ground of investigation, replicability, and similarity of method.

> To be a science, psychology must use the same material that all sciences use. Its facts must be capable of verification by other capable investigators everywhere. Its methods must be the methods of science in general.[44]

Psychologists writing in these forums spoke, in fact, to two separate audiences; they used the magazines as platforms from which to "preach back" to the scientific community, as well as from which to plead their cause with the public. They aimed to win over skeptics, to dispel the scorn with which many natural and physical scientists greeted psychology, and to refute the accusation that psychology had been embraced and distorted by amateurs, commercial psychology counselors, and hucksters. As practitioners and expositors of pop psychology—such as spiritualists and character analysts—flourished, their notoriety fueled reactions from scientists outside of psychology. The resulting hubbub encouraged many mainstream psychologists to respond publicly: in "Psychology Goldbricks," a professor of psychology set out to "debunk" the practice of commercial character analysis because it was not "real" psychology.[45] In proof, the professor described how character readers refused to participate in a process set up by the Psychology Division of the American Association for the Advancement of Science to require the licensing of all persons who practiced or taught "applied psychology."[46] Had these people been legitimate scientists, he implied, they would have cooperated with the established organizations.

The growing use of psychoanalysis stimulated further magazine criticism of both psychology and psychiatry. *Scribner's* noted that the public often perceived analysts as members of a "mystic cult" who used a "quack method of treatment," but the same article criticized the field as a whole for not yet using a "scientific method in the laboratory sense."[47] Some critics expressed the opinion that none of the social sciences could ever "reach solid conclusions or yield much sound advice for years to come," even though a "hierarchy of priests of reason has arisen to decry instinct and custom and insist that science and reason are sufficient lamps for our feet."[48] Central to this debate was whether the psychologists' object of study—the human mind—was an appropriate topic for scientific investigation. As George Draper wrote in *Scribner's:*

To use the term *scientific* in connection with the existing methods of analytical psychology at once arouses controversy. It is stoutly maintained by some that science being really a matter of numerical measurement cannot possibly concern itself with imponderables.[49]

To many physical scientists, the "humanistic sciences," sociology and psychology, could never be objective, despite their claims to the contrary. Experiments and analysis of data in the social sciences could not be value-free (as they were in the other sciences, these critics implied), because "the presentation of their truths must necessarily show the active influence of the human temperament" that they study.[50] Physicist Erwin Schroedinger, like many other popularizers, simplistically divided all science into two separate "groups of sciences."[51] In one group he placed what he called "the 'exact' sciences"; in the other, fields such as sociology and psychology "that deal with the human spirit and its activities." He tied legitimacy to the use of a definable (although not explicitly defined) group of methods.

Although a few physical and life scientists declared in the magazines that the social sciences "can and must become a full-blown science [*sic*]," these observations always seemed to be made grudgingly.[52] Writers carefully pointed out that achieving status as a real science—that is, knowing "how to effect the transformation" to legitimacy—would be difficult. The problem lay in the social sciences' ability (or inability) to increase the accuracy, objectivity, and replicability of their methods, as well as to diminish what writers like Schroedinger termed "the influence of the human temperament."

The drive for more quantitative methods and for what was called a value-free social science conflicted with other influences within the social sciences, which in the early twentieth century were frequently characterized as "a mixture of social service, ethics, and liberal Christianity."[53] Psychology and the rest of the social sciences were regarded as a set of fledgling disciplines, well-intentioned and socially-directed but immature and unsophisticated. The social sciences still searched for acceptably rigorous methods; they imitated the language of the physical sciences, and they had a supposedly unscientific preoccupation with human emotion. Society seemed to regard the social sciences as having questionable validity, even though the topics they addressed were tied to problems that all agreed were important.

The legacy of these public conflicts continued after the war, and demonstrates just how popular images can influence policy making.[54] In the late 1940s, the public image of the social sciences as less than legitimate seriously inhibited their quest for a share of public funding. As the U.S. Congress considered legislation to establish the National Science

Foundation (NSF), the definition of what actually constituted *science* became a heated political issue.[55] Because the establishment of the NSF derived from an initiative present in a letter President Franklin Roosevelt had written to Vannevar Bush (which had prompted the writing of *Science— The Endless Frontier*), debate arose over, among other things, the appropriate interpretation of that directive.[56] Should the proposed agency include the social sciences as well as the natural and physical sciences? In the late 1940s and early 1950s, American social scientists had insufficient status and support within the research community as a whole to maintain a strong position in the political jockeying. American voters and the Congress also apparently did not recognize the practical potential of social science research.[57] As research disciplines, the social sciences may have seemed immature compared to such fields as physics. Critics also exploited the controversial nature of some social science research, such as Alfred Kinsey's studies of sexual behavior. Others condemned sociologists for being apologists for criminals.

As a consequence of such attitudes, which were amply represented among members of Congress, many proponents of the NSF feared that including the social sciences in the enabling legislation would endanger political support for the entire proposal. During the legislative hearings, witnesses expressed "a general sense of uneasiness that the potential—or actual—results of social science research might challenge deeply entrenched value-centered beliefs."[58] As an analysis of the debates later concluded,

> the social sciences tended to have unfavorable connotations for many people: as connected with socialism, authoritarianism, and improper manipulation of people; as an attempt to apply scientific methods to a field that lay beyond the reach of science; as connected with 'isms' and 'crackpot ideas.'[59]

Although the initial legislation actually included the social sciences, President Truman vetoed that bill (for unrelated reasons), and the social science lobby had less success in subsequent legislative drives. When the act establishing the National Science Foundation was finally made law in 1950, it did not explicitly mention the social sciences, and those fields continue to experience an uneasy existence within the agency and throughout American science.[60]

Quick Steps

Popularizers in the magazines, both journalists and scientists, sought to present scientific research as a process different from all other processes, at once worthy of respect, yet also simply a more complicated version of ordinary ways of thinking and analysis. Thus, ornithologists "looked at birds" and astronomers "looked at stars." When writers attempted just such superficial explanations of research methods, their prose nevertheless implied that *looking* meant something entirely different—and therefore perhaps all the more mysterious. This descriptive approach was not confined to sensationalistic articles or to scientifically unsophisticated writers; science journalists and scientists alike used such terms and techniques. Their intent may have been to simplify and demystify science, but the effect—because nothing was ever really explained—was to increase the appearance of unintelligibility and to impart an air of magic. Although the linguistic straining sought to make science appear simpler, it reinforced the image of "differentness." No rhetorical tap dance could effectively explain away the complexity that confronted the uninitiated.

This situation inadvertently worked to the scientists' advantage in government policy making. When scientific advisors in the 1940s and 1950s used the imagery of science's unusual labors to support their arguments for self-governance instead of tight government control, the apparent complexity of the enterprise discouraged closer scrutiny by the politicians. This defensive obscurity was especially important in securing a postwar support structure for science based on a model of scientific autonomy as well as authority. In the popular magazines of the late 1950s, however, writers began to argue that the public should question this autonomy and consider social regulation of scientific activity. As the next chapter will show, these proposals, too, were influenced by powerful images, present since earlier in the century, of what might happen if society imposed limits on research.

8

Slowing the Bicycle:
Risks and Restrictions

Science is never static, never stagnant, never content with the
boundary it has reached. It is always dynamic, always breaking
bounds. . . . Science . . . abhors a limitation . . .
L. P. Jacks, 1924[1]

American national culture tends to regard movement and change as virtues. Even as Americans hold fast to traditional social and political values,
they move forward and see such progress as natural and good. As an intellectual enterprise, twentieth-century science fit this cultural image well,
for it seemed to have an "inertia of motion."[2] "Like a man on a bicycle,"
E. E. Free wrote in 1924, "science cannot stop; it must progress or collapse."[3] Science was a "powerful motor," propelling society along a road
of "indefinitely expanding prosperity."[4] Never content with any boundary
they reached, scientists continually redefined the edge, pushed forward,
and, in consequence, discovered new things.

This image became an important rallying metaphor in the debates
during the 1940s over government funding of scientific research. When
Vannevar Bush and his advisors chose "Science—The Endless Frontier"
as the title for what became the central planning document for postwar
science, they apparently intended to evoke dreams of new industries and
new jobs that would prevent a postwar depression; but the phrase also
neatly fit a public image of research that permeated twentieth-century popular culture.[5] Since Colonial times, Americans had regarded the frontier
as a place where old ideas met new possibilities; at the frontier, pioneers
found open land waiting to be explored, mapped, and conquered.[6] Borders
in the new nation changed rapidly, and fences thus served more than one
purpose. Sometimes wood or wire barriers defined the edge of civilization,

containing a society's wealth and resources; sometimes fences kept out predators or enemies. Whatever their purpose, such barriers were always constructed for some common good, if not always by unanimous consent. When farmers in the American West erected fences to prevent grazing cattle from damaging their crops and enable settlement, the cattlemen complained that barbed wire restricted *their* freedom to move herds along their traditional routes to market.[7]

For scientific research, the twentieth-century debate was framed in similar conflicts of interest: whenever society asserted its right to control research done under its auspices (or supported by its largess), scientists asserted their right to intellectual freedom, to progress freely along an endless intellectual frontier. Both argued that their position represented the common good. Early in the century this conflict seemed less important for the overall political relationship of science and society. Popular discussion downplayed the risks of research, primarily because the risks were perceived to be small (or to affect small numbers of people) and researchers could be trusted to act responsibly. Research seemed a private not a public matter, funded more by private or commercial groups than by the public. As the century progressed and the research enterprise grew, criticism of science increased in the magazines. Scientists' own popular writings demonstrated the research community's awareness of this criticism; they increasingly argued that any constraints on research freedom would slow science-based progress. Some limitations might be imposed for the greater good, they conceded, but restrictions should not be made frivolously and should be imposed only with the advice and consent of those most expert about science, that is, the scientists.

Both scientists and critics believed science to be bursting with new ideas. Images of intellectual restlessness (e.g., "Science is the pursuer; life is the pursued . . ."[8]) and endless production of new knowledge (e.g., "The gap between the now knowable and the unknowable is vast . . ."[9]) filled the writings of all types of commentators. Neither scientists nor critics disputed the range and quality of the benefits of research, and most accepted that the inhibition of all scientific progress would harm society. As one journalist expressed it, "in limiting science we are also limiting ourselves."[10] After World War II, however, more writers, both scientists and science critics, began to question this assumption; they mentioned the risks of research, and some even suggested, cautiously, that society must begin to monitor the conduct and results of scientific research. In the political debates of the time, those who lobbied for tighter government oversight of research funding argued that such control was appropriate because society not only would finance research but also would suffer any unforeseen negative consequences. Although this argument did not at first prevail, the images gained strength in the subsequent mass-media discussions.

This debate over limiting research centered, in fact, on one of the remarkable incongruities of the twentieth-century public images of science: the idea that science is *in* but not *of* society. Writers worked hard to connect even the most esoteric research or eccentric researchers to some social context, to ground them in commonplaces; yet the very same popular descriptions would often state unequivocally that science and scientists were *different*. When critics proposed constraints on research—on its topics, methods, or communication—they used this perceived difference to support the argument that scientists should be governed by different political rules or that, at the least, scientists should be left to control their own activities because they best understood science. If there were to be intellectual fences restricting science, then *scientists* should design, build, and site them. Any arguments for political constraints on research, therefore, contradicted strong existing cultural images of scientists as trustworthy and of externally-imposed limits as unnatural. Those who supported restrictions were forced to prove that, in a political sense at least, scientists were *not* different and should abide by the same rules of political accountability and ethical behavior that were imposed on other professionals. It was not a popular message and, as the history of postwar science shows, it was not widely accepted until the 1960s and 1970s, as reported abuses of that trust grew, and the image began to conflict dramatically with the reality.

Natural and Unnatural Limits

Popular discussion of science divided restrictions on science into natural and unnatural limits. The nature of science itself imposed certain limits, such as the inherent potential of scientific knowledge. Although scientists continually tested the edge, within these *natural* boundaries only imagination constrained innovative researchers: "The limits of science are not limits of its methods, but limits of its spheres."[11]

Scientists could, for example, only study a certain range of topics. The physical world was finite, even if it appeared to stretch over the horizon; the universe, too, had certain finite aspects. Scientists could study only what existed: the otherworldly, the supernatural, the fantastic, were off-limits to authentic science. Awareness of where these natural boundaries of science lay was said to be one of a researcher's vital skills.

Writers sometimes linked these intrinsic limits to the modesty and humility of scientists. "Science," one biologist observed, "does not assume that it knows—despite the great deal that it does know—more than a small part of the order of nature." [12] The same scientist wrote elsewhere that "all that the naturalist can claim is that he knows a part of the order of nature." [13] Scientists did not manufacture supernatural objects and could not indulge in alchemy; they could "create" only in that they synthesized or reassembled existing elements, materials, or lifeforms. Similar distinctions between real scientists and wizards dominated other discussions, many writers implying that the nature of science, rather than any failure of human abilities, set these limits.

This notion of identifiable internal boundaries became a favorite hobbyhorse of magazine critics of science in the 1930s, especially when writers would often associate science with disturbing effects on society. Many of the presumed negative effects came from scientific knowledge, for example, psychology's reshaping of beliefs about the human mind. When science exceeded its natural limits, that is, when it attempted to study unobservable or unmeasurable objects or theories, the argument ran, then it somehow threatened social stability, but it did so in ways not clearly articulated by the critics.

Journalists and social critics, perhaps mimicking the views of the scientists, tended to regard externally imposed restrictions as the most dangerous to science. If controls on science's agenda, methods, or communication were applied inappropriately by those who misunderstood science, they could inhibit scientific ingenuity and hence slow scientific progress. No one really argued that externally imposed restrictions should be avoided entirely, but constraints that were too tight, or imposed too soon or too frequently might damage valuable scientific research. Moreover, these externally imposed limits were frequently imposed by people uneducated in science and hence considered to be insensitive to researchers' needs. If the engines of progress were to be slowed, then scientists alone should apply the brakes.

Early in the century, magazine arguments against these external unnatural, limits were based mostly on the need to protect science's intrinsic worth; they asserted that restricting scientific research was wrong because science was basically good and rarely harmful. From the 1920s on, however, more serious proposals to restrict research could be found in the magazines, indicating that some shift in public attitudes took place about then.

One radical proposal to halt research altogether received considerable attention in American popular magazines. Speaking in 1927 to members of the British Association for the Advancement of Science, Edgar Arthur Burroughs, an Anglican bishop, suggested that "the sum of human happiness . . . would not necessarily be reduced if for, say, ten years, every physical and chemical laboratory were closed" and if the effort of the scientists were transferred to improving human life, thereby enabling society "to assimilate the staggering amounts of new scientific knowledge." [14] Many articles mentioned the Burroughs proposal of a "holiday for science," but it was never given serious consideration. Some scientists vigorously opposed the idea, and many others regarded it with amusement. By the 1930s, however, scientists could not blithely continue "to pursue science while disregarding any social problems associated with its use," historian William McGucken writes. [15]

The proposal did signal a change in open criticism of science, and it challenged the scientists' resistance to public comments. The "ritual incantation of science," another historian observes, seemed to have "lost much of its magic." [16] The strength of media attention in the United States alone demonstrated that Burroughs had inadvertently touched a nerve and exposed a growing uneasiness with the idea of unchecked scientific growth. [17]

By the 1950s, arguments against externally imposed controls had clearly shifted from the idea that science was intrinsically good and were centered on assertions that limiting science would harm not science but *society.* The defenders of science admitted that not all research results were positive but they argued that "When you lock the laboratory door, you lock out more than you lock in." [18] Society needed the benefits that science would bring.

Some defenders of unrestricted research emphasized threats related to military control of research, especially in physics. Astronomer Fred Hoyle predicted in 1951, for example, that if scientists could not freely investigate what they wished, and if government controlled the agenda for research, then an emphasis on the destructive uses of science would ensue. Describing an "increasing tendency to rivet scientific inquiry in fetters," both in the United States and elsewhere in the world, he warned of terrible consequences:

> Secrecy, nationalism, the Marxist ideology—these are some of the things that are threatening to choke the life out of science. . . . What will happen if science declines is that there will be more work, not less, on the comparatively easy problems of destruction. It will be the real science, where the adversary is not man but the Universe itself, that will suffer. [19]

The Consequences of Science

Those who favored some type of controls on research implied that restrictions would prevent harm, either to certain individuals or to society in general. On the other side, few argued for no controls at all, but most believed that only the scientists should design the regulations, and all these writers implied that inappropriate restrictions would harm society because they would inhibit scientific progress. Both positions relied on vague and often inaccurate images of the costs, rewards, and risks of research.

Popular discussions centered on one implicit question: Is this particular risk worth this particular reward? The response varied considerably, depending upon whether the author focused more on the costs, risks, and rewards *for researchers* or on the costs, risks, and rewards *for society*. From the 1910s to the 1940s, magazine articles focused on the risks to the individual researchers and usually dismissed or ignored any rewards to those scientists other than intellectual satisfaction. When articles examined the effects of science on society, they most often emphasized the social benefits of research and minimized the risks. By the 1950s, these emphases were reversed. Writers no longer ignored the potential risks to society, and they increasingly acknowledged that scientists could profit in ways beyond simply the so-called thrill of discovery.

Changes in these images reflected subtle changes in the public's assessment of scientists' social responsibility. Expressed in descriptions implying that researchers were "disembodied" from normal human society and thus reluctant to accept public responsibility for controlling their own work, these beliefs drew on accounts of scientists' wartime contributions, most of which were initially assessed as positive but later questioned as negative.

Costs, Risks, and Rewards for the Individual Scientist

If one were to judge by the content of mass magazines alone, then all scientists paid a heavy price to do their work, a cost that was primarily physical and involved social inconvenience as well as extraordinary physical and intellectual efforts. Every time writers emphasized that researchers "worked day and night" with little rest, they contributed to the impression that all scientists worked (or overworked) in that way. Scientists could simply not conduct real research, they implied, without being martyrs to their work.

Some scientists toiled in smelly laboratories or unheated observatories; others paid a cost of social isolation in order to avoid distractions or interruptions. The accounts often seemed like appeals for sympathy; consider, for example, this 1927 account of an astronomer working in Washington, D.C.:

> In a concrete room thirty-five feet below the street, a man sat and looked through a small telescope. . . . All day he watched. . . . Outside, the Sat-

urday traffic of the National Capital went on as usual. . . . But the man at the telescope saw none of these things, heard none of them, felt nothing. His locked door shut the world out of his underground chamber. . . . [20]

The need for privacy somehow "required" scientists to abdicate routine emotional interactions and normal family lives; articles implied that the situation was imposed on scientists.[21] Authors almost invariably described these supposed sacrifices with admiration, rarely questioning whether the research could proceed without antisocial behavior. Journalists described inconvenience and social isolation as normal practice. They never seemed to wonder whether the researchers had exaggerated or overdramatized their plight or had manufactured such costs as excuses for an inability or unwillingness to participate as family members, for example.

The courageous magazine scientist also faced and overcame risks to personal safety or health in the name of progress. Sensationalized accounts of fieldwork—unimaginably hostile aboriginal tribes, wriggling multitudes of poisonous reptiles, extremes of weather or terrain—enlivened articles by explorers and anthropologists. Biologists, too, routinely confronted the risks involved in studying infectious diseases:

> Under his easygoing manner lies the fortitude that has helped him face, almost every day for twenty-five years, the risk of infection and possible death, and has kept the dangerous work going despite the loss of one staff member after another.[22]

Such descriptions glorified the scientist as tough, brave, and altruistic, apparently willing to risk injury and death solely for the sake of acquiring useful knowledge.

When authors implied that scientists' rewards for their work were mainly intellectual—such as the "thrill" of discovery or the satisfaction of acquiring new knowledge—they reinforced a picture of altruistic sacrifice.[23] Scientists in the magazines rarely performed their research for money, power, or fame; instead, their rewards were intangible. This image fit a general stereotype for heroes. Fictional magazine heroes of the 1930s, of all types, tended to seek similar reward symbols—"recognition or deference from others"—in their fight for moral virtue.[24] This emphasis on intellectual rewards is present in a myth still strong within science today: that "scientific virtue is its own reward."[25] The magazine researcher's satisfaction came from solving a problem, especially if one could be the first to do it: "The highest reward of science [is] the secret satisfaction of standing where no mortal man has ever stood before . . ."[26]

Here, again, the image reflected only partial reality, of course. Most scientists sought some money, power, and prestige from their research, and it is difficult to accept that journalists did not recognize these motives. More likely, the ideas presented in the magazines parroted the scientists' self-perceptions, perpetuating an image of the scientist as a professional who gains much from his job beyond monetary compensation. As we know from the sociology of science, the research community has helped to sustain this image of intellectual satisfaction by continually reminding its members that their role is "to advance knowledge" and that the best fulfillment of that role is "to advance knowledge greatly"; moreover, esteem and recognition have accrued "to those who have best fulfilled their roles."[27] Thus, awards given for *scientific* accomplishments, rather than for, say, public service, have carried the most prestige among scientists.

The financial rewards of a scientific career were the least discussed of all, and certainly until mid-century, university scientists were not as well-paid as members of most other professions. Popular magazines rarely mentioned the possibility that even the most successful and well-known scientists (and even those with ties to industry) might have made money from their science. Writers did not necessarily condemn scientists who openly profited from their work, but they emphasized carefully that economic motives were rare. Sometimes writers even hinted that a certain scientist's lack of business skills should be regarded as proof of altruism (rather than of inability to handle money). This type of treatment existed even in the 1930s, when many magazines endorsed stronger links between science and industry. Descriptions of "unbusinesslike" scientists uninterested in financial reward, especially as expressed in their own words, helped reinforce an image of them as worthy of public trust because they practiced science for altruistic reasons.

Costs, Risks, and Rewards for Society

No aspect of science received as much attention from the magazines as the number and diversity of scientific accomplishments. Science was the inexhaustible cornucopia. Both scientists and journalists listed all that science gave to society, the "amazing fruits that have been plucked from the tree of knowledge."[28] Authors had less interest, however, especially early in the century, in identifying and analyzing the potential risks, costs, or harms to society that either the research process itself or the application of scientific knowledge created.

Some praised intangible benefits: for example, that the "scientific spirit has created for us a new worldview" or that "science . . . makes it easier for human beings to satisfy the desires they already have."[29] Others extolled the importance of such promising scientific gifts as new fabrics, exotic fruit, and world peace:

Practically everything you eat, taste, wear, smell and see has resulted in some way from the ingenuity of chemists.[30]

[Scientists] are continually developing healthier and more prolific strains of seed—Wonders that have been done with wheat, pineapples, fruit trees, and other plants. . . . [31]

[The scientist's] discoveries have conquered disease, provided vast export markets, made America rich.[32]

Lists of past and promised boons dominated magazine coverage of science, sometimes as an introductory justification for the research, sometimes as a stirring and sentimental conclusion to an article.

Few authors bothered to distinguish carefully between the planned-for products of directed (*applied*) research and the unexpected applications of undirected (*pure* or *basic*) research. The image remained the same: Society supported all research not for the intrinsic worth of its scholarship but for the usefulness of what it found. Every discovery and every new product of technology was said to represent a "valuable consequence" of some scientist's work. Moreover, articles continually overdramatized the ramifications of a single project, as in this exaggerated prose:

Scores of other inventions and discoveries, which he has either tossed off personally or supervised, are already affecting the lives of all of us. . . . Taken as a whole, his contributions to science are saving hundreds of lives and millions of dollars every year.[33]

This tendency to conflate the images of science and technology in part reflected the American magazines' preoccupation with practical results and industrial progress. Although some authors acknowledged that scientists themselves believed in the importance of undirected research "of a more fundamental character," articles more often traced basic research directly to some potential application. Again, both scientists and journalists indulged in this practice. "In fact, all truly great advances are . . . derived from fundamental science, and the future progress of the world will be largely dependent upon the provision made for scientific research," George Ellery Hale argued.[34] The "practical man" who distrusts pure science need not, Hale continued, "resent investments made for the purpose of advancing our knowledge of such fundamental subjects as physics and chemistry."[35]

This image of some assured return on society's investment contributed to a common justification for industrial sponsorship of pure research; because of the substantial financial returns on successful research, industry could afford to invest occasionally in research that yielded nothing. In American industrial laboratories, therefore, "pure science" was said to go "hand in hand with that which is applied."[36] The same scientific community that promoted a public image of scientists as uninterested in commercially based research also espoused an investment model for the support of pure research, although most scientists appeared reluctant to calculate precisely what the return might be.

Realizing a profit from such investment, conjuring something out of nothing, turning ideas into dollars—these and similar images filled the magazine descriptions of inventors as well. The work of "hard-head, practical" inventors, of course, promised immediate value, for they could seemingly connect science with everyday life.[37] In a *Cosmopolitan* article, Henry Ford outlined the 1930s distinction between ancient science and modern invention. "The older scientists," he wrote,

> made their discoveries as things of themselves and were so far away from the daily workaday world that they would have lost standing had they even suggested the possibility that their studies could have any commercial application.[38]

Then Thomas Edison came along and, according to Ford, became "a greater scientist than any of them" because he was not "bound by the old scientific traditions" and because he "thought of science as an aid to mankind."[39] Moreover, science's utility was inevitable, not accidental, and therefore could be planned. As Julian S. Huxley observed, "the investigation of any problem, however apparently remote from everyday life, may be fraught with the most valuable consequences."[40] Even those who set out to do "pure research," another author warned, must be ever-vigilant because of the "inevitability" of application:

> They cannot remain indefinitely in any field of pure research. For every time they come upon a new bit of knowledge, almost instantly they discover some practical application. Thus the dividing line between pure science and applied science becomes thin.[41]

This concept of a thin or disappearing dividing line between pure science and its application recurred often in the magazines. When authors distorted the timespan between discovery and application, or gave the impression that every scientific idea would be applied and applied rapidly (e.g., "the scientific discovery of to-day becomes the working device of to-morrow"[42]), they cultivated exaggerated expectations of science. Although a few writers conscientiously explained that "it always takes some time before an experiment can be translated from the purely scientific stage to that of practice,"[43] far more implied that all scientific discoveries could be turned quickly into working devices. In most cases, therefore, popularizers not only misrepresented the connection between a discrete basic research project and some practical application, but also stated that pure research was always automatically transformed into practical technology.

Even though such a connection flattered science, it was based on fundamental misunderstandings of the nature of research and of the predictability of research application. It promoted an ambiguous image: that basic research should be tolerated when it produced seemingly useless knowledge, although it was undertaken in the first place because it might produce something useful.

Fundamental, undirected research represented, of course, an economic risk. No one could guarantee that sponsors would reap sufficient gain to offset their investments. Early in the century, in fact, popular science writers tended not to analyze the harsh economic reality of an investment-based model for science. Even in the mid-1940s, as federal money for research increased, few articles addressed the financial risks.

In an age of billion-dollar deficits, such omission now seems naive, if not also socially irresponsible. A few conscientious journalists in the 1930s investigated both the economics and the potential risks of research. As long as the amount of public funds going into science was relatively small and the potential gain high, however, the image of scientists as intrinsically altruistic, as unconcerned with financial rewards or the implications of their work, probably seemed correct to both journalists and readers. The investor, whether industry or government, might stake money in research of seemingly "no tangible gain," only to find that the investment is repaid a "hundredfold."[44]

After World War II, these images changed, as both journalists and scientists identified more precisely the risks that all types of research posed. The harsh reality of the Cold War and the nuclear arms race refigured the initial euphoric image of atomic physics as having won the war. Magazines recorded these gradual changes in their accounts of the social assessment of research risks and benefits.

Scientists, the magazines made clear, could not always predict or prevent "the chain of events which an epic discovery will set in motion";[45] moreover, the Manhattan Project demonstrated that scientific success could have terrible consequences for humanity. Through the mass media, Americans learned about the accuracy of both scientific potential and scientific prophecy. They learned how scientific research could bring harm even where it may have intended to bring benefit. Writers began to use such evocative metaphors as "a scientific gamble"; they no longer presented scientific benefits as a "sure thing." This image—more alert to uncertainty, more sensitive to the risks accompanying benefits, and changed greatly from how magazines in the 1910s had shown the consequences of science—emerged decisively after World War II, although its evolution rested on decades of confused explanations of scientific methods and on exaggerated warnings of the consequences of restrictions.

Developing Regulation

These and other images infused and influenced the social and political attitudes toward research regulation that have developed more strongly in the last few decades. First, the popular writers' failure to distinguish clearly between science and technology undoubtedly increased the benefits that their audiences attributed to basic science. Each time a journalist rewrote the popular history of science and attributed new commercial products to scientific achievement, the true technical geneology of the developments was lost. In return, of course, science gained prestige and authority; scientists could seemingly deliver on promises at will. We do not dare to doubt any scientist, one commentator wrote, for "when he tells us that soon we shall be doing this or that we know from experience that we had best believe him."[46] By the 1930s, scientists were the "one trustworthy authority"; science, "the one source of truth."[47]

Second, images of scientists' inherent restlessness reinforced a general uneasiness with science-induced change, as did also their insistence that progress should be the prerogative of science. If scientists were the ones who best understood what controls were needed, some observers astutely asked, then why did they allow negative effects? In this case, the scientists' intellectual impatience, their inclination to push the limits of knowledge ever farther, could also be interpreted as irresponsibility if they appeared unwilling to consider what might happen as a result of that progress. This mistrust perhaps also came from what John Wright Buckham called science's "inability to accomplish what was expected of it, . . . its inner limitations and inadequacy."[48]

Two particular situations in the late 1940s and 1950s also influenced public support for sociopolitical regulation of research. After World War II, as Congress considered legislation to regulate atomic energy research and development, the mass media covered extensively the debate over who should control the atom. Many scientists argued publicly that restricting free communication among scientists, through government classification of data, for example, might thwart foreign espionage but would also hinder basic research. They played extensively on the theme of the inhibition of scientific progress. To nurture scientific genius, they argued, freedom in research and in research communication was vital. Yet it was clear throughout the magazines that public concern did not favor such a plea of special cause, for, as the McCarthyites warned, even scientists could betray their country.[49] These debates may have helped to foster suspicions of the scientists' trustworthiness.

Another influence on attitudes came from journalistic attention to how human subjects were used for scientific research and testing. Following World War II, revelations of how the Nazis had abused prisoners "in the name of science" provided repulsive images of cruel scientific experimentation. As biomedical research grew in size and scope in the United States, and as more and more people were needed to test experimental drugs and procedures, U.S. scientists carefully pointed out that their research was different. The German doctors had not been engaged in normal science, they argued. Nevertheless, increased journalistic attention to research subjects, referred to as "human guinea pigs" and often portrayed as manipulated for seemingly unimportant research, fueled political scrutiny of the decades-old plea that "scientists know best."

Many magazine articles addressed the delicate issue of secrecy (e.g., should patients be told the nature of the test and the risks they might run?), but even interviews with the scientists themselves did not always help to place the research in a favorable light, especially when researchers appeared to be ignoring the potential harm to human subjects. In a 1949 article on tuberculosis research, for example, a science writer described experimentation on patients in a Veterans Administration hospital.[50] "Its promise is staggering, although to date, its performance has been shrouded in secrecy," the author noted.[51] At the article's conclusion, he explained that the researchers had imposed such secrecy out of fear of "Congressional chastisement from publicity-conscious members of the House and Senate who might have screamed 'You can't experiment on our heroes.' "[52]

Similar descriptions of how scientists kept certain aspects of research quiet in order to avoid political criticism or social control could be found in a 1951 article on research to develop a polio vaccine. "Should we try to do our experiment as quietly as possible and later be accused of attempting to cover our evil deeds," an epidemiology professor asked, "or shall we welcome publicity and run the risk of losing our control group of unvaccinated children . . . ?"[53] "Many an experiment has been ruined," he complained, "when the public got wind of it and insisted that no treatment or preventative with even *possible* merit could be withheld."[54]

Since early in the century, scientists had successfully argued for self-governance by pointing to the risks and difficulties of research. Popular images had reflected a mood of unqualified trust in scientists' judgment, a willingness to let scientists decide how to conduct their work. By mid-century, however, mass magazines contained modest but assertive questioning of such autonomy, alongside their strong support for science.

Many authors began to suggest that the public should play a role in regulating scientific activity after all, and these assertions signaled a critical change in public attitudes. Earlier considerations of limits on research focused on what might happen if scientific progress was inhibited; by mid-century, mass media attention had turned to the consequences of unrestrained progress. The following chapter describes some of the specific criticisms that had also helped to justify public skepticism and suspicion.

9

The Critical Message:
Rejection and Embrace

> Science . . . has builded us a new house . . . a much finer, more spacious and commodious house . . . but new, new, all bright and hard and unfamiliar . . .
>
> John Burroughs, 1912[1]

Readers of American popular magazines early in this century might reasonably have concluded that scientists stood poised to overturn every traditional social value, every known fact, every cherished belief. The essence of science's public image was challenge and change; the stereotyped scientists, impatient with the status quo, rubbed their hands greedily as old myths crumbled. Science's record certainly supported this image. Evolutionary science had pummeled conventional religious beliefs about the age and origins of the natural world, until even some theologians admitted that the biologists' explanations had merit. Physicists, astronomers, and psychologists attempted to stretch the borders of the physical and nonphysical universe beyond even the wild imaginings of novelists.

At first, popular sentiment, as expressed in the magazines, greeted each new intellectual manifesto as part of a desirable, natural drive for progress, but by mid-century many influential critics endorsed a more skeptical approach to science. Change through scientific progress remained desirable, but not as many popular authors accepted either change or challenge as automatically beneficial. A new "public ambivalence toward science" struggled to visibility in the magazines.[2]

Some of the most prominent social movements—naturalism, aestheticism, mysticism, scientific management, technocracy, progressivism—enfolded science into their ideologies. Even mainstream theologians attempted to reconcile the "mysteries" of science and religion. Often, the

141

commentators, like neurotic lovers, rejected and embraced science at the same time. Typically, they would excoriate science for some allegedly offensive action or attribute, and then later in the same article use scientific evidence to support their position.

Although both promoters and critics of science discussed essentially the same subjects—scientific knowledge and the effect of that knowledge on society and the human spirit—they offered dramatically different interpretations. Promoters sought to probe science's value; they assumed first that it was good. Critics searched beneath the surface data of scientific accomplishment, measuring their effects on social or moral values and assigning it responsibility for all undesirable effects. This discrepancy in view did not derive from the subject itself but from the observer's initial assumptions. Raw scientific data, uninterpreted and unused, presented neither threat nor promise. Science's promoters dismissed the possibility of harm and emphasized the promise. Critics acknowledged such promise but emphasized the potential harm.

The proportion of popular magazine articles openly critical of science—between 5% and 10% of all articles on science—began to rise in the 1920s (see Figure 9.1).[3] This increase may have reflected general social reassessment and criticism of the 1920s and 1930s. As American society later embraced the promise of science for wartime usefulness, there was much less criticism published in the magazines.

Despite slight variations in the amount of criticism published, certain major themes appeared consistently in these magazines throughout the century. One important theme focused on how scientists communicated with the public, arguing that researchers deliberately used terms that few nonscientists could understand and that scientists' obscure language reflected their social values. A second theme criticized how scientists worked: because researchers examined only narrow aspects of a problem, they neglected the whole and ignored the implications of their work. Many critics argued that such tunnel vision was deliberate; it allowed scientists also to ignore their responsibility for how scientific knowledge was used and to blame society for any misuse. The third and strongest critical theme accused scientists of debasing and destroying human values. When scientists presumptuously proposed science as an object of social faith, then they were attempting to subvert the moral authority of religion. Each of these themes was amply represented in the mass magazines.

Obscure Language

Many of the liveliest critical articles focused on scientific communication. In "Should Language Be Abolished?" (1918), for example, Harold God-

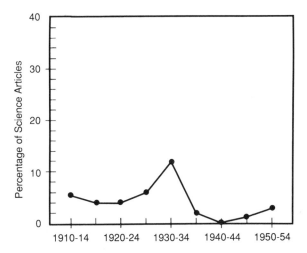

Figure 9.1. Articles critical of science, 1910–54 ($n = 27$). Data are taken from a sample of eleven U.S. mass-circulation magazines and are given as a percentage of all science articles published in those magazines during each five-year period.

dard, a professor of English, accused scientists of replacing proper language with sign and symbol, and of thinking with "things instead of words." Goddard's scorn for scientists was unrelenting: The scientist represented "a pioneer" in the movement to abolish language. Moreover, scientists were using technical language deliberately in order to erect a barrier around science and thus to confuse nonscientists and discourage criticism.[4] This theme of deliberate obscurantism appears throughout popular magazines, even in articles otherwise sympathetic to science. Even some scientists admitted that they had indeed "evolved a preposterous and terrifying language of their own" which was "not ideally adapted to the interchange of confidences in ordinary human intercourse."[5]

Magazine satires sometimes began by portraying scientists as different because they spoke a foreign language that had to be translated into ordinary English before it could be understood. Although these writers intended their comments as humor, more often, their criticism had serious intent: scientists refused to talk in "plain English." Even the most earnest defenders of science had to admit that obscurantism existed. Science, E. E. Slosson wrote, "is mostly printed in a foreign language not only when it appears in French . . . or Japanese, but also when it seems at first sight to be in ordinary English."[6] Most defenders, however, excused such practices and explained that popularizers would fulfill the role of translating the scientists' "negative exponents into human language."[7]

To the critics, perhaps predictably, *all* technical terms seemed to be "utterly indefensible jargon"; they were too complicated, too long, or too esoteric. When writers suspected that scientists were engaging in gratuitous complexity, they asked rhetorically, "Why won't these scientists talk in plain terms?"[8] The assumption that most scientists were poor communicators was so pervasive that scientists who deviated from the norm and spoke in clear, understandable terms drew considerable praise. One biographer attempted to prove that his subject, a biologist, did not fit "the conventional stereotype" precisely because he "speaks the United States language freely."[9] Another writer attributed one scientist's popularity to his "gift of being able to talk to the public in the public's own tongue."[10]

Certain journalistic practices reinforced this image of intentionally obscure communication. Journalists would often describe how they had requested interview subjects to "be good enough to furnish some plain answers to a few simple questions."[11] By recounting the circumstances of such requests, journalists implied that scientists would not willingly choose ordinary language but instead must be persuaded or pushed to do so. As one writer summarized, "I asked him to let me cut out all the scientific and technical language and to use plain, simple terms."[12] Journalists further reinforced the image when they applauded as socially responsible those scientists who explained the "complexities of the universe" in nontechnical language and castigated those who chose technical jargon:[13]

> the biologist seems unable to escape from the use of a terminology that is to be found only in the larger dictionaries—and these dictionaries are at home, while the public is in the lecture-hall.[14]

Although critics sometimes ridiculed or satirized scientific language, laughter did not necessarily indicate that they dismissed it as unimportant. Instead, it masked the embarrassment of ignorance—and the anger of frustration. Although a few scientists painstakingly explained that what seemed like obscurantism was actually precision and was necessary "to secure accuracy of definition and expression" in research, most journalists appeared to suspect that the obscurity was deliberate.[15] Moreover, they hinted that the scientists had an ulterior motive: secrecy. By intentionally imposing a language barrier, the scientist could make a nonscientist feel like an outsider unworthy of being trusted with secret knowledge. Even journalists could not be part of the trusted inner circle. Such explanations just fueled the critics of science: secrecy was undemocratic and counterproductive to the widespread implementation of scientific ideas.

Each time scientists pleaded that their pronouncements be accepted on faith, they inadvertently fueled the public's uneasiness. The extent of the magazines' discussion of this topic throughout the period studied showed that few readers (and few journalists) believed that they could really understand scientific theories; most were convinced that they would never understand. They felt discouraged, they felt "locked out" from being able to assess the ramifications of scientific advances, and they saw no easy means by which to change this situation.

One expository technique that science writers frequently used to enliven their prose—metaphors and similes—further contributed to this sense of isolation. Comparative devices, which were quite common in magazine articles on science and which the writers (and their interview subjects) may have intended as helpful, inadvertently supported the impression that scientific concepts were being translated from a foreign language and they contributed to the sense that readers and scientists lived in different worlds. Philosopher Hannah Arendt has suggested that scientific obscurantism may in fact represent just another cost of scientific and technological advance, for "the 'truths' of the modern scientific world view, though they can be demonstrated in mathematical formulas and proved technologically, . . . no longer lend themselves to normal expression in speech and thought."[16] It could be "that we . . . will forever be unable to understand, that is, to think and speak about the things which nevertheless we are able to do."[17] Moreover, she continues, because science is always cast in "objective form," its ex cathedra announcements carry a weight and legitimacy that discourage nonscientists' attempts to analyze or question them.

One field in particular—mathematics—exemplified the impossibility of comprehensive public understanding. In mathematics, researchers routinely used symbols that, although intended as abbreviations for spoken statements, contained statements that, as Arendt has phrased it, "in no way can be translated back into speech."[18] Fears that human language would be abolished and sign and symbol substituted were exacerbated by increasingly abstract mathematics, and by the celebratory use of such mathematics by theoretical physics and molecular biology in the 1930s. Magazine writers in fact often placed the fault for many communication problems directly at the mathematicians' feet. Although some writers praised the "certainty of a mathematical demonstration,"[19] admired the "pyrotechnics of higher mathematics,"[20] or called mathematics "vital universal speech,"[21] the majority regarded it as the most cabalistic of the sciences, divorced from all human attributes. Mathematics, to these critics, "had a striking resemblance to the working of a machine, clean, precise, cold."[22] The powerful mathematics employed by theoretical physicists only reinforced a worsening image. As hard as they tried, the audience could not decipher the messages: "People stand reverently before [science's] pundits, listening hard, trying to understand, but what they hear is ever less intelligible."[23] By the 1950s, even such an avowed science booster as Vannevar Bush accused the physicists of "speaking a mathematical language which completely bars the unsophisticated from participating in the excitement of their delving."[24]

Because this point could be neither conceded nor changed, science's promoters had to acknowledge that incomprehensibility was indefensible, and the critics had a reliable source of fuel for their hostility. The language of mathematics represented an insurmountable barrier even to the best-educated nonscientist. Comprehensive understanding of science seemed denied to all but a few. In addition, as the technical complexity increased, each scientist, too, became an amateur in all fields but one. All readers—even those with considerable scientific education—were forced to rely on specialists for help in translation. And this reliance on experts became another reason for uneasiness and fear of the scientific unknown, accompanied by wary hope that scientists would indeed do the right thing. Even the doyens of science, the heads of the scientific establishment, seemed bewildered by the complexity—and obtuseness—of some of their fellow scientists' work; on occasion, scientists complained that such language barriers could endanger public support for science. Bush expressed a universal fear when, in 1955, he wrote about his young colleagues in physics: "We can merely hope they will later come up for air and tell us in a common language what it is all about."[25]

Tunnel Vision

Science's disciplinary overspecialization affected more than its language. The so-called standard approach to research—ever more specialized, ever more narrow—put intellectual blinders on the researchers, limiting their vision. What ordinary people saw as a romantic vista of mountains and sky, the scientists regarded as sources for data. "The geologic ages are dealt with by pick and hammer and reduced to slides," one journalist observed, "and the lore of the stars has become a pure matter of mathematical formulae."[26] When researchers focused thus on only one narrow part of a puzzle, they risked ignoring the implications of their work.

To the critics, "sweeping and positive utterances regarding the all-knowingness and all-mightiness of modern science" represented false statements because of the deficiencies in scientific expertise.[27] Most scientists simply could not estimate with any accuracy or certainty "the varying degrees of practicalness" of their knowledge because they only knew about their narrow scientific field.[28] Moreover, by retreating into their specialties, they ignored questions of social responsibility.

Critics regarded this abdication of responsibility as intrinsic to science and as intentional. Scientists seemed "almost pathetically powerless" before the complexity of their own creations:

> The point where responsibility rests upon us all lies just ahead of the last point reached by advancing science, and is continually being thrust forward by the forces behind it. . . . This inability of science to overtake responsibility is what I mean by its limitation.[29]

Because of this inability or unwillingness to consider the consequences of their research, some argued those who sponsored or instigated research must share (or shoulder) the burden of controlling it.[30]

In addition to specialization, science had several negative associations stemming from research conducted for military purposes. Following World War I, the image of the field of chemistry overall was affected by chemists' participation in war-related research. Before the war, the chemist seemed harmless; then, as Leo Baekeland observed in 1917, "almost overnight . . . came the discovery that chemists are indispensable to a nation, whether for the needs of war or peace."[31] The result was a revised public image. "Truly the chemical plant is the very factory of war!" Samuel Hopkins Adams cried in 1919.[32]

The Allied propaganda campaign painted a picture of the German chemist as a devious war-monger:

> The little, bespectacled German chemist toiled in his laboratory, building up colors, scores of them, hundreds of them, thousands of them. He had thought that he was making dyestuffs. But all the time it was really he who was making war. And if they had let him alone a little longer . . . he might have made, there in his secluded laboratory, victory as well as war.[33]

When postwar articles accused German scientists of having contributed "as much, if not more, to the success of the [Axis] campaign than the strategist, the army and the navy," then *all* scientists, regardless of nationality, became associated with the negative effects of war.[34] Scientists could not only be easily duped by political regimes, this image implied, but they could also work without apparent concern for the moral consequences of their actions.

U.S. scientists who had been involved in wartime research at first eagerly claimed credit for their work. A tongue-in-cheek account of the academic scientist's war effort, for example, was given in "The Demobilized Professor" (1919), in which the author proposed a march down New York City's Fifth Avenue:

> There should be floats bearing the trophies, the death-dealing gases and explosives, the life-saving surgical and medicinal devices, the new offensive and defensive engines of war, which have sprung from the professor's inventive brain.[35]

Magazine coverage of military research in general, however, linked approval of science more with assessment of science's good and bad effects than with scientists' nationality or citizenship. Instead of praising U.S. scientists for "blocking the war," critics were more likely to cry that a stateless entity called *science* had fed war's fires "with new methods of propaganda and multiplied its destructive agencies a hundredfold, devising deadly explosives and poisons that threatened the extinction of civilization itself."[36] In these and similar commentaries published in the 1920s, the sense was, as historian Roy MacLeod phrases it, "that scientists were increasingly indifferent to the misapplication of their discoveries."[37] As the uses became more visible (and more destructive), the scientists appeared to be hiding their heads in their laboratories, and the image of denied responsibility was strengthened.

Harper's, Atlantic, and similar publications gave considerable attention in the interwar period to the intellectual upheavals provoked by theoretical physics. In this case, too, the long-term effects of popular reaction were not confined to just that field but were extended to all scientists. Heisenberg's uncertainty principle, for example, disturbed many philosophers writing for popular audiences. Within physics, Selig Hecht wrote, the principle had had disorienting but ultimately positive effects; but outside physics, "the devastation produced has been pitiful."[38] Physicists had proposed ideas that, if accepted, disturbed the "natural order" and that showed the foundations of all life to be unsteady. The floor seemed solid and reliable but it was not. Everything was composed of particles too small to be seen, these particles heaved in constant motion, and all matter moved in some state of mathematical uncertainty. Such popular descriptions could only provoke anxiety among some readers, especially when the popularizers held out little hope that researchers could ever control or change these forces.

After 1945, stories about the Manhattan Project reinforced these images. The atomic physicists had deliberately designed a lethal weapon; but they, too, seemed powerless to control it. Moreover, they seemed unwilling to accept full responsibility for their creation: their words sometimes implied that they felt themselves to be only pawns in the political game. One fictional atomic physicist romanticized thus in a 1955 *Harper's* short story:

> It was idyllic. Those were the days, remember, when you could be a physicist without feeling guilty; the days when it was still possible to believe that

you were working for the greater glory of God. Now they won't even allow you the comfort of self-deception. You're paid by the Navy and trailed by the FBI.[39]

The scientists' postwar efforts to ban atomic weapons, much of it visible in the popular magazines and likened by some in its political naïveté to a "children's crusade," further heightened the image of irresponsibility. Scientists seemed like creators who had decided to lock up their horrible creation only after it was out of the cage.

The Destruction of Human Values

Many social critics held no sympathetic brief for science—to them, it was an unwelcome intruder, a party crasher in a civilized society. They described science as a vicious force intent on debasing or destroying human values, as antithetical to the goodness in human nature. To these writers, scientists appeared to flaunt their lack of emotion, discarding human feelings as irrelevant to research. When scientists eliminated "the local, the individual" and favored "the general, the universal," then they diminished "sympathy, love, appreciation."[40] "We study botany so hard," even naturalist John Burroughs complained, "that we miss the charm of the flower entirely."[41]

In their search for ways to convey this undesirable aspect of science, critics sometimes used multilayered metaphors. In one type of image, they likened research to a spotlight: it revealed imperfection, destroyed illusion, and, if sufficiently powerful, harmed life as well. Science, the "broad, all-revealing noon-day," subjected gentle life to the glaring, unflattering light of discovery. But this light brought only false revelation; ultimately, science failed "to throw any real light upon the meaning of human existence and of the universe."[42] Science revealed all yet revealed nothing and, in the process of revealing, could destroy as scientists restructured and reordered social ideals without concern for tradition or history:

> Science has made or is making the world over for us. It has builded us a new house—builded it over our heads while we were yet living in the old, and the confusion and disruption and the wiping-out of the old features and the old associations, have been, and still are, a sore trial—a much finer, more spacious and commodious house . . . but new, new, all bright and hard and unfamiliar . . .[43]

Criticism such as this, widespread in the 1920s and 1930s, resembled a moan of despair. Knowledge brought facts, not wisdom; it only showed us what we did not know.[44] Science achieved. Science studied. Yet science neglected the very core of human existence. As physicists pushed "farther and farther into the nature of matter," they robbed life of the "attributes that are most familiar and most comfortable" and left "a world of units all alike save in positive or negative nature, impalpable, invisible, without taste or smell . . ."[45]

The science criticism of the 1920s contained many of the same images found in the literary and social criticism of the time; for example, environmental desolation, a crumbling of former civilizations, and a deterioration of outmoded philosophies. In "The Waste Land" (1922), for example, poet and critic T. S. Eliot painted a stark landscape of human life that was now "stony rubbish," "a heap of broken images," an "unreal city."[46] His poem eulogized something that once was but was no longer, a pastiche of faded hope and despair, of ruined glory, of the scent of decay. The intellectual destruction to which the popular science critics pointed came from a similar desolation of dreams, tradition, and moral certainty. Not at all critics blamed science for instigating this process of cultural disintegration, but all seemed to believe that science had accelerated it. Science's "skeptical attitude" questioned matters of nature, time, and life which had "long been thought settled" and which many believed were best left alone.[47]

To the scientist, the elimination of preconceived ideas (or outmoded theories) represented only a "starting point," properly followed by "genuine analysis, and the patient accumulation of all relevant data."[48] If nonscientists looked only at scientific analysis, in which traditional beliefs were challenged and discarded, then it was understandable, popularizers observed, that they saw only intellectual destruction ("the wasteland so created remains a wasteland"); whereas the scientists wanted to take the next step: to rebuild on the ground they had cleared.[49]

The critics could not accept such explanations. To them, science seemed to want to evict humanity from its palace of ideals:

> Science . . . has not only turned her face outwards from man, but stripped him of all the robes of his divinity, turned him out of the palace that he had so laboriously built in the center of the world, and left him in rags, pitiably insignificant and suddenly transported to an outlying corner of the cosmos.[50]

When similar images appeared in scientists' writings, they surely did little to alleviate the audience's concern.

Joseph Wood Krutch, editor of *The Nation,* synthesized many of these contemporary attitudes in *The Modern Temper: A Study and a Confession,* which was serialized in *Atlantic* in 1927 and 1928.[51] Krutch attempted "to describe the mood generated in me by the intellectual convictions current in my time,"[52] examining the roots of what he saw as philosophical despair. As he traced the development of scientific faith and the public's unquestioning acceptance of all that science offered, he showed how this faith was undermined when science achieved less than it promised yet continued to promise more.[53] Krutch did not perceive science as either deliberately malicious or intrinsically malign; rather, it had unwittingly begun "to destroy more than it knew it was destroying . . ."[54] Because science no longer offered absolute interpretations of the world but now admitted uncertainty, it revealed the universe as an uncomfortable home for the human spirit.[55] The universe that science revealed (and the "pattern of nature" it mapped out) had, to Krutch, "no relation to the pattern of human needs and feelings."[56] Although science once seemed to be helping humanity toward some type of social progress, it did not seem, by the late 1920s, "so surely as once it did, to be helping us very rapidly along the road we wish to travel."[57] These qualified realizations held a hidden message: The fault lay in ourselves. Humanity traveled the road of scientific progress without prior planning; society had neglected its duty to observe and be watchful as the scientists moved forward.

Krutch's series prompted responses such as Paul Laubenstein's "The Modern Well-Tempered Mind" in the February 1928 *Atlantic*. More reluctant than Krutch to place the entire blame on science, Laubenstein argued that the fault lay in society's interpretation and use of science rather than in science's inherent evil nature, and his softened defense epitomized another prevalent interpretation of science's social role. Laubenstein concurred with two of Krutch's assertions. One was the extent of society's "submission to a new dogmatism of science."[58] Science, Laubenstein agreed, was fallible: "It is high time we stop talking of the 'certitudes of science'."[59] Science—especially psychology—could not describe human experience as accurately or completely as it claimed it could. He also agreed with Krutch's complaints about the overuse and idolization of scientific experts: scientific training and knowledge were not automatically transferable to other circumstances.[60] Science did not contain the "only valid and legitimate [methods] for the discovery of truth . . ."[61] Because of science, Laubenstein asserted, human values might eventually face "extinction" and most certainly would suffer diminished prestige; but this submission to science, this "kow-towing" to scientific authority, was not without an element of choice.[62] As Laubenstein, Krutch, and many other critics emphasized, society must direct science to appropriate goals.

A Rival to Religion

To Laubenstein, religion, not science, deserved society's first loyalty, a suggestion shared by many critics in the interwar years.[63] As theologian

Harry Emerson Fosdick decided in the 1920s, "There is a real conflict between those whom science has led to a materialistic philosophy and those who interpret life in terms of its spiritual values."[64] Fosdick, as did most critics, carefully explained that not all scientists were on the "other side." "This is not a conflict between science and religion," he emphasized, "this is a conflict between most scientists and all religionists on one side and a few scientists upon the other."[65] Nevertheless, the intricate and occasionally acrimonious relations between scientists and theologians attracted the steady interest of magazines throughout the early twentieth century. During the 1920s, however, as Figures 9.2 and 9.3 show, discussion of religion, science, and evolution intensified as the antievolutionists used the mass media to disseminate their views. Almost one-third of the lead articles on science published during the period 1925–29 were, in fact, on the relations between science and religion. This finding coincides with other content analyses that have recorded a rise in the number of all magazine articles on religion from 1925–28 and a decline thereafter.[66]

Ironically, the use of theological language in science articles reinforced an appearance of conflict. All sorts of authors spoke of "faith" in science, "worship of science," and the "commandments of the new decalogue of science."[67] Many placed science and religion on equal footing as similar things and hence as potential rivals for allegiance. Many asked whether science could "save" humanity from specific scourges, calamities, or diseases.[68] The general theme running through these articles implied that scientists' advice must be taken "on faith." Science possessed strength and authority (inherent in its methods and data) that were unavailable to religion. Science represented the "inscrutable processes or forces in the natural"; religion represented "the supernatural."[69]

> The mysteries of religion are of a different order from those of science; they are parts of an arbitrary system of man's own creation; they contradict our reason and our experience, while the mysteries of science are revealed by our reason, and transcend our experience.[70]

The popular discussion of how science related to religion thus had a curious duality. At the heart of the religious objection to science was a conviction that scientific arrogance insulted God and threatened divine authority. Many religious people believed that scientists were attempting to sell an alternate religion and to advocate faith in "the discoveries and achievements of science." Scientists planned to supplant conventional religion; science's alternate set of beliefs would become the "new religion." Yet, the theologians—especially those representing more well-educated constituencies—acknowledged that they were caught in a dilemma: they were unwilling to accept science but unable to ignore it. Even for the devout,

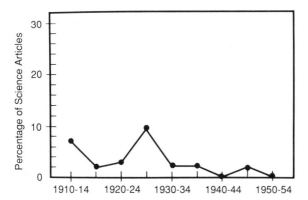

Figure 9.2. Articles on science and religion, 1910–54. The proportion of all articles which discussed the relationship between science and religion (*n* = 23). Data are taken from a sample of eleven U.S. mass-circulation magazines and are given as a percentage of all science articles published in those magazines during each five-year period.

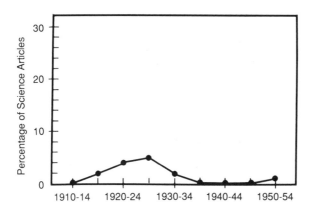

Figure 9.3. Articles on Darwin and evolution, 1910–54. The proportion of articles which discussed the work and life of Charles Darwin or evolutionary theory, either favorably or unfavorably, (n = 12). Data are taken from a sample of eleven U.S. mass-circulation magazines and are given as a percentage of all science articles published in those magazines during each five-year period.

to reject scientific knowledge seemed "heresy to the faith of the age."[71] So these theologians argued that they must accept science's dogma without question, just as the devout accepted religious dogma. John Burroughs observed that nonscientists must take certain scientific explanations "on faith" and must believe them even when they seemed incomprehensible.[72] To Burroughs, faith in the truths of science was "waxing in proportion as theological faith is waning."[73] As he and many other authors explained, this change in social dominance intensified the animosity between science and religion.

Especially in the 1910s and 1920s, many magazine writers seemed to be trying to accept science, even though it bothered them intellectually and spiritually. They struggled to explain the new science in the context of their faith; but the harder they tried, the more questions they raised.[74] A few theologians judged the struggle to be hopeless, for science was intrinsically incompatible with religion:

> The old explanation of a mysterious thing as due to God interfering with the laws of the universe . . . is to science the one incredible thing. . . . Science does not deny the mystery. What it denies is the explanation of it as a suspension of law.[75]

Even some scientists and promoters of science argued much the same point. Burroughs wrote that

> The miracles of religion are to be discredited, not because we cannot conceive of them, but because they run counter to all the rest of our knowledge; while the mysteries of science, such as chemical affinity, the conservation of energy, the indivisibility of the atom, the change of the non-living into the living . . . extend the boundaries of our knowledge, though the *modus operandi* of these changes remains hidden.[76]

Writings such as these implied that, correct or not, science and religion sat in warring camps, even though many scientists, seeking reconciliation, called the threat imaginary. Science did not seek to destroy religion, they argued.[77] Earnest efforts to support this view often involved articles by or interviews with prominent scientists. Vernon Kellogg, Secretary of the National Research Council, pointed to "Some Things Science Doesn't Know,"[78] such as immortality, the human spirit, and the soul. Science, Kellogg argued, harbored no antagonism to religion; even though science developed knowledge of the "manner of things," God remained "the cause of things."[79] A 1927 interview with physicist Michael Pupin attempted to show how "Science Is Leading Us Closer to God," not only "making us better Christians" but also "teaching men what God's laws are and how to obey them."[80] Pupin was quoted as speaking of "a spiritually developed scientist" who acknowledged that "science is . . . the highest form of human theology" and will "strengthen religion." The purpose of science is not, he asserted, "merely to make material things" but to provide "a better understanding of the Creator, and a closer personal relationship with him"; if science could not do that, he stated, "then I am a failure as a scientist."[81]

Such essays could not dispel the perception of open intellectual warfare that hovered about the 1925 Scopes trial in Dayton, Tennessee. The successful prosecution of John Scopes, a high school teacher who had taught about evolution in his biology class, provided a cause célèbre around which fundamentalist Christians and other religious groups could rally.[82] Contrary to what one might expect, the general magazine coverage was not slanted for or against Darwinism, or for or against Scopes. Some magazines appeared to make a real effort at even-handed coverage. Calling the trial "Monkey Business in Tennessee,"[83] *Collier's* published in the summer of 1925 articles by both the son of Charles Darwin (" 'You Can't Make a Silk Purse Out of a Sow's Ear' "[84]) and fundamentalist politician William Jennings Bryan ("The Bible's Good Enough for Me"[85]); then, in the October issue the magazine ran an interview with a physicist which focused on his religious beliefs.[86]

In a post-Scopes assessment in 1926, theologian Harry Emerson Fosdick urged restraint in the publication of criticism and condemnation of science. Science should not be stopped altogether, he argued; rather the scientists and the theologians should attempt to define common ground. Fosdick recognized that accommodation would be difficult; religious beliefs and religious texts, for example, relied on knowledge about the natural world that was contemporary to Biblical times, when those writers "supposed they were living on a flat earth covered by the solid firmament of the sky." "There is no peace for religion in its relationship with science," Fosdick wrote, "until we recognize that of course the Bible is not an inerrant book."[87] By the 1930s, even evangelist Elmer Davis considered in print how a "new Bible" could be reconciled with science.[88] Complaining that science continually changed, Davis concluded that "it may seem a waste of time to try to write a scientific Bible at all" but he did not rule out such an exercise.[89] In 1933, one biologist proposed that a "completed Christianity of Science" would soon become dominant.[90]

Pleading for more tolerance on both sides, Fosdick offered definitions of the two value systems which attempted to accommodate their intrinsic differences and allow peaceful coexistence. Science incorporated "interpretation of man's existence," study of the specific parts of life, and formulation of "the laws by which they are put together to make a complex unity," he wrote. Religion was "the appreciation of life's spiritual values and the interpretation of life, its origin, its purpose, and its destiny in terms of them."[91] Fosdick dismissed the Biblical story of creation as neither "pro-scientific" nor "anti-scientific . . . for the simple reason that it is not scientific at all."[92]

By the 1930s and 1940s, resignation to essential differences permeated popular discussion of science and religion, and most authors es-

chewed aggressive, confrontational criticism. The image of two competing intellectual or philosophical systems has remained relatively steady
ever since, but the level of widespread hostility expressed by organized
religion appears far less, at least on the surface, in the United States. Just
as Burroughs predicted, science dominated as the legitimizer of truth and
as the premier authority for social and political action; religious movements in America today appear to feel forced either to accommodate their
theology to scientific explanations of the natural world, or to reject modern
science altogether and possibly even to propose an alternative science.[93]

As proof of how entrenched these ambiguous attitudes have become,
we need only look at the more recent U.S. court battles over *creationism*.
The creationists, primarily representing fundamentalist sects, oppose any
explanations for the origin of the universe which conflict with literal interpretation of the Bible (and, in particular, with the book of Genesis). The
modern creationist movement has attempted to eliminate the teaching of
evolution from U.S. public schools or, at minimum, introduce "equal-
time" teaching of lessons on fundamentalist explanations of creation and
the development of life. Many of their recent efforts have been directed at
changing state or local laws governing school curricula. The published
reactions to these battles exemplify how entrenched certain images of science have become.

In writing about the 1981–82 legal challenge to creationism legislation in Arkansas, for example, most journalists depicted creationists as a
sincere but disadvantaged minority forced to battle the overwhelming authority of modern science.[94] They described creationists as only seeking
fair play for their ideas and equal time for their potentially legitimate interpretation of the history of the natural world. Even when newspaper
editorials called the creationists "religious zealots" and found their arguments unpersuasive, they did not throw all their support to the scientists.
Editors and journalists may not themselves have agreed with the creationists' views, but the public image of scientific authority was so strong that
fair reporting required them to present creationists as underdogs. The
plaintiffs in the Arkansas case (those who supported the teaching of evolution) in fact skillfully used these same images of authority in their legal
briefs, which emphasized the differences between the "legitimate" methods of evolutionary biology and the "pseudoscience" of creationists. Science, not religion, was the touchstone of legitimacy.

Most news coverage of the case in fact reinforced an image of a
battle between David and Goliath, especially when journalists called
scientists "angry" or "scornful" or quoted scientists' hostile characteriza-
tions of the religious fundamentalists. The scientists' statements usually
criticized the creationists on all counts: scientists were rarely quoted as

supporting the creationists' basic right to believe as they wished. The coverage also consistently (and unsympathetically) portrayed science as an "autocratic arbiter of its own rules"—no democratic participation allowed.

Unlike the 1920s coverage of the Scopes trial, which took place at a time when science had yet to achieve the social status, prestige, or authority it enjoys today, the 1980s coverage of creationism portrayed a battle between unequal forces. The cumulative effect of such popular attention has affected the stability and positiveness of the public image of science. As Americans began in this century to question the credibility and reliability of scientific authority, they also began to question whose interests the scientists promoted first, those of society or those of science.

10

The End of Progress:
Promises and Expectations

> Opposition has raised its head in vain. 'Make way for science and for
> light!' has cleared obstruction from every path. If there have been
> doubters they have been branded as foes to progress . . .
>
> The Editors of *Cosmopolitan*, 1910[1]

When science's cheerleaders cried "Make way for science and for light!,"
they employed a metaphor common throughout twentieth-century popular
science. Science sought to shed light on "the never-to-be-accepted darkness" of ignorance.[2] The scientific imagination incorporated a series of
visions that "flashed before the mind" of a researcher.[3] Scientists' eyes
were "windows of intelligence," enhanced by such instruments as telescopes and microscopes. Popularizers even accused science's critics of
proposing to return society to the "dark ages" when there was no science.

To these writers—and probably to most readers of the popular magazines—the light of science and its incessant search for new knowledge
seemed unequivocally positive. As part of this assessment, popularizers
tied the metaphor of light to the equally powerful metaphor of progress.
To shade or to dim the light of science risked inhibiting progress and en-
dangering the flow of benefits. If scientists were to illuminate the forests
of ignorance, then they must work without restraints. Writers did not question science's authority as a body of knowledge, as a social system, or as
a method; instead there was "a general tendency to regard the scientific
man as the one trustworthy authority."[4]

These images of enlightenment and authority enhanced the effect
when scientists repeatedly promised benefits from research. Because
scientists possessed intelligence and stamina, they seemed able to do almost anything. Early in this century, the popular press effused a stream of

promises that science's extraordinary success would never stop, as long as scientists were free to do their work. Even today, scientists' writings and public speeches, and the official reports of scientific advisory committees routinely promote research benefits but they rarely question the inevitability of such benefits.

Attention to science's "report card" is not, of course, necessarily bad. Many other groups and professions spend considerable money and time promoting their own accomplishments. For scientists, however, the exploitation of science's products created an unreasonable level of public expectation of cures and technical solutions and, over the course of this century, contributed to a politically volatile tug-of-war between control and freedom of research.[5]

The power of those promises derived in part from the popular images that surrounded them. As described in the previous chapter, each article on science reiterated traditional images—in metaphors, descriptions, and tone—of scientists as hardworking and intelligent, scientific methods as reliable, and scientific knowledge as authority. The effect of the roll-call of promised benefits must be measured therefore against the background of such stereotyped attributes, none more complex than the allocation of social authority.

Science: The True Authority

From one perspective, it could seem that, in this century, science received much of its praise by mistake. As engineers, managers, and industrialists did their work, the stack of benefits attributed to science grew in the popular press. Even when a new product—automobiles, radio, electrical appliances, vaccines, synthetic materials—was correctly assigned to a clever designer or inventor, there was at least a nod to its scientific foundations. The praise for science's contribution to modern technology was often quite sweeping. One *Century* author asserted in 1924 that "most of the new ideas of the last two decades have been in some way or other scientific in character. Anything that goes under the aegis of science gains a special claim to consideration."[6]

In part, this contradiction in the allocation of credit stemmed from science's unusual social prestige. The ordinary person, one writer observed, "speaks mistily about the men working in science as 'THEY'" and gives to scientists the place of authority once reserved for political or ecclesiastical rulers.[7] This authority is more dangerous, he added, because it is unquestioning, and because the scientists are so remote. The ordinary citizen "does not even know the names of these intellectual leaders, and probably has never come into contact with one of them," even though he speaks "hopefully about the way in which 'They' are sure to master the secrets of Nature." [8]

Such confusion of science and technology (and their combined record of success) formed a litany repeated endlessly in the magazines, a theme that reinforced science as an unquestionable authority. To doubt scientists' recommendations or promises betrayed a lack of faith in science, popularizers accused; they dismissed skepticism as not only inappropriate but possibly dangerous. The scientists' "boasted power to foretell and control upon the basis of [their] hypotheses has been too often vindicated to permit a skepticism . . ."[9]

Scientific authority also rested, as discussed in Chapter 7, on the acceptance of research methods as the only legitimate routes "for the discovery of truth and for its explanation and description." [10] Reflection in tranquility might not guarantee understanding of the human mind, but the experiments of psychology definitely would. Some critics blamed scientists for deliberately promoting such an image, for deluding society "into believing that the only proof worthy of the name, adequate and true, is proof set up in scientific formulae," [11] but such accusations were rare in the popular magazines. *Science,* for most writers, represented "a prestige word of great potency"; when attached to a topic, a method, or a program, the term awarded an "honorific significance." [12] Expressing attitudes widespread at the time, sociologist Robert K. Merton observed in a 1937 speech that there existed "an increasing gap between the scientist and the laity. The layman must take on faith the publicized statements about relativity or quanta or other such esoteric subjects." As a result, Merton continued, "science and esoteric terminology become indissolubly linked" and thus when "apparently scientific jargon" clothes mysticisms or political ideology, the layperson cannot judge its authenticity. "The borrowed authority of science," Merton noted, "becomes a powerful prestige symbol . . ."[13]

The dangers inherent in allocating unquestioned authority to every scientific pronouncement concerned many observers. J. W. N. Sullivan, the great British science writer, speculated that in the absence of more specialized information, nonscientists initially assessed scientific theories by the degree to which those theories "squared with common sense" (that is, by whether the theories agreed with what they already knew). As theoretical constructs moved farther from everyday experience, he noted, readers easily developed an "uncritical credulity" toward science. As instruments became more complicated, the objects of scrutiny smaller, and the theories more abstract, nonscientists willingly gave "a measure of credence to almost anything that professe[d] to be scientific," and thereby intensified the influence of pseudoscience labeled as science.[14] Even if an idea was far-fetched, Sullivan wrote, simply labeling it as *scientific* would ensure its acceptance; most laypersons would not risk dismissing a scientific theory "merely because it sounds ridiculous." [15] A few journalists retained some "shallow" skepticism in the face of such pressure, but most presented science as "the one key to knowledge, the one source of truth, in the modern world." [16]

When scientists spoke authoritatively on topics outside their field of expertise, they relied on these and related popular beliefs for acceptance. Writing in 1921, entomologist Vernon Kellogg asserted, for example, that there were many areas of human life in which, although the biologist might be inexperienced, he might nevertheless "believe he has at least as much right as anyone else to venture." [17] By the late 1920s, some scientists seemed inclined to become self-appointed experts on almost everything. The practice attracted considerable criticism but continued nonetheless. Magazinists warned their readers against assuming that "the specialist in any particular science is ipso facto also well qualified to speak with equal authority on religion and philosophy." [18] As one journalist wrote, in such a climate there appeared to be little difference between "a scientist adrift in religion and a Methodist bishop floundering in Geology." [19]

The overreaching scientific expert became even more of a political problem in the 1940s. Both the scientists lobbying for *and* those lobbying against federal policy on atomic weapons used their scientific reputations to attract public support for their political views, although many of their colleagues found such practices inappropriate. In 1945, sociologist George Lundberg, for example, attacked scientists who knowingly used their scientific reputations to gain a public hearing:

> Both scientists and the public have frequently assumed that when scientists engage in ordinary pressure group activity, that activity somehow becomes science or scientific activity. It is not surprising, perhaps, that the public should be confused on this point, because it may not always be clear when a scientist is expressing a scientific conclusion and when he is expressing a personal preference. [20]

Lundberg argued that it was "unpardonable" of scientists to confuse statements based on what they knew as scientists with statements based on their personal beliefs about religion, morals, or politics. "To pose as distinguished scientists announcing scientific conclusions when in fact they are merely expressing personal or group preferences is simple fraud." [21] No one argued that scientists should make no public statements about science-related political issues; rather, commentators pointed out that scientists had a responsibility in such situations to acknowledge the social or political nature of the issue and to clarify that they spoke as citizens, but not necessarily as experts.[22]

Other scientists agreed more with the view, espoused by chemist Harold C. Urey in the 1940s, that although scientists should indeed speak as citizens on certain public issues, their citizenship carried special privileges and responsibilities. Urey unfortunately demonstrated in his writings some of the same narrow-minded attitudes that he condemned. "Most scientists," he wrote, "prefer to view their present interest as 'social awareness' ":

> It is as if a bacteriologist had discovered a dread disease which might lead to a disastrous epidemic. He would not be a 'politician' if he asked that the city health commission take measures to deal with a plague. He would merely be demonstrating common decency and social awareness of what his discovery meant to human lives.[23]

To readers in 1946, that analogy probably seemed farfetched; surely the bacteriologists would know best about epidemics and public health decisions. Today, after such episodes as the swine flu vaccination program (in which epidemiologists' advice influenced a premature and inadvertently harmful program of mass inoculations), we have ample evidence that even the most well-intentioned scientific announcements can sometimes provoke unforeseen and terrible political and social consequences, and can even result in loss of life.[24] Urey's suggestion that it would be both advisable and responsible for scientists to use their authority as scientists to stimulate political action represented attitudes prevalent in the scientific community at the time and helps to explain why even skeptical journalists allocated such unwarranted universal authority to scientists.

Promises

The chain of authority linking the legitimacy of scientific methods and the authenticity of scientific knowledge to the personal opinions of scientists also tied together the promises of science and the public's expectations. The popular magazines record an extraordinary message communicated throughout this century, a litany of promises that science would cure every disease, fix every problem, and brush away every tear—if only research was kept free of undue restraint. This "song of science," when viewed en masse in the texts of thousands of magazines, showed a public image of science that was not only inconsistent with reality but also politically unstable.

It is easy to understand why so many journalists inadvertently treated the scientists as able to predict the outcome of all their research; as anthropologist and science writer Loren Eiseley has written, people "have an insatiable demand for soothsayers and oracles to assure them and comfort them about the insubstantial road they tread."[25] Whether portrayed as hero, wizard, or expert, the magazine scientist was a man in motion, ever seeking the new.[26] Even when standing still, he stretched to peer over the next horizon. He thus became both prophet and producer.

Sensitive to the dangers of inflated public expectations, a few scientists tempered their remarks with qualifications. In 1912, astronomer Edward Arthur Fath wrote that the possibilities of his research were "endless, but, in view of the fact that our actual knowledge is practically nil, such speculation is largely fruitless."[27] Similarly, a biologist commented in 1921 that naturalists could claim only that they know "a part of the order of nature."[28] But far more articles painted a different picture, and both journalists and scientists participated in developing those expectations. Journalists in fact often seemed to lean forward and encourage scientists to make predictions. Each time a scientist complied, it reinforced the journalists' expectation of such behavior.

If scientists had limited those responses to cautious and qualified predictions, science's real achievements would in fact have afforded ample prestige; but, as hundreds of articles show, they rarely did so. Contrary to what some historians have argued, most scientists participated extensively (and apparently willingly) in the cycle of promises.[29] Perhaps out of enthusiasm for their work, perhaps out of some naive desire to please the journalists who were interviewing them, or perhaps out of a spirit of self-confidence, the scientists promised benefits from all they did. In article after article, they abandoned the usual tentative language of their scientific papers and adopted the popular rhetoric of "the sure thing."

Several years ago, in commenting on the evolution of public attitudes to science, Charles Spencer divided the 1970s "rebellion against science" into two separate influences: one he identified as the counterculture's "humanistic view"; the other as changes in "what people believe science can do for them or for society."[30] The 1970s disillusionment, he believed, derived from the combination of images of science as "the key to utopia" and the realization that utopia was no longer within reach. Spencer suggested that to study the roots of this attitude, one might review systematically "what science promised society." In fact, by analyzing the texts of articles in twentieth-century popular magazines, it was possible to do just that.

The magazine's promises ranged from the modest ("You'll be able to walk through a downpour after the war without losing the crease in your pants"[31]) to the fantastic ("Out of the test tube comes a thrilling age of magic, in which you will melt your unwashed dishes down the drain, buy fifty new suits of clothes and throw them away unlaundered"[32]). In 1910,

readers were told that "every hour is pregnant with promise of other discoveries";[33] in 1920, they were reminded of "the unlimited possibilities of
future scientific productivity";[34] and in 1946 they were assured that if a
solution existed to any problem, then scientists would eventually find it.[35]
A physicist was quoted in 1950 as saying that he thought "scientific research is the answer to every material problem now facing us."[36] Even
J. D. Bernal, the British crystallographer and Marxist critic, predicted that
"we may judge from the history of science that even greater possibilities
lie in new discoveries of which at present we have no idea."[37] The promises involved about every conceivable solution to human problems or fulfillment of human desires. A *Cosmopolitan* article in 1912 outlined scientists' ultimate promise—"the conquest of death itself"—as it described
their attempts to provide "immortality" for all people.[38]

Promises sometimes involved the use of new technologies. Articles
in the 1910s and 1920s hinted at the social changes that radio would bring,
for example.[39] Although some of those predictions represented plausible
ideas, others represented magnificent fantasies. Radio "both fitted into and
extended Americans' notions of how the future would be made better,
maybe even perfect, through technology," one historian observes, by helping to deliver society "from a troubled present to a utopian future."[40] In
1924, Waldemar Kaempffert described "To-Morrow's Wireless" thus:

> As a wine-glass vibrates with sound when its rim is rubbed, so the earth will
> vibrate electrically when it is subjected to the action of millions of impulses
> correctly timed. And those impulses will be imparted by gigantic induction-
> coils incorporated in immense towering steel cages. . . . In every large city,
> you will see such a steel frame, projecting far up into the sky, overtopping
> houses and buildings. . . . [41]

Kaempffert reported that Nicholas Tesla, inventor of the induction coil,
imagined that his device would enable the world to unite in a "community
of interest" for a "harmonious existence" in the future, a promise repeated
in another article which predicted that radio would bring "education and
happiness and democracy" as well as cultural, social, and political unifi-
cation.[42]

One of the most prominent "boosters" of science and engineering in
the 1920s, Floyd W. Parsons, believed that people could not be "sheltered
from the effects of scientific advance," for science was "revolutionizing"
industry and "transforming business from a routine grind into a romantic
adventure."[43] He was certain that the scientific advances of the next decades would "represent more progress than had previously been made in all
recorded history." His articles mixed impossible or implausible examples
with some that now we take for granted. Parsons predicted that "surface

cars" would "go out of business"; there would be "power transmission without wires"; airplanes would sell for $150; accurate earthquake and flood predictions would minimize damage; sidewalks would be "arcaded under the buildings"; there would be color motion pictures; and there would be radios on all trains.[44]

Promises regarding the production or processing of food were common. Articles predicted that science would "so increase productivity" that starvation would be eliminated and that synthetic food would soon become a reality.[45] In the 1940s and 1950s, *Collier's* authors predicted such wonders as "new bread from the sea," a sea algae that would provide "an inexhaustible supply of food."[46] In another *Collier's* article, the staff writer advocated a "Manhattan Project" to meet international food needs: with such a crash research effort, he argued, Western society could "win the stakes" in the "food race" and grow "enough food for the millions today and those to come."[47]

Some promises were linked to ongoing research. In describing weather forecasting, authors declared that "physicists are brewing sample patches of the weather we'll enjoy tomorrow" and that scientists could already "produce rain or snow virtually at will."[48] Once the space program was underway, authors made many promises about its success. "The Army Air Force has announced that research underway might produce a rocket to the moon within the next eighteen months," Eugene H. Kone wrote in 1946.[49]

Postwar debates over two scientific issues—atomic energy research and cancer research—exemplified how promises that continued from decade to decade throughout this century could build a foundation of essentially unfulfillable public expectations.

The Promises of Atomic Energy

Long before Alamogordo gave proof of atomic energy's terrible potential, journalists had publicized the promises inherent in the research (see Figure 10.1).[50] In 1933, Charles F. Kettering wrote, "Suppose that, within twelve months, scientists, using the tools already in their hands, begin to blow atoms to pieces."[51] A 1934 *Harper's* article explained the newest "Discoveries within the Atom" and promised many new uses.[52] And *Collier's* editors described in 1940 "the new and fascinating way of life that lies within the immediate grasp of man through utilization of Uranium-235, the long-sought, parochial source of atomic power."[53] "War itself will become obsolete," the author of that article predicted: "Although engineers would apply this new power, some of the glory must be reserved for the physicists," he insisted with unforeseen irony.[54]

In the *Post* in 1940, William L. Laurence told breathlessly how the

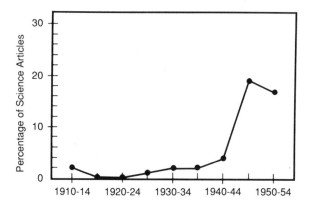

Figure 10.1. Articles on atomic energy, 1910–54. The proportion of all articles which discussed atomic physics research or research related to atomic energy ($n = 45$). Data are taken from a sample of eleven U.S. mass-circulation magazines and are given as a percentage of all science articles published in those magazines during each five-year period.

atom had already given up its secrets; he described the newest work of Otto Hahn, Lise Meitner, Enrico Fermi, Niels Bohr, and other physicists, and then outlined what their research could mean for society.[55] (Figure 7.3 shows the opening pages from that article.) Although Laurence and other journalists knew of suggestions that atomic energy would have considerable military usefulness, they optimistically emphasized the domestic uses of atomic physics. In *Harper's,* John J. O'Neill wrote that, after weighing the possible benefits and the dangers of atomic energy, "the net results appear to be an indication that the discovery of the Uranium 235 process for the release of atomic energy promises the dawn of a new era for mankind."[56] In the early 1940s, most popular commentators regarded the "new era" as one to be welcomed, not feared.

After the American public learned about the terrible destruction at Hiroshima and Nagasaki, they could not ignore the other side of this gift from the scientists. Even the most optimistic booster of science could see what the new dawn had revealed; in the magazines, themes of destruction and death increased. And, as historian Paul Boyer describes in *By the Bomb's Early Light,* this tone of fear pervaded all of American culture.[57] Although magazines continued to praise scientists for having helped to win the war in the Pacific, the cheers had a hollow ring.

Some of this change resulted from scientists' own public statements about government programs for atomic energy research and from their participation in the debate over military control. Manhattan Project scientists had soon realized that they could not pack the moral and political implications of atomic weapons away with the uniforms and campaign ribbons, and some of them began nationwide lobbying efforts to inform public decision making.[58] Because they knew that research on ever more destructive weapons was moving forward, physicists sensed the urgency of affecting political plans to expand the research and to restrict international cooperation.

Public concern, as reflected in the tone of magazine coverage, developed slowly, however, perhaps because the initial expectations had been so high. The boosters of atomic power also continued to exaggerate its potential. Even after the war, optimistic outlines of the peaceful uses of atomic energy continued.[59] When sociologist Steven Del Sesto analyzed postwar reception to atomic power, he found that the idea of "unlimited power" captured the imagination of all sorts of writers—politicians, political scientists, and scientists—who promoted it as, among other things, potentially reducing manual labor, propelling automobiles and ocean liners, and assuring world peace.[60]

Within a year or so, positive expressions gave way to mixed messages of expectation and fear, as more and more articles described the lingering physiological effects of radiation, the "deplorable" state of current civil defense, and the implications of the new "nuclear politics."[61] Some of this change coincided with deteriorating relations between the United States and the Soviet Union and the consequent demands of the Cold War.[62] In 1947, lawyer and science writer James R. Newman reconstructed the process then taking place within the scientific community. The scientists, he said, "were certain that the use of fissionable and radioactive materials would lead to further significant discoveries in basic science, which in time would produce innumerable and unpredictable technological devices," but that they believed such benefits were far away.[63] In the near term, he said, there were "limited" medical applications and possibly some domestic energy production. Newman then identified the issue that still lies at the heart of public attitudes to nuclear energy: the unpredictability of its use. Something about this product of science seemed different, its ambiguity unmistakable. Biologists had made startling and uncomfortable discoveries; chemists had developed chemicals of alarming toxicity; but any of these results seemed more controllable than the new atomic physics. The atomic and hydrogen bombs made suspect all previous generalizations about research applications and about whether researchers could control their science. Newman attributed public disillusionment to the scientists' apparent inability to predict what research would bring. The same people who demonstrated startling insight "into the heart of the atom," he wrote, "can only guess at the scope of the application of the power they have won; and they profess no confidence at all in predicting the social, economic, and political consequences of their discovery."[64]

In fact, uncontrollability, not technical unpredictability, raised the level of fear. Scientists could predict accurately the technical limits of their work (e.g., the range of a bomb's destruction, its so-called killing power) but they could not predict the social and political aspects of its use, such as whether, when, how, or by whom it might be used.

Such descriptions as Newman's portrayed scientists as failed magicians. Some scientists might continue to predict that some day "wholesale blessings will flow from the atom," and others might call atomic energy "a gift richer by far than the gift of Promethean fire that started man on his slow march from the cave on the road to the stars"; but, face to face with their own discovery, the scientists appeared powerless to live up to their own promises.[65]

The ambiguity apparent in magazine discussion of atomic and nuclear power through the 1950s persists today. As recorded in many social surveys, a majority of Americans can identify some benefits from the production of nuclear energy, but most also see possible harmful consequences from the work. In the mid-1980s, Americans were almost equally divided on whether the benefits outweighed the harms or vice versa.[66]

Cures for Cancer

The promises of atomic energy encompassed the fate of the whole world; biology, on the other hand, promised results of concern to each individual reader.[67] In 1954 *Collier's* observed that

> A little more than a decade ago scientists unraveled the mystery of the atom and began the atomic age. Today an equally basic mystery is being solved— that is the living cell, indeed the secret of life itself. As a result, we may be on the threshold of a hopeful new era in which cancer, mental illness, and, in fact, nearly all diseases now regarded as incurable will cease to torment man.[68]

Postwar biology in fact provided science with some of its most notable successes and its longest unfulfilled promise. In the 1940s and 1950s, descriptions of discoveries that might cure some disease or relieve some painful condition filled the magazines. Many promises proved correct, although not always in the time predicted:

1941   In a few more years . . . chemotherapy—will give us a cure for tuberculosis.[69]

1944   The magic which will eradicate leprosy and tuberculosis may be just around the corner.[70]

1949   In the four years since its discovery, streptomycin has become rec-
       ognized as the best of all known drugs for combating tuberculo-
       sis. . . . Its promise is staggering.[71]
1950   We are also apparently on the verge of discovering a vaccine for
       polio.[72]

On occasion, a journalist might emphasize that a researcher was reluctant to say anything "which might arouse false hopes in the ill"; in
interviews, some scientists carefully stressed the "serious shortcomings"
of their work or warned that it might not live up to its early promise.[73]
Neither journalists nor readers could ignore the impressive advances that
medical research had already made, however, and it always seemed that
even better things were to come. No matter how cautiously they phrased
the first part of an article, few writers seemed able to resist adding stirring,
hope-filled conclusions. "They no longer apply the word 'hopeless' to any
disease," one journalist wrote in 1950:

> During the last few years they have made greater discoveries than during all
> the long history of medicine. They are now digging deeper into the unknown
> than ever before. They still have a long way to go before they discover
> remedies for all our ills, but they are marching steadily toward that goal.[74]

In the midst of all this optimism, one longtime promise of medical
research remained conspicuously unfulfilled: a cure for cancer. Few science topics were covered by the magazines with such consistency throughout the period studied. Each of the eleven magazines published many articles on the treatment and cure of cancer (see Figures 10.2 and 10.3).
From "Conquest of Cancer" (*Cosmopolitan,* August 1912) to "Chemicals
for Cancer" (*Atlantic,* March 1954), journalists and scientists alike recounted "the latest and most authoritative statements on the subject."[75]
They told readers about "the recent gains . . . and the further moves necessary" and described how "the great ring of science [was] slowly surrounding the greatest disease killer of the present day."[76]
    Early in the century, writers routinely repeated inflated promises
made by scientists. In the 1920s, one author remonstrated, "I am happy to
assure my readers that cancer is curable, *provided* the advice of those who
have been in constant contact with this terrible disease is sought and followed."[77] Even in 1954, the head of a major research group boasted that,
despite the inadequacy of current research methods, the development of a
cure was inevitable: "The basic advances which have been made foretell
the future development of more effective treatment as certainly as the day
follows the night."[78] Later in the same article, he used more cautious lan-

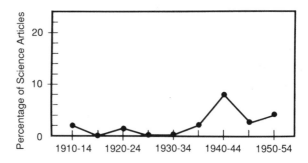

Figure 10.2. Articles on cancer research, 1910–54. The proportion of all articles which discussed research on cancer ($n = 14$). Data are taken from a sample of eleven U.S. mass-circulation magazines and are given as a percentage of all science articles published in those magazines during each five-year period.

guage, but such reticence did not dampen public expectations, fueled by decades of medical progress.[79] The Gallup Poll for December 1949 reported that 88% of Americans believed that "a cure for cancer" would be found within the next fifty years.[80] In the late 1940s, writers even linked the promises of peaceful atomic energy with cancer research: "No scientist now would dare predict just where or when in the struggle against cancer the final break will come. We can be sure, however, that atomic energy in its various forms will contribute heavily to the final victory."[81]

After decades of promises about a cure for cancer, the tone of discourse slowly changed. A note of caution—slight but perceptible—had appeared in the magazines by the 1950s. Journalists still cheerfully assured readers that cures would be found, but they also appraised the time and effort required to achieve such cures with a more jaundiced eye. Fewer and fewer articles trumpeted the small steps forward. The level of promise and excitement remained high (compared to discussions of other research fields), but writers were more cautious about predicting universal cures. The tone changed noticeably from nervous impatience to wary appraisal.

Perhaps improvements in the quality of medical reporting overall influenced this change. Perhaps the writers simply had a better idea of the realistic potential of the research. By then, the researchers themselves were also acknowledging how complicated the scientific questions were; their statements to journalists may have reflected their own reassessments of whether a cure was possible.[82] More likely, better reporting and the scientists' caution combined with shifting public attitudes toward science in general to produce a more tempered perspective on the research potential in this field.

This interpretation is consistent with data from social surveys conducted in the 1950s, which showed public confidence in all types of research to be relatively strong. A 1957 survey by the National Association of Science Writers, for example, concluded that the public "believed that science and technology had won the war, created 'miracle' drugs, and would continue to produce a cornucopia of benefits to American society."[83] Most people thought that science made their lives "healthier, easier, and more comfortable."[84]

Similar continuity may be seen in public estimates that are neither Pollyannaish nor thoroughly supportive of the success of cancer research. The 1985 National Science Foundation survey found that 55% of the public thought it "very likely" that researchers would discover a cure for common forms of cancer in the next twenty-five years or so, down slightly from optimism of previous years but still high; 37% thought it "possible"; and 6% thought it not likely at all.[85] Even though estimates of the likelihood of a cure are now more realistic (and therefore more pessimistic) than fifty years ago, the general image of medical research has not changed all that much and still translates into a poignant hope for the cure of all sorts of diseases and conditions. A mood of yearning optimism, now tempered with pragmatic caution, remains the principal metaphor, probably because the researchers themselves consistently endorsed this image.[86]

Developing Expectations

No dramatic sea change took place in the public presentation of science from the 1910s through the 1950s; it did not shift abruptly from positive to negative (or vice versa). Clusters of images all fit together to create a

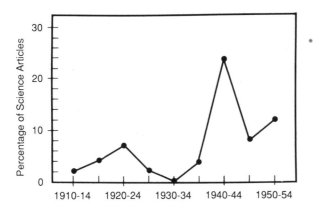

Figure 10.3. Articles on medical research, 1910–54. The proportion of articles which discussed research on all types of diseases or medical conditions, including cancer ($n = 34$). Data are taken from a sample of eleven U.S. mass-circulation magazines and are given as a percentage of all science articles published in those magazines during each five-year period.

portrait of something called *science* conducted by some people called *scientists.*

Nevertheless, one common message echoed throughout these magazine articles. It was elusive (and unmeasurable in any quantitative sense) but persistent. There was an unmistakable tone of expectation—not anticipation of any one benefit, or fear of any specific harm, but a shared expectation that science would not be passive, and that scientific research would produce a better world. Americans surely did not believe that scientists would solve all problems. They did not really believe that science could wash away hunger, poverty, and disease, or that it could be "the very death of death." They did, however, appear to expect that *something* would happen and that in most cases the benefit would be large.

Several distinct characteristics of the popular presentation of science contributed to this tone of expectation. First, repeated descriptions of research success and a constant, unquestioning emphasis on the reliability and accuracy of scientific methods (Salomon's *science as technique*) reinforced an image of science's strong cultural authority. Second, each time they failed to question a scientist's claim to universal expertise, journalists inadvertently strengthened the social prestige of all scientists. Third, when popularizers' emphasized science as power, by listing its products and describing the productivity of scientists, they boosted expectations of its potential usefulness. Fourth, describing scientists as different, as simultaneously apart from and superior to the rest of society, made them appear to be subject to different rules. Fifth, the repeated assertion that scientists were motivated only by altruism or intellectual curiosity made them appear to be trustworthy and reliable in all their promises. And, sixth, the omnipresence of science in all parts of popular culture, not only through specific descriptions, but also through multiple references to science or scientific methods in discussions of most other topics, increased its seeming importance.

The authority, power, prestige, complexity, and bounty of science so overwhelmed nonscientists that even naturally inquisitive journalists, as well as unsympathetic social commentators and critics of science, accepted without question most of what scientists said. The skepticism inherent in political reporting was rarely applied to science, at least in the first part of the century. Muckraking magazines like *Cosmopolitan* and *Collier's,* which excoriated corrupt politicians in almost every issue early in the century, let scientists appear to be without fault.

Perhaps this tendency represented a human predisposition to choose the rosy promise rather than admit the gloomy possibility. The magazine scientists seemed optimistic and well-meaning; they looked toward the future, not the past, and worked with confidence and boundless energy.

Perhaps both the journalists and their audiences wanted to believe in the scientists' best intentions and, even though they knew that it was impossible, also wanted to believe that science might eventually dispel all evils. The optimism inherent in every act of research undoubtedly fueled the hope—especially in the years before and after the great wars—that science would rescue society from the morass of difficulties facing the world. Science would do what politicians seemed unable to do: provide sufficient food, make war obsolete, prevent natural disasters, and eliminate disease. Journalists and scientists alike endorsed research as the universal panacea.

This concurrence of promise and potential also helped to maintain the public's faith in science through the 1950s and 1960s, even though many promises went unfulfilled, and unpredicted side effects seemed to threaten human life and well-being. Cancer research had yet to find a cure; Rachel Carson showed that chemical pesticides harmed more than insects; but the public's expectations and enthusiasm remained unabated.

Loren Eiseley has argued that unfocused waiting (i.e., waiting for nothing in particular) is symptomatic of this century's confusion and despair and that confusion over what society wants comes from its failure to control its own institutions.[87] Certainly this seems true for science. Americans allowed scientists both to predict what bounty they would produce and to choose which research areas they would pursue. Convinced that science was incomprehensible and that scientists were the only ones who should control science, society could only watch and wait. As critic Roy Kenneth Hack wrote in an *Atlantic* short story in 1916, "The modern world has persuaded itself that all it has to do is to hand over its fortune to science. Science has accepted the trust."[88] Until mid-century, few journalists or politicians questioned the wisdom of that trust. The tone of anticipation observed in the magazines thus represented the failure of both the journalists *and* their audiences to question science and scientists. All too often, they both accepted science's promises at face value.

11

Continuity and Change

In the 1910s, science fit smoothly, if untrumpeted, into national life. Today, it cannot be dismissed, disregarded, or ignored. Sometimes thrilling, sometimes thorny, never neutral, science in American culture seems neither good nor bad but somehow both, an institution we simultaneously need and fear, appreciate and suspect.

The political incorporation of science in the United States—connecting research to national needs, financing the education of scientists, and subsidizing research institutions—intensified across the century, but our beliefs about science (and especially our expectations of its potential) have remained significantly stable. As social analyst Daniel Yankelovich has observed, "Change is the one constant we expect in our history, and yet, despite all the changes, certain themes in American culture persist generation after generation."[1] During the first fifty years of this century, science itself changed radically—in funding, instrumentation, policy implications, and personnel—but the public images of science exhibited strong continuity of interpretation, consolidating oft-repeated subthemes of authority, usefulness, complexity, and bounty. Public opinion surveys since the 1950s show the continued stability of many of these themes. Americans still approve of science and respect scientific genius, and they still expect great benefits from research; they do, however, now freely question the uses of science and, on occasion, question scientists' actions. This situation has several implications for public policy on science and for the communicators who mediate between scientists and the public.

Images and Attitudes after 1955: Implications for Policy

In the decades since the 1950s, the mass media in the United States have consistently expressed mixed messages about science. Discussions of the positive benefits of research appear side by side with those of such gifts as nuclear waste and pesticide pollution. Promises of universal cures for disease follow news stories about cancers linked to once-promising industrial chemicals. The message seems clear: Science gives, but science also takes. Nevertheless, public attitude surveys show that most Americans still have a positive image of science and scientific research overall.[2] Americans surveyed in the late 1950s assigned high value to science; the world was better and people were healthier because of science, they believed, and those who discerned some threat in scientific research (e.g., science "makes life change too fast") were in the minority.[3] When Karen Oppenheim compared 1950s data with surveys run in 1964, she detected a slight increase in negative assessments of science; by then, over half of the American public thought that science was causing some social changes and doing so too swiftly (a strengthening of the image of science as a runaway engine of progress), and similar majorities believed that science was breaking down traditional ethical boundaries between right and wrong.[4] These data did not indicate widespread rejection of science, however, and comparisons of surveys from the 1950s and 1960s with those sponsored by the National Science Board (NSB) since 1972 show continued strong belief in the beneficial nature of science. In the 1950s, over four-fifths of the public thought the world "better off" because of science; in 1985, a National Science Foundation survey asked whether, on balance, Americans thought the benefits of scientific research outweighed harmful results, and a majority agreed, to greater or lesser degrees.[5] That same survey concluded that people continue to expect "significant outcomes" from science and found that three-quarters of the public believes that, even if it brings no immediate benefits, scientific research should receive federal support.[6]

Confidence in scientific institutions plays an important role in the depth of public enthusiasm for scientific research and in Americans' willingness to trust the overall goals of that research. Since 1966, two major public opinion organizations, as part of their general surveys on trust in all types of national social and political institutions (e.g., the press, the Supreme Court, religion), have asked Americans to assess their feelings of confidence in "the people running the scientific community." On the basis of those data, which indicate declining levels of confidence, many members of the scientific community began in the 1970s to be concerned about trust in science in general and to warn of invidious antiscience feelings.[7] Examination of those surveys shows, however, that respect for leaders of *all* American institutions is declining. Science has, in fact, actually gained in status since the 1960s, having steadily maintained position as the second most respected institution (after medicine) since 1978.[8]

Like attitudes toward most other institutions or professions, attitudes toward science include complex judgments tagged to social values and to beliefs about the importance (or lack of importance) and inherent usefulness of certain activities, but large social surveys are not the only means of measuring such attitudes. In 1982, I worked with John Doble, Gerald Holton, and Daniel Yankelovich in developing a pilot research project to measure such beliefs, in regard to how Americans assessed the importance of different types of research.[9] Using a focus group format developed by Yankelovich's Public Agenda Foundation, the project assembled six groups of ten to fifteen people in different cities across the United States. Participants were chosen, through standard small-group techniques, to approximate the general population and, although slightly better educated than the national average (53% had one or more college degrees), they were sufficiently representative on other characteristics (e.g., age, gender, race) to reflect the views of mainstream Americans.

Each group met for several hours. First given pretests of their attitudes toward science and social issues, they were then asked to discuss and rate hypothetical scientific and technological research proposals that had been written to exemplify specific evaluative criteria, such as offering practical but long-term benefits (e.g., research on photosynthesis in green plants) or having potentially high but uncalculated risks (e.g., research on laser isotope separation of uranium). After some group discussion of arguments for and against funding, each person rated the priority of the projects. Other tests designed by Public Agenda measured such factors as attitude change, attentiveness to science in general, and individual value systems.

The project showed that people often utilize more than one criterion when asked to rate their support for specific scientific projects, and they apply different criteria to different projects. When deciding whether research should continue, they do not view science monolithically, according to some rigid stereotype; instead, they focus on a proposed project, initially biased toward funding but then, after they learn more about it, assessing benefits or risks according to their own value system. Perhaps because most media coverage is oriented around results and projects, people do not automatically view science as a unified structure; they certainly do not readily perceive relationships between projects or regard scientific fields as interdependent.

Americans also appear to assign little or no intrinsic value to science as a cultural institution. That majestic edifice that scientists (and science writers) praise with such sympathy simply may not exist in the minds of most Americans. Instead, they see "science" as instrumentally valuable, just one among many human activities that can improve the quality of life. This practical view of science might well help to explain the conflation of science and technology so prominent in American popular culture: science appears as a more esoteric but nonetheless practical initiator of technology. Other survey data from the 1970s and 1980s, for example, show that the images of science and technology have either merged or are continually confused; moreover, basic research attracts "little independent support" in the polls and instead "the public priorities for science strongly emphasize immediate practical contributions to everyday life and well-being."[10] Our project concluded that rather than being a form of "crude utilitarianism," the instrumental image indicated that the public approves of research because of its promise and potential. Participants in the focus groups often interpreted the phrase *science for its own sake*, for example, as implying some practical benefit nonetheless.

Americans also assign greatest importance to research that, if successful, will be useful (and hence used). These attitudes coincide with earlier public images of science as best when it is of use, and they help to explain continually weak support for the social sciences and the more esoteric basic research fields. As one participant in the focus groups phrased it, "You're talking about the quality of life for your children and grandchildren, and the more practical kinds of research will have much more bearing on that than studying quasars, as much as we would like to know more about them."[11]

When asked to establish criteria for scientific choice, Americans also believe that they have a right to be involved—experts alone should not choose what benefits should be sought and what risks the research might acceptably pose. The participants in our project, for example, were not antiscience on any of the measures applied. They often argued strongly that science and technology had made the world better, and they showed respect for scientists and great faith in science's ability to help in solving great national problems. They did not, however, feel that scientists alone should determine research priorities and felt that it was both appropriate and, in some cases, necessary to impose limits on research agenda and methods. They believed that citizens have every right to participate in decisions about the directions and practices of science because of the risks and benefits involved and, most importantly, because such participation is consistent with democratic principles. Such attitudes, in fact, contribute to declining trust in the leaders of the scientific community, which in turn now justifies increased public control over the direction and goals of science.

Many people believe that certain aspects of human life should be off-limits for science, not just in whether or how research knowledge is used but also in how research data is gathered. When participants in our survey negatively assessed an applied social science proposal, they often used arguments similar to those made forty years earlier in the mass magazines about the appropriateness and legitimacy of the social sciences. The public still may not regard the social sciences as equal to other research fields in their legitimacy, authority, and importance.

Despite continued strong support for science and scientists, Americans increasingly express beliefs, through social surveys and through political actions, that research should not progress unrestrained, especially on certain topics or employing certain methods. Minor but strong opposition exists to research on longevity and to research that uses animals.[12] About one-third of the public responding to the 1987 NSB survey oppose studies that might lead to precise weather control and modification (indicating that some people recognize that even benign-sounding research in meteorology could produce negative effects). Opposition also exists to research to create new forms of animal and plant life (42% of respondents in the 1985 NSB survey) and to create new biological and chemical weapons (66% opposed). Most people feel that the level of government regulation at present is appropriate, but surveys in the 1980s show that as many as one-fifth of the public believe that regulation of genetic research is "too low." Over one-tenth think that regulation of all basic research is "too high," however, indicating strong political support for research regulation.

The impulse to control scientific research concurs with attitude shifts found throughout American culture, which appears to be moving from "an optimistic expectation of an open-ended and unlimited future to a fear of instability and a new sense of limits."[13] Americans still support growth in science, but they are skeptical about science's ever-expanding progress and unlimited benefits. By the late 1970s, general social surveys such as those run by the Gallup and the Yankelovich organizations showed increasing concern about the nation's economic future and strong beliefs that personal well-being might not be automatic.[14] It should not be surprising then that many Americans believe that scientists should share in the shortfall and the sacrifices. The majority no longer believe that scientists work for knowledge's sake, for example, thereby acknowledging the economic connection of science and obliterating the old myths of altruism. As the nature of the relationship between science and society undergoes tougher political scrutiny and reassessment, science moves into a regulatory environment of social or political controls, limits, and restrictions on all parts of the research process.[15] Some of these changes in public attitudes draw on social fears of new types of research; some react to real abuses. Some cultural attitudes may also be the result of continued tension between science and moral philosophy, such as that between science and fundamentalism.[16]

The images of scientists as individuals also have special implications for science policymakers. Many of the characteristic stereotypes found in twentieth-century magazines have been measured in social surveys conducted since that time. Research in the 1950s, for example, showed that most Americans perceived scientists as useful and well-meaning and wanting "to work on things that will make life better for the average person"; but a significant minority (under one-quarter) saw scientists as overly curious, as prying into parts of life best left unstudied.[17] Over 40% believed scientists to be "odd and peculiar people," and most thought that they worked harder than the average person.[18] Only a minority (slightly over one-quarter) agreed with the statement that "scientists are mainly interested in knowledge for its own sake" and have no interest in the practical value of research.

In the late 1970s, a replication of the classic 1950s survey conducted by Margaret Mead and Rhoda Métraux found that students' images of scientists had not changed; most high-school students (and their teachers) still believed that scientists have disaffected personalities, few hobbies, and little social life because they are so wrapped up in their work.[19] Around the same time, a British survey of science-attentive magazine readers found that most regarded scientists as "remote, withdrawn, secretive, unpopular, and singular-minded."[20] In reviewing research on attitudes to scientists, Georgine Pion and Mark W. Lipsey concluded in 1981 that modern American images of scientists are clearly "stereotypical and distorted."[21] The National Science Foundation surveys confirm this further; in 1985, four-fifths of the public regarded scientific researchers as "dedicated people who work for the good of humanity," yet slightly over half believed that scientific knowledge gave those same researchers "a power that makes them dangerous."[22]

None of these surveys emphasize the gender or race of the images, perhaps because the image of scientists as white and male is so dominant and obvious, and therefore statistically uninteresting to survey analysts. Certainly when studies do look at such issues (as in those cited at the end of Chapter 5), they confirm the strength of the stereotype. If these images are allowed to continue, important opportunities for attracting more women and minority group members to scientific careers will be lost, however. The persistence and, in some cases, cultivation of a vicious, counterproductive stereotype will serve no one well. Cultural images depicting scientists as different, for example, contradict the ideals of an open and democratic science that would attract bright, energetic, dedicated, but well-rounded students. We may all want to seem special, but science should not be portrayed as a private club, especially when it is now supported substantially by the federal government.

Other stereotypes of scientists affect the viability of science in its policy settings as well as recruitment to science courses. Stereotypes of scientists as always rational, always logical, and, by implication, deficient in ordinary human emotionality may help to sustain science's cultural authority, but they falsely encourage citizens to expect automatic answers and quick fixes from science. The Royal Society, in a wide-ranging study of public understanding of science in Great Britain, noted that one factor inhibiting better public communication efforts is the public's "view of science as a simple logical process producing unequivocal answers, and of scientists as correspondingly always logical, unemotional and somehow impersonal individuals removed from the messiness of 'real life'."[23] In public debates, the study pointed out, the public that retains such false ideas of scientists may ignore or dismiss very real differences in scientific opinion, or choose implausible but quick technical fixes as solutions to what are inherently complex social dilemmas.[24]

The tension between positive support and wary assertions of control has significant implications for science's political context. Public acceptance affects the political support for and funding of research. It influences the extent of regulation or social control of how research is conducted and communicated. And it affects whether scientific conclusions are wisely used, or are rejected in favor of religious or other nonscientific explanations.

Implications for the Public Communication of Science

The double-edged attitudes toward science will also affect strategies for the public communication of science in the future. As Pion and Lipsey concluded, "public support for science is 'soft' " because opinions on this topic are not strongly held: images therefore are "readily subject to the influence of new events, information, or persuasion by a respected referent group."[25] Events such as technologically linked accidents or spectacular discoveries will always affect public attitudes, although surveys conducted before and after Sputnik, Challenger, and Chernobyl measured less substantial changes than we might expect.[26] When organizations and political movements, such as the creation-scientists or the animal rights groups, question the values of science, they, too, have a powerful effect on public attitudes, depending on the audience's sympathy for the group's message overall.

My concern in this book has been with the third influence—that of information about science, especially as disseminated through the mass media. Editors, producers, and reporters in all parts of the mass media influence public opinion because they shape the messages about science; they not only translate and interpret technical information but also inform their audiences about the values and intentions of science. As they are doing this, they can choose their roles freely: to be investigators, skeptics, passive reporters, or promoters of science.

In most cases, modern science journalism fails not because it is biased for or against science but because it covers the social structure and social implications of science inadequately or incompletely. We need far more emphasis on how scientific research is conducted and on what can be realistically expected from conventional research techniques and standards (e.g., in levels of proof or how risk is calculated). Research projects can be described in ways that dispel myths and inform policy debates, but most often they are not. Science writer Isaac Asimov, addressing the shortcomings of televised science programming for children, for example, advised that more programs should concentrate on methodology. The process, not the answers, should be emphasized, he argued: "Show them how the answer is reached, to get them used not to scientific conclusion, but to the scientific method."[27]

The bias, the perspective from which the communicator approaches science—as supporter or skeptic—most determines the message the audience will receive. The great magazines of the early twentieth century integrated science into American culture and acknowledged the complexity of research, but they were rarely skeptical and they did not initially regard any aspect of science as suspect. Only a few social and political critics investigated science's activities and motives with vigor and suspicion.

Even a cursory examination of modern news media reveals that American science journalism has changed over the decades, in both topic and tone. Where journalists of the 1920s may have ignored the economic aspects of research, their modern counterparts routinely report on costs and projected returns. They also investigate side effects, error, fraud, and greed in science. Few journalists appear to regard scientific research as automatically beneficent.

In their anger at the implications of stories about the sordid side of science, many scientists blame journalists for the intensity of public scrutiny, accusing reporters of misinterpreting facts, concentrating on unimportant internal controversies and personalities, or fueling the flames of trivial debates in order to boost sales or ratings. For certain, today's science writers regard both science and scientists more critically, but they are far from hostile to scientific ideals. Like the popular magazine writers early in the century, modern journalists place science in its social context and relate it to politics, economics, social customs, and morality; they do not, however, accept scientists as altruistic Knights of Research. Reporters no longer automatically adopt the scientists' version as the only truth for "yesterday, to-day, and forever." Up through the 1940s, journalists tended to choose images proposed by or acceptable to the researchers. Today, they are more likely to scrutinize and occasionally to reject the scientists' myths in favor of the images widespread in American society.

Without question, daily interactions between journalists and scientists seem quite different from when reporters regarded Einstein and Edison with unqualified awe. One particular controversy, which significantly rearranged the relationships between most scientists and science journalists, shows how these changes can come about.

In the 1970s, fears over premature release of organisms from recombinant DNA research prompted energetic political debate about the efficacy of laboratory controls and, in particular, about who would set those controls, when, and why. Communications problems erupted early in the controversy because of the diversity of viewpoints represented; each side framed the issues differently. Opponents of the research believed that no experimentation should proceed without regulation, although they disagreed about the degree of acceptable restriction. Proponents of the research cried that even minor restrictions would hobble projects destined to bring great medical advances. Other participants in the debate argued that restraints on university basic research would violate principles of academic freedom. Commercial firms (and their contractors within the universities) warned that local regulations originally intended for universities could eventually inhibit industrial research (and, hence, industrial development) as the field matured.

The extensive media attention drew criticism from scientists who considered the debate to be an internal one, a matter for scientists to decide; some even blamed the media for provoking what they called public hysteria. Such criticism seems to have awakened many science journalists to their responsibility to investigate science as thoroughly as the media routinely investigated other American institutions. They could not be friends with the scientists and maintain their objectivity.

The RDNA controversy, like many subsequent ones over other types of research, also focused attention on the interdependence of the scientists, the science journalists, and the public. Scientists in the late twentieth century, unlike their predecessors in 1910, cannot plead political independence; most researchers receive at least some of their education and/or employment through government grants and contracts to universities and industry. Society first supports science, not vice versa. To obtain and sustain that support, scientists must convince the public of the value and importance of science. The public image that scientists have carefully tended throughout the century reinforces political deference to scientists on how these research activities should be funded and controlled. Earlier in the century, the science journalists, too, adopted this image and drew back from sharp criticism.

When Roy Kenneth Hack wondered in 1916 why society was allowing science to define the science-society relationship, he proposed one simple explanation.[28] The benefits of science, he argued, simply distracted society's attention from the real issues, away from how science works, and away from the decision-making process.[29] Only when the harms became so great that they could not be ignored did society pay attention to its own responsibilities. Likewise, since the 1950s, science journalists have begun to reject blanket acceptance of science and realign their responsibilities to their audiences.

Hack's words seem uncannily prescient in predicting the dilemma for modern public communication of science. "In the pursuit of gain," he wrote, "we have not only suffered ourselves to be enslaved by science, which is our tool, but we have done so because we had our attention so concentrated upon the material advantages which we could procure by the use of the tool, that we totally overlooked the disadvantages, both material and spiritual, that result from misuse of the tool."[30] When journalists hailed each scientific discovery as a "whisper of salvation"[31] and cited each success as proof that more good things would come, they reflected and reinforced the general public's own expectations. These attitudes toward scientists—automatic and unquestioning and too often coupled with muddy descriptions of how science really worked—dressed scientists in a mantle of mystery, immune from criticism. Eventually, however, the popular images of science did not match what science was bringing. Idealistic exaggerations of benefit could not obscure the magnitude of unpredicted harms. It was that discrepancy, rather than any specific negative image or set of images, that created the philosophical and political tension now existing between science and the public, and that is expressed in increased government and social regulation.

The scientific community, however innocently, fostered this situation through its own attitudes and actions toward popularization and through its actions to facilitate (or inhibit) public understanding; for, although magazine journalists and editors selected for their readers, the information made available to them was, first and foremost, what the scientists produced. When scientists controlled the flow of information, they could set the tone of public discussion and public acceptance. As long as the journalists relied on scientists' cooperation in interpreting technical material, the scientists' willingness to cooperate either facilitated or inhibited coverage.

Thus dependent upon their sources, the early science journalists became friendly with and sometimes protective of the scientists, even though contemporary commentators warned of the dangers of such a "camp-follower" relationship.[32] E. E. Slosson wrote in 1922 that "popular science need not be incorrect, but has to be somewhat indifferent. The would-be popularizer is always confronted by the dilemma of comprehensible inaccuracy or incomprehensible accuracy."[33] Slosson, himself an unabashed promoter of science, thus identified a crucial question: whose interests should science journalism serve—those of the audience or those of the source? This problem resembled that pondered by journalists on all beats, but the question contained special implications for science early in the century because the scientists themselves so tightly controlled the gateways of information. Journalists could be easily drawn into seeing scientific data from only the scientist's perspective, whether it be to take a number's multiple-place accuracy too seriously or to refrain from warning of suspected but scientifically unproven risks. Slosson admonished science journalists not to get "too close" to their subjects, to stand somewhat aloof from science, to write as observers, not as members of the community. Such rules of emotional detachment were good advice, but they were not always followed.[34]

A new generation of science communicators and journalists, alert to the moral, economic, and political implications of research, may succeed in conveying a realistic image and in supplying their audiences with the information necessary to accept or dismiss scientific advice wisely. When science-linked issues like nuclear proliferation, environmental degradation, and AIDS dominate the headlines, it is worth the effort. Certainly the modern science journalists appear less dependent upon the willingness of scientists and more able to uncover and interpret quite technical information on their own. Although many well-meaning scientists express disgust at *any* media coverage that exposes the research enterprise or scientific expertise to tough scrutiny, the time for rosy illusions is past. Given the past consequences of allowing an obscured, inaccurate image to dominate, and given the seriousness of the issues facing the world, a clearer view will be healthy for all concerned—for scientists as well as for the public.

APPENDIX 1 *Magazine Circulation*

The highest average per issue circulation for the years 1910, 1923, 1943, and 1953, for eleven American magazines. Circulation data were taken from the *N.W. Ayer and Son's Directory of Newspapers and Periodicals* (n/p = not published in that year).

Magazine	1910	1923	1943	1953
American	287,181	1,742,651	2,432,134	2,564,910
American Mercury	n/p	n/p	50,017	no data
Atlantic	25,000	117,352	106,989	199,306
Century	125,000	48,979	n/p	n/p
Collier's	500,000	992,035	2,938,306	3,119,753
Cosmopolitan	425,000	994,366	1,992,526	1,865,869
Everybody's	500,000	280,000*	n/p	n/p
Harper's	125,000	70,986	106,733	150,194
Scribner's	200,000	83,088	n/p	n/p
Post	1,246,720	2,202,927	3,403,534	4,224,339
World's Work	104,000	116,316	n/p	n/p

*By this date, *Everybody's Magazine* had switched to an all-fiction format.

APPENDIX 2 *Sampling data for each magazine*

	Number of All Issues Published, 1910–1955	Number of Issues Analyzed for Study	Percent of Issues Sampled	Number of Science Articles Published	Index*
Frame 1:					
Atlantic	552	216	39.1%	80	37
Century	239	107	44.8	16	15
Cosmopolitan	550	215	39.1	31	14
Everybody's	144	72	50.0	10	14
Collier's	2318	893	38.5	104	12
Frame 2					
World's Work	270	102	37.8	52	51
American	552	222	40.2	103	47
Harper's	552	222	40.2	100	45
Scribner's	353	138	39.1	48	35
American Mercury	372	160	43.2	31	19
Post	2398	968	40.4	112	12
Total	8300	3316	39.9	687	21

*The index is the number of science articles found in a publication, divided by the number of issues of the publication sampled. An index of 100 would indicate that, on average across the period studied, there was one science article in every issue; an index of 50, one in every two.

APPENDIX 3 *The science articles published by each magazine, 1910–55*

The index adjusts for the number of issues sampled for each year ($n = 687$). A score of 100 indicates that, in that year, the magazine published about one science article in every issue; a score of 50, in half the issues. (In the 1920s, *World's Work*'s index exceeded 100.) Dotted lines indicate that no issues were sampled during the intervening year.

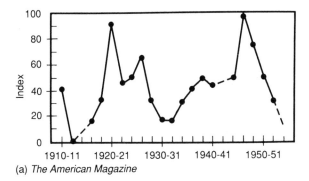

(a) *The American Magazine*

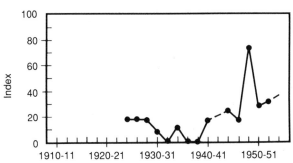

(b) *The American Mercury*

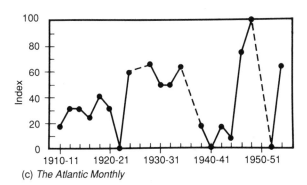

(c) *The Atlantic Monthly*

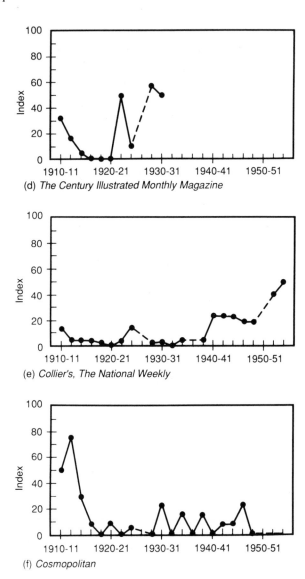

(d) *The Century Illustrated Monthly Magazine*

(e) *Collier's, The National Weekly*

(f) *Cosmopolitan*

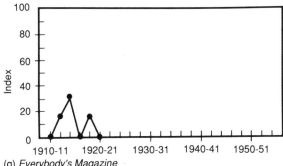

(g) *Everybody's Magazine*

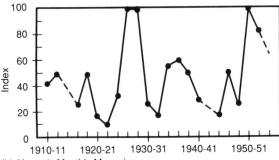

(h) *Harper's Monthly Magazine*

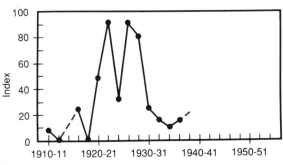

(i) *Scribner's Magazine*

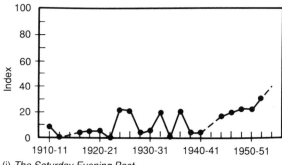

(j) *The Saturday Evening Post*

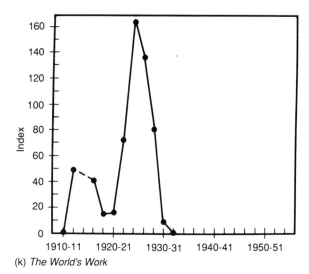

(k) *The World's Work*

APPENDIX 4   *Articles on (a) archeology or paleontology, (b) astronomy, (c) chemistry, (d) geology or earth sciences, or (e) social sciences, 1910–55.*

The proportion of all science articles which discussed archeology or paleontology (*n* = 26), astronomy (*n* = 47), chemistry (*n* = 49), geology or earth sciences (*n* = 12), or social or behavioral sciences (*n* = 20). Data are taken from a sample of eleven U.S. mass-circulation magazines and are given as a percentage of all science articles published in those magazines during each two-year period.

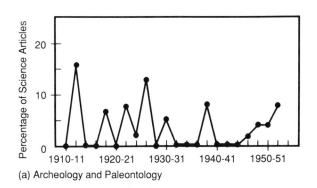

(a) Archeology and Paleontology

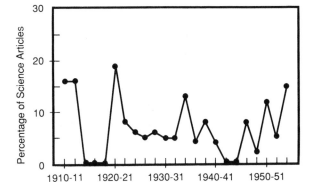

(b) Astronomy

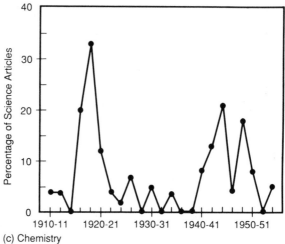

(c) Chemistry

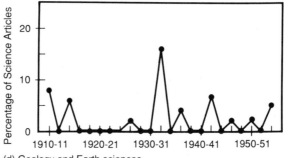

(d) Geology and Earth sciences

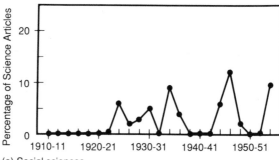

(e) Social sciences

APPENDIX 5 *Changes in styles of popular magazine science, 1910–54*

Over the entire period, narratives by all authors accounted for 65.5% of all articles; commentaries, 16.7%; first-person narratives (by scientists and others), 9.2%; and interviews with scientists, 8.3%. Data are taken from a sample of eleven U.S. mass-circulation magazines and are given as a percentage of all science articles published in those magazines during each five-year period. Similar trends are shown when science articles are plotted as a function of all articles on all subjects.

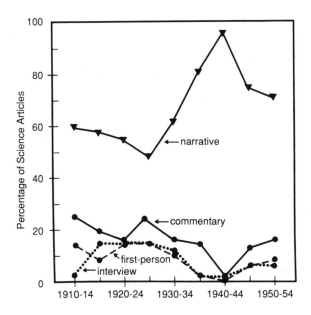

APPENDIX 6   *Article orientation, classified by author's occupation*

The orientation of popular magazine articles on science, classified by the occupation of the author ($n = 676$). Data are taken from a sample of eleven American magazines, 1910–1955. The classification system adapts a content analysis scheme described in Michael Ryan and Dorothea Owen, "A Content Analysis of Metropolitan Newspaper Coverage of Social Issues," *Journalism Quarterly*, 53 (Winter 1976): 634–40.

	Scientists %	Journalists %	Others %
Specific events	82.1	14.3	3.6
Announcement	18.2	81.8	0
Scientists' accounts of current research	100.0	0	0
Predictions	72.0	16.0	12.0
Analyses of trends or results	42.2	61.5	4.3
Social or political aspects	49.6	28.0	22.4
Biographies	12.0	57.6	30.4
Descriptions of equipment or labs	35.0	58.3	6.7
All cases	40.0%	46.6%	13.4%

APPENDIX 7 *Articles written by (a) astronomers, (b) biologists, (c) chemists, or (d) physicists, 1910–55*

The proportion of articles written by scientists which were written by astronomers ($n = 32$), biologists ($n = 59$), chemists ($n = 24$), and physicists ($n = 41$). Data are taken from a sample of eleven U.S. mass-circulation magazines and are given as a percentage of all science articles published in those magazines during each two-year period.

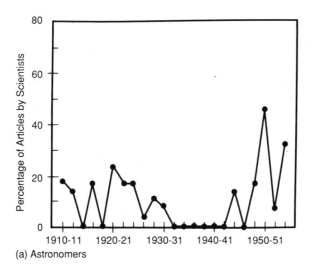

(a) Astronomers

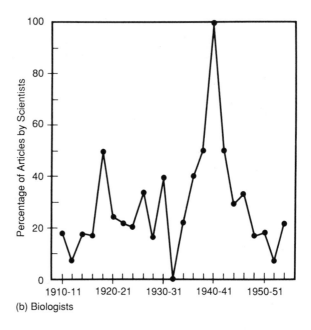

(b) Biologists

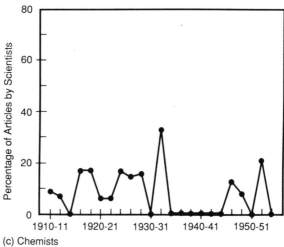

(c) Chemists

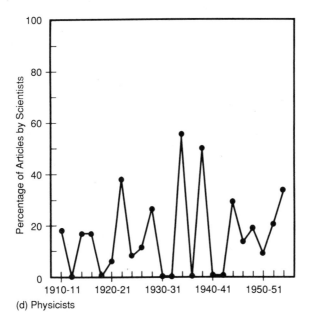

(d) Physicists

APPENDIX 8   *Author's Expertise, by Magazine*

The percentage of articles written by scientists on topics within the known expertise of the author, as measured by education or research experience in the topic discussed; data are for first authors only (*n* = 259). Data are taken from a sample of eleven U.S. mass-market magazines, 1910–55. For some magazines, rows do not total to 100% because of missing data. Only one *Everybody's* article on science was written by a scientist, and that was on a topic outside the author's field of expertise.

Magazine	Article Not in Author's Field %	Article in Author's Field %
Collier's	0.0	95.2
Post	13.3	33.3
American Mercury	16.7	83.3
Cosmopolitan	20.0	53.3
Century	22.2	66.7
Harper's	28.8	67.8
Scribner's	28.9	65.8
Atlantic	35.4	41.7
American	35.7	64.3
World's Work	44.4	33.3
Everybody's	100.0	0.0
Average for all magazines	31.1	68.9

Notes

Chapter One

1. Walter Lippmann, *Public Opinion* (New York: Macmillan, 1960), Chapter 1.

2. Vincent Price and Donald F. Roberts, "Public Opinion Processes," in Charles R. Berger and Steven H. Chaffee, eds., *Handbook of Communication Science* (Newbury Park, Calif.: Sage Publications, 1987), 806.

3. Jean-Jacques Salomon makes the distinction between these three aspects of science in *Science and Politics,* trans. Noël Lindsay (Cambridge: The MIT Press, 1973).

4. Elisabeth Noelle-Neumann, *The Spiral of Silence: Public Opinion—Our Second Skin* (Chicago: The University of Chicago Press, 1984), esp. chapters 18–20.

5. Kurt Lang and Gladys Engel Lang, "In the Plural," *Journal of Communication* 38 (Summer 1988): 130 [a review of Berger and Chaffee, *Communication Science*].

6. Price and Roberts, "Public Opinion Processes," 806.

7. Lang and Lang, "In the Plural," 131.

8. Ibid.

9. George Ellery Hale, "How Men of Science Will Help in Our War," *Scribner's Magazine,* June 1917, 722.

10. Frank P. Stockbridge, "Creating Life in the Laboratory," *Cosmopolitan,* May 1912, 781.

11. Growth in this period can be measured by many yardsticks, for example,

the number of graduate degrees in the sciences, the number of scientists working in research, increased research budgets, or increased membership in scientific professional societies.

12. Edwin E. Slosson, "Science Remaking the World," *The World's Work,* November 1922, 39.

13. See James Penick, Jr., et al., eds., *The Politics of American Science, 1939 to Present* (Cambridge: The MIT Press, 1972), 7.

14. Don K. Price, "Endless Frontier or Bureaucratic Morass?" in Gerald Holton and Robert S. Morison, eds., *Limits to Scientific Inquiry* (New York: W. W. Norton, 1979), 75–92.

15. See Bernard Brodie and Fawn W. Brodie, *From Crossbow to H-Bomb* (Bloomington: Indiana University Press, 1973).

16. Hale, "Men of Science," 721–26.

17. Ibid., 722.

18. James H. Collins, "Something Yet Again: Chemical Control," *The Saturday Evening Post,* 10 February 1917, 17.

19. For example, Samuel Hopkins Adams, "The Color Scheme of War," *Collier's,* 7 June 1919, 11.

20. Samuel Crowther, "Our Kings of Chemistry," *The World's Work,* February 1921, 349.

21. Carroll W. Pursell, Jr., "Science and Government Agencies," in David D. Van Tassel and Michael G. Hall, eds., *Science and Society in the United States* (Homewood, Ill.: The Dorsey Press, 1966), 236.

22. Frederick Lewis Allen defined Technocracy as "governance by science," implying "a state of affairs in which everything will be done scientifically . . ." (Frederick Lewis Allen, "What About Technocracy?" *The American Magazine,* March 1930, 34.)

23. Henry F. May, *The End of American Innocence, A Study of the First Years of Our Own Time, 1912–1917* (New York: Alfred A. Knopf, 1959), 20. Robert Nisbet, *History of the Idea of Progress* (New York: Basic Books, 1980) also discusses this point.

24. May, *End of American Innocence,* 132. Also see William E. Akin, *Technocracy and the American Dream: The Technocratic Movement, 1900–1941* (Berkeley: University of California Press, 1977); and Samuel Haber, *Efficiency and Uplift: Scientific Management in the Progressive Era, 1890–1920* (Chicago: University of Chicago Press, 1964).

25. "Science in Industry," *The Saturday Evening Post,* 28 March 1931, 24.

26. See Daniel J. Kevles, *The Physicists: The History of a Scientific Community in Modern America* (New York: Alfred A. Knopf, 1978), chapters 12 and 13; and Daniel J. Kevles, "Robert A. Millikan," *Scientific American* 240 (January 1979), 143. Also see Ronald C. Tobey, *The American Ideology of National Science, 1919–1930* (Pittsburgh: University of Pittsburgh Press, 1971); and Lance E. Davis and Daniel J. Kevles, "The National Research Fund: A Case Study in the Industrial Support of Academic Science," *Minerva* 12 (April 1974).

27. Tobey says that Robert Millikan opposed the idea because he believed existing publications accomplished the goal just as well. (Tobey, *Ideology of National Science,* 62 and 64.) Also see Kevles, *The Physicists,* chapter 12.

28. Tobey, *Ideology of National Science*, 62. Also see David J. Rhees' work on chemists during World War I.

29. Kevles, *The Physicists*, 171 and chapter 12. Also see Tobey, *Ideology of National Science*, chapter 3. David J. Rhees, "A New Voice for Science: Science Service under Edwin E. Slosson, 1921–1929," (M.A. thesis, University of North Carolina, 1979) is the best history of the founding of the Service.

30. Kevles, *The Physicists*, 178. Slosson directed many of his own articles in general-content popular magazines at publicizing the new organization. For example, Edwin E. Slosson, "Science from the Sidelines," *The Century Illustrated Monthly Magazine*, January 1922, 471–76; Edwin E. Slosson, "Science Remaking the World," *The World's Work*, November 1922, 39–50; and Edwin E. Slosson, "Science Remaking Everyday Life," *The World's Work*, December 1922, 162–175.

31. Kevles, *The Physicists*, 269.

32. George Ellery Hale, "A National Focus of Science and Research," *Scribner's Monthly*, November 1922, 516.

33. Tobey, *Ideology of National Science*, 7. See Kendall Birr, "Industrial Research Laboratories," in Nathan Reingold, ed., *The Sciences in the American Context: New Perspectives* (Washington: Smithsonian Institution Press, 1979), 193–208. Birr states that by 1931, according to the National Research Council, more than 1,600 companies had laboratories employing nearly 33,000 people; by 1940, there were 2,000 industrial laboratories employing over 70,000 people (p. 199).

34. Nathan Reingold and Ida H. Reingold, eds., *Science in America: A Documentary History, 1900–1939* (Chicago: The University of Chicago Press, 1981), 3.

35. One of the best discussions of these attitudes may be found in Price, "Endless Frontier," 75–92.

36. Tobey, *Ideology of National Science*, 199. Kevles, *The Physicists*, 185–89. Also see Robert Kargon and Elizabeth Hodes, "Karl Compton, Isaiah Bowman, and the Politics of Science in the Great Depression," *Isis* 76 (September 1985): 301–18.

37. Kevles, *The Physicists*, 188.

38. Nathan Reingold, "The Scientist as Troubled American," *American Industrial Hygiene Association Journal* 40 (December 1979): 1111.

39. Pursell, "Science and Government Agencies," 239. Also see Lewis E. Auerbach, "Scientists in the New Deal: A Pre-War Episode in the Relations between Science and Government in the United States," *Minerva* 3 (Summer 1965): 457–82.

40. Pursell, "Science and Government Agencies," 240.

41. Salomon, *Science and Politics*, 31.

42. Although the rumors later proved to be wrong, many of the Manhattan Project scientists were convinced that the Germans were close to building an atomic bomb.

43. Even as late as 1945, Manhattan Project scientists argued that they had "no claim to special competence in solving the political, social and military problems which are presented by the advent of atomic power." (Quoted in Salomon, *Science and Politics*, 45.)

44. William Haynes, "The Battle of Synthetics," *Collier's,* 30 September 1944, 56.

45. Ibid., 56.

46. Ibid.

47. Salomon, *Science and Politics,* 47.

48. "Physics in the Contemporary World," reprinted in J. Robert Oppenheimer, *The Open Mind* (New York: Simon and Schuster, 1955), 91.

49. Federal R&D expenditures had gone from $74 million in 1940 to $1,590 million in 1945. By 1955, they had reached $6,182 million. (Birr, "Industrial Research Laboratories," 202.)

50. See House Committee on Science and Technology, *A History of Science Policy in the United States, 1940–1985,* Science Policy Study Background Report No. 1, 99th Cong., 2d sess. (Washington: Government Printing Office, 1986); and J. Merton England, *A Patron for Pure Science: The National Science Foundation's Formative Years, 1945–57* (Washington: National Science Foundation, 1982).

51. Historian Alex Roland described this approach in testimony before the Science Policy Task Force, House Committee on Science and Technology, 7 March 1985.

52. Vannevar Bush, *Science—The Endless Frontier: A Report to the President on a Program for Postwar Scientific Research* (Washington: Government Printing Office, 1945), 12.

53. Ibid.

54. John R. Steelman, *Science and Public Policy: A Report to the President,* vol. 1 (Washington: Government Printing Office, 1947), 31.

55. House Committee on Science and Technology, *The Regulatory Environment for Science,* Science Policy Study Background Report No. 10, 99th Cong., 2d sess. (Washington: Government Printing Office, 1986); also published by the Office of Technology Assessment under the same title.

56. House Committee on Science and Technology, *The Regulatory Environment,* chapter 2; Paul A. Fruend, ed., *Experimentation with Human Subjects* (New York: George Braziller, 1969); Murray L. Wax and Joan Cassell, eds., *Federal Regulations, Ethical Issues and Social Research* (Boulder, Colo.: Westview Press, 1979); Keith M. Wulff, ed., *Regulation of Scientific Inquiry* (Boulder, Colo.: Westview Press, 1979).

57. See the surveys sponsored by the National Science Foundation and summarized in annual reports to the National Science Board. For example, National Science Board, *Science and Engineering Indicators—1987* (Washington: Government Printing Office, 1987), chapter 8, and other reports in the same series.

58. See, for example, two special issues of *Daedalus,* published as Gerald Holton and William A. Blanpied, eds., *Science and Its Public: The Changing Relationship* (Boston: D. Reidel, 1976), and Holton and Morison, eds., *Limits to Scientific Inquiry* (see n.14).

59. Irwin Edman, "We Superstitious Moderns," *The Century Illustrated Monthly Magazine,* June 1924, 190.

60. Salomon, *Science and Politics,* xii.

61. See House Committee on Science and Technology, *The Regulatory Environment.*

Chapter Two

1. See, for example, the discussion in the special issue on "Scientific Literacy," *Daedalus* (Spring 1983) issued as vol. 112, no. 2 of the *Proceedings of the American Academy of Arts and Sciences*. Numerous reports published by the National Science Foundation, the American Association for the Advancement of Science, and the Congressional Office of Technology Assessment, among others, describe the narrow range of most science curricula.

2. John C. Burnham showed me a new way to see this point (personal communication). Arthur Lucas has written an excellent review of current work on this topic. See A. M. Lucas, "Scientific Literacy and Informal Learning," *Studies in Science Education* 10 (1983): 1–36.

3. See Annette M. Woodlief, "Science in Popular Culture," in M. Thomas Inge, ed., *Handbook of American Popular Culture,* vol. 3 (Westport, Conn.: Greenwood Press, 1981), 429–58. Woodlief reviews the central scholarship and includes a general bibliography of sources. For a comprehensive review of the popular presentation of science in the nineteenth and early twentieth centuries, see John C. Burnham, *How Superstition Won and Science Lost: Popularizing Science and Health in the United States* (New Brunswick, N.J.: Rutgers University Press, 1987).

4. Krieghbaum and many others have described the coverage of science (usually natural history or medicine) from colonial newspapers to the present. See Hillier Krieghbaum, *Science and the Mass Media* (New York: New York University Press, 1967); Woodlief, "Science in Popular Culture"; and Burnham, *Superstition Won.*

5. David Rhees says that the American Chemical Society, for example, began its own news service in 1919. See David J. Rhees, "A New Voice for Science: Science Service under Edwin E. Slosson, 1921–29," (M.A. thesis, University of North Carolina, 1979).

6. See Marcel C. LaFollette, "Science and Technology Museums as Policy Tools—An Overview of the Issues," *Science, Technology, & Human Values* 8, no. 3 (Summer 1983): 41–46.

7. The definitive histories of broadcasting in this period are Erik Barnouw, *A Tower in Babel: A History of Broadcasting in the United States to 1933* (New York: Oxford University Press, 1966) and Erik Barnouw, *The Golden Web: A History of Broadcasting in the United States, 1933–1953* (New York: Oxford University Press, 1968). There is, to date, no good, short history of science programming on radio in the United States (news or informational, not drama). John Burnham includes occasional discussion of how radio was used to disseminate technical information on psychology and health (Burnham, *Superstition Won*). The Smithsonian Institution Archives contain some of the records of radio broadcasts produced by Science Service.

8. Although there are some good analyses of science fiction in the movies, little work has been done on radio plays or movies dramatizing the lives of real scientists. Burnham, for example, mentions the health films but does not point toward any comprehensive history of this topic. See Burnham, *Superstition Won.* For description of the interaction of scientists and film makers, see Nathan Rein-

gold, "Metro-Goldwyn-Mayer Meets the Atom Bomb," in Terry Shinn and Richard Whitley, eds., *Expository Science: Forms and Functions of Popularization* (Dordrecht, Holland: D. Reidel, 1985), 229–45.

9. Television viewing rises dramatically in the 1950s. In 1950, average daily television use per household was only around thirty-five minutes; by 1955, it was slightly over three and one-half hours; by 1959, it had exceeded five hours per day. To the best of my knowledge, there exists no comprehensive study of science on television in the 1950s. The broad-based content studies from that time do not give a separate category to science or nature programming, however, and that may indicate contemporary assessment of its lesser importance. See, for example, the studies commissioned by the National Association of Educational Broadcasters in the early 1950s. Also see Marcel C. LaFollette, "Science on Television: Influences and Strategies," *Daedalus* (Fall 1982): 183–98.

10. Martin U. Martel and George J. McCall, "Reality-Orientation and the Pleasure Principle: A Study of American Mass-Periodical Fiction (1890–1955)," in Lewis Anthony Dexter and David Manning White, eds., *People, Society, and Mass Communications* (New York: The Free Press, 1964), 290, n. 4.

11. "Popular Magazines," *The Saturday Evening Post*, 10 December 1910, 18.

12. Terry Hynes, "Magazine Portrayal of Women, 1911–1930," *Journalism Monographs* no. 72 (May 1981): 3, citing observations by Theodore Peterson and other magazine historians.

13. As Terry Hynes observes, commercial magazines, "under pressure to build the widest possible audience, would be unlikely proponents of changes which might threaten or alienate their readers." (Hynes, "Magazine Portrayal," 3.) Patricke Johns-Heine and Hans H. Gerth aptly note that in magazines there is a "complex interaction between reader, writer, and publisher which results in the reader getting what he wants and wanting what he gets" (p. 226). See Patricke Johns-Heine and Hans H. Gerth, "Values in Mass Periodical Fiction, 1921–1940," in Bernard Rosenberg and David Manning White, eds., *Mass Culture: The Popular Arts in America* (Glencoe, Ill.: The Free Press, 1957), 226–34.

14. See Herbert J. Gans, *Deciding What's News: A Study of CBS Evening News, NBC Nightly News, Newsweek, and Time* (New York: Pantheon Books, 1979), especially chapter 2, "Values in the News".

15. "The publisher is a merchant, and the editorial art is largely one of merchandising . . ." While editors and publishers may have strong personal opinions on public issues, they must provide "satisfaction for the desires and tastes" of their audience. (Frank Luther Mott, "Trends in Newspaper Content" (1942), reprinted in Wilbur Schramm, ed., *Mass Communications*, 2d ed. [Urbana: University of Illinois Press, 1960], 371.)

16. Because this is not a book on editorial decision making, I discuss here the images that were selected, not those that were rejected. Many scientists tend to assume that every person wants to know every piece of information that science has produced, and that all science stories, therefore, are interesting and important; but not all ideas and not all information available to every editor are published. As Deems Taylor observed in 1917: "A great many things go on in the world that are

important and deserving of record, but in which the average man is not interested at all." (Deems Taylor, "The Very Human Magazine," *The Century Illustrated Monthly Magazine,* July 1917, 425.)

17. Ray Long (1932), quoted in Frank Luther Mott, *A History of American Magazines,* vol. 4 (Cambridge: The Belknap Press of Harvard University Press, 1957), 498.

18. "Popular Magazines," *The Saturday Evening Post,* 10 December 1910, 18.

19. Kenneth E. Boulding, *The Image: Knowledge in Life and Society* (Ann Arbor: The University of Michigan Press, 1961), paperback edition, 67.

20. Roland Marchand, *Advertising the American Dream: Making Way for Modernity, 1920–1940* (Berkeley: University of California Press, 1985), xvii. In regard to images in magazine advertising, Marchand cites Jacques Ellul's notion of "integration propaganda"—that is, "ideas and images that reinforce and intensify existing patterns and conceptions" (p. xviii).

21. Nathan Reingold, "Reflections on 200 Years of Science in the United States," in Nathan Reingold, ed., *The Sciences in the American Context: New Perspectives* (Washington: Smithsonian Institution Press, 1979), 14.

22. Herbert J. Gans describes this activity for the electronic media and newsmagazines. See Gans, *Deciding What's News,* 80.

23. Gitlin proposed that media "frames" shaped the 1960s news coverage of the political left, but the concept is applicable also to science coverage. See Todd Gitlin, *The Whole World is Watching: Mass Media in the Making and Unmaking of the New Left* (Berkeley: University of California Press, 1980), 7.

24. There is an extensive literature, from Warren Breed's descriptive classic "Social Control in the News Room" (1955) to modern quantitative studies, on the relationships between an editor and her authors. These influences are complex and important, and while not the subject of this book, deserve future study in regard to the shaping of science content.

25. Perhaps some future work could compare the image discussed here to the images presented to specialized audiences; such analyses would have to take into account the personal agendas of the editors and publishers, especially for smaller publications with strong political allegiances.

26. The table in Appendix 1 gives representative circulations for these magazines.

27. Mass communications research has clearly shown that there is usually significant audience overlap for popular media and that people "highly-exposed" to one medium tend to be "highly-exposed" to other media as well. See, for example, the classic study of 1940s radio listeners by Paul F. Lazarsfeld and Patricia Kendall, "The Communications Behavior of the Average American" (originally published in 1948), in Schramm, *Mass Communications,* 425–37.

28. Two sampling frames were used to control for the possibility of coincidental editorial choices and for news coverage of major events. Magazines owned by the same publisher, for example, were assigned to different frames. Random samples of six-month periods were then chosen for each frame across the forty-five-year analysis period. For each issue of a magazine examined, the total number

of all nonfiction articles (on all subjects) was also recorded. Appendixes 1 and 2 contain further information on the sampling techniques and some representative circulation figures. For additional discussion of the content analysis, see Marcel Chotkowski LaFollette, "Authority, Promise, and Expectation: The Images of Science and Scientists in American Popular Magazines, 1910–1955" (Ph.D. diss., Indiana University, 1979).

29. Some years ago, in an unpublished study, I analyzed all the fiction (short stories and novellas) published in 216 issues of *American, Cosmopolitan,* and *Harper's* for the years 1930, 1935, 1940, 1945, 1950, and 1955. Only twenty-four of the characters in hundreds of short stories and novellas were scientists. All were male, with Anglo-Saxon surnames, shy or eccentric personalities, and some type of tall or wiry appearance. Most worked (or had worked) in universities and all were described as highly intelligent, hard-working, and devoted to science.

Walter Hirsch analyzed scientist characters in science-fiction magazines published between 1926 and 1950 and found that although the proportion of scientists who were heroes declined, the proportion of villains remained steady. He also found that, across the period, scientists were more and more placed in bureaucratic settings. See Walter Hirsch, "The Image of the Scientist in Science Fiction: A Content Analysis," in Bernard Barber and Walter Hirsch, eds., *The Sociology of Science* (New York: The Free Press, 1962), 259–68. George Basalla's analysis of comic strips published during 1945–75 found that scientists were "rarely the heroes" and were often manipulated by stronger characters, but he gives little data on change over time. See George Basalla, "Pop Science: The Depiction of Science in Popular Culture," in Gerald Holton and William A. Blanpied, eds., *Science and Its Public: The Changing Relationship* (Boston: D. Reidel, 1976).

30. A brief content analysis of fiction in some of these same magazines (see note 29) and my observations during the nonfiction study lead me to believe that there was far less fictional than nonfictional attention to science during this period, and that there were probably only minor differences in the images of scientists depicted in the two types of content.

31. Marchand found in his study of advertising that "themes and motifs remained remarkably consistent. The social content of the ads changed far less than did the styles of layout and illustration; in fact, the attitudes and values conveyed by the ads proved exceptionally consistent." See Marchand, *Advertising the American Dream,* xvi.

32. In the following two sections, I have supplemented my own study of these eleven magazines with information on publishing histories from Frank Luther Mott's *A History of American Magazines,* vols. 1–5 (Cambridge: The Belknap Press of Harvard University Press, 1930, 1938, 1938, 1957, and 1968), the most authoritative source on magazine publishing. All conclusions on science coverage are mine, however, unless otherwise noted.

33. Mott, *A History,* vol. 4, 2.

34. Ibid., 698.

35. A. J. van Zuilen, *The Life Cycle of Magazines: A Historical Study of the Decline and Fall of the General Interest Mass Audience Magazine in the United States during the Period 1946–1972* (Uithoorn, The Netherlands: Graduate Press, n.d.), 3.

36. "About Magazines—Quick and Dead," *The World's Work,* May 1910, 12877.

37. Ibid.

38. van Zuilen, *Life Cycle,* 4.

39. Appendix 2 contains data on the number of science articles published in each magazine, across the period studied.

40. *The Saturday Evening Post* (1821–1830, 1839–1842, and 1845–1969); there were other titles in the intervening years. See Mott, *A History,* 4:671–716, for a history of the *Post* to 1957.

41. Mott, *A History,* 4:686–87, describes the Curtis changes.

42. Ibid., 688, discusses this content in detail.

43. Ibid., 692.

44. From 1910 to 1955, almost one-third of all the *Post* articles on science were biographical or autobiographical. In the late 1930s, as much as 80% of the science articles in a year were biographies; from 1915 to 1924, none.

45. Mott, *A History,* 4:703. Such apparently different articles as "Dethroning King Cotton" (2 July 1910) and "The Life History of an A-Bomb" (5 December 1953) demonstrated the consistency of this approach. Both articles discussed government-funded research programs; both pragmatically weighed the value of such programs. See Harris Dickson, "Dethroning King Cotton," *The Saturday Evening Post,* 2 July 1910, 12–14, 46; and Harold H. Martin, "The Life History of an A-Bomb," *The Saturday Evening Post,* 5 December 1953, 36, 172–174.

46. For example, an article on the Massachusetts Institute of Technology: Robert M. Yoder, "Buck Rogers Would Love It Here," *The Saturday Evening Post,* 20 October 1951, 32–33, 124.

47. The *Post* was revived in 1971 as a bimonthly nostalgia periodical, but its circulation, content, and editorial goals differed substantially from those of the *Post* in its heyday as a dominant source of family entertainment and information. See van Zuilen, *Life Cycle,* for an exhaustive account of the demise and a brief analysis of the revival.

48. *Everybody's Magazine* (1896–1923) and *Everybody's* (1923–1929). See Mott, *A History,* vol. 5.

49. *Frank Leslie's Popular Monthly* (1876–1904), *Leslie's Monthly Magazine* (1904–1905), *American Illustrated Magazine* (1905–1906), and *The American Magazine* (1906–1956). For a complete history, see Mott, *A History,* 3:510–16.

50. Ibid., 514.

51. Ibid., 515.

52. Biographies represented almost 60% of all of *American's* science articles.

53. Science was frequently named as one of the agencies that could help lead society out of the Depression. For example, Charles F. Kettering with Beverly Smith, "Ten Paths to Fame and Fortune," *The American Magazine,* December 1937, 14–15.

54. *Collier's Once A Week* (1888–89), *Once A Week, An Illustrated Weekly Newspaper* (1889–95), *Collier's Weekly, An Illustrated Journal* (1895–1904), and *Collier's, The National Weekly* (1905–57). For a complete history of *Collier's,* see Mott, *A History,* 4:453–79.

55. Mott, *A History*, 4:465 describes the effect of this sale.

56. Waldemar Kaempffert, "The Most Famous of Comets," *Collier's*, 2 April 1910, 21–22, and Joseph Jastrow, "The Unmasking of Paladino," *Collier's*, 14 May 1910, 21–22, 40, 42.

57. Mott, *A History*, 4:471; Mott is quoting Chennery.

58. Ibid., 472.

59. Ibid., 475.

60. "Against the *Post's* newsboy solicitation *Collier's* pitted its salesmen," who pushed an installment plan. "*Collier's* sometimes lured *Post* contributors into its own pages, and vice versa." (Mott, *A History*, 4:475.)

61. Ibid., 478–79.

62. *Cosmopolitan Magazine* (1886–1925), *Hearst's International Combined with Cosmopolitan* (1925–52), *Cosmopolitan* (1952–present). See Mott, *A History*, 4:480–505 for a history of *Cosmopolitan* to the mid-1950s.

63. Ibid., 482, 484.

64. Carlin Philips, "Smiling Surgery," *Cosmopolitan*, March 1910, 529–32; Peter Clark Macfarlane, "The Conquest of Cancer," *Cosmopolitan*, August 1912, 306–15.

65. Antonio Sagliano, "Probing Pompeii," *Cosmopolitan*, November 1912, 760–65; G. A. Reisner, "Solving the Riddle of the Sphinx," *Cosmopolitan*, June 1912, 4–13.

66. Ella Wheeler Wilcox, "The Madness of Vivisection," *Cosmopolitan*, May 1910, 713–18; Elie Metchnikoff and Henry Smith Williams, "Why Not Live Forever?," *Cosmopolitan*, September 1912, 436–46.

67. In 1930–34, biographies accounted for three-quarters of *Cosmopolitan* science articles; in 1935–39, one-half; and in 1940–44, all. Scientists wrote one-fifth of the science articles in that decade in a first-person style.

68. Elizabeth Shepley Sergeant, "Cosmopolite of the Month: Dr. Carl G. Jung," *Cosmopolitan*, January 1939, 6, 15.

69. Henry F. May, *The End of American Innocence, A Study of the First Years of Our Time, 1912–1917* (New York: Alfred A. Knopf, 1959), 75.

70. *The World's Work, A History of Our Time* (1900–32). For a complete history, see Mott, *A History*, 4:773–88.

71. Mott, *A History*, 4:774, quoting Page. *The World's Work* carried an average of one science article in every two issues.

72. Ibid., 783.

73. Floyd W. Parsons, "Looking Ahead in Industry. II.," *The World's Work*, July 1922, 279–91.

74. The result of this merger, *The Review of Reviews and World's Work*, folded in 1937. See Mott, *A History*, 4:788.

75. *Scribner's Monthly, An Illustrated Magazine for the People* (1870–81) and *Scribner's Magazine* (1887–1939). Mott, *A History*, 4:717–32, describes the history of *Scribner's Magazine*.

76. Mott, *A History*, 3:468.

77. From 1920 to 1931, the percentage of articles written by scientists fluctuated between 66% and 100%.

78. Mott, *A History*, 4:730–31.

79. First published under *The Century Illustrated Monthly Magazine* (1881–1929); later, *The Century Quarterly* (1929–30). For a complete history of *The Century,* see Mott, *A History,* 3:468–80.

80. Mott, *A History,* 3:479.

81. Julian S. Huxley, "Searching for the Elixir of Life," *The Century Illustrated Monthly Magazine,* February 1922, 621–24.

82. See Ronald C. Tobey, *The American Ideology of National Science, 1919–1930* (Pittsburgh: The University of Pittsburgh Press, 1971), 62–95.

83. For example, Morris Fishbein, "Twenty-five Years of Medical Progress," *The Century Illustrated Monthly Magazine,* February 1928, 408–20.

84. Mott, *A History,* 3:479.

85. *The American Mercury* (1924–present). For a history of *The American Mercury* to 1960, see Mott, *A History,* 5:3–26.

86. Mott, *A History,* 5:17. Mott reports that circulation dropped from 62,000 in 1930 to about half that in 1933.

87. Ibid., 19–20, describes this changeover.

88. Ibid., 22, 24.

89. William Bradford Huie, "Who Gave Russia the A-Bomb?" *The American Mercury,* April 1951, 413–21.

90. Julien Steinberg, "Who Gave Russia the A-Bomb? Part II (The Case of Clarence Hiskey)," *The American Mercury,* May 1951, 593–602.

91. *The Atlantic Monthly: A Magazine of Literature, Art and Politics* (1857–65) and *The Atlantic Monthly: A Magazine of Literature, Science, Art, and Politics* (1865–present). For a history of *Atlantic* through the late 1930s, see Mott, *A History,* 2:493–515.

92. Ibid., 506, quoting Howells in the November 1907 *Atlantic.*

93. Ibid., 513.

94. Alfred North Whitehead, "Religion and Science," *The Atlantic Monthly,* August 1925, 200; Joseph Wood Krutch, "The Modern Well-Tempered Mind," *The Atlantic Monthly,* February 1928, 190–204; Joseph Wood Krutch, "Disillusionment with the Laboratory," *The Atlantic Monthly,* March 1928, 367–72.

95. For example, Hans Zinsser, "The Deadly Arts," *The Atlantic Monthly,* November 1934, 530–43. This was an excerpt from his forthcoming book: Hans Zinsser, *Rats, Lice and History: A Study in Biography* (Boston: Atlantic Monthly Press, 1935).

96. For example, Sumner Welles, "The Atomic Bomb and World Government," *The Atlantic Monthly,* January 1946, 39–42, responding to Einstein's article in the November 1945 issue.

97. *Harper's New Monthly Magazine* (1850–1900) and *Harper's Monthly Magazine* (1900–present). See Mott, *A History,* 2:383–405, for a history of *Harper's* through the late 1930s.

98. Theodore Peterson, *Magazines in the Twentieth Century,* 2d ed. (Urbana: University of Illinois Press, 1964), 410.

99. A. D. Hall, "The Soil as a Battleground," *Harper's Monthly Magazine,* October 1910, 680–87; Harris Dickson, "Dethroning King Cotton," *The Saturday Evening Post,* 2 July 1910, 12–14, 46.

100. For example, when Harry Emerson Fosdick talked about science and

religion, zoologist Julian Huxley responded a few issues later that science would indeed not "destroy religion." See Harry Emerson Fosdick, "Science and Religion," *Harper's Monthly Magazine,* February 1926, 296–300; Julian Huxley, "Will Science Destroy Religion?," *Harper's Monthly Magazine,* April 1926, 531–39.

101. Mott, *A History,* 2:404.

102. "Personal and Otherwise" (column), *Harper's Monthly Magazine,* March 1934.

103. In 1936, for example, Gray published an exceptionally good analysis of science's economic base, which included attention to such issues as the commercialization of research and how modern research universities would be financed. See George W. Gray, "Science and Profits," *Harper's Monthly Magazine,* April 1936, 539–49.

104. Peterson, *Magazines in the Twentieth Century,* 412.

105. In one article, Harlow Shapley, for example, urged scientists to become more directly involved in the political discussions over postwar federal science funding and organization. Harlow Shapley, "Status Quo or Pioneer? The Fate of American Science," *Harper's Monthly Magazine,* October 1945, 312–17.

106. Robert Littell, "The Voice of the Apple," *Harper's Monthly Magazine,* September 1946, 221–28; Henry L. Stimson, "The Decision to Use the Atomic Bomb," *Harper's Monthly Magazine,* February 1947, 97–107; Gerald Wendt, "A New Job for the Atom," *Harper's Monthly Magazine,* May 1947, 21–27; and Henry Schacht, "Cancer and the Atom," *Harper's Monthly Magazine,* August 1949, 83–87.

107. When the number of lead stories are indexed to the number of issues sampled, the data again show a pattern of increased attention to science in the 1920s and show that attention appeared to be increasing in the mid-1950s to an all-time high.

108. This conclusion is confirmed by other data; for example, the number of article series that discussed physics or physicists increased during the 1940s and early 1950s.

Chapter Three

1. Roy Chapman Andrews, "Explorers and Their Work," *The Saturday Evening Post,* 22 August 1931, 85.

2. "About Magazines—Quick and Dead," *The World's Work,* May 1910, 12878.

3. See, for example, Dorothy Nelkin, *Selling Science* (New York: W. H. Freeman, 1987).

4. Michael Schudson, *Discovering the News: A Social History of American Newspapers* (New York: Basic Books, 1978), 72.

5. Hillier Kreighbaum, "The Background and Training of Science Writers," *Journalism Quarterly* 17 (1940): 15–18. In 1975, Ryan and Dunwoody reported a figure of 13%. See Michael Ryan and Sharon L. Dunwoody, "Academic and Professional Training Patterns of Science Writers," *Journalism Quarterly* 52 (1975): 239–46, 290.

6. Some of these changes may have been affected by activity in particular research fields; for example, biologists made a number of exciting discoveries in the mid-1920s, and this probably influenced the 1926 peak, over half of which were biographies of biologists. Likewise, the 1939 peak undoubtedly reflected the publicity given to Einstein and to developments in physics; one-third of those biographies described physicists. By 1949–50, however, biographies described researchers from every part of science (although the greatest proportion were biographies of physicists, chemists, and biologists), and this data most likely indicates heightened interest in science in general.

7. Rae Goodell, *The Visible Scientists* (Boston: Little, Brown, 1977).

8. All these scientists appeared on radio and gave interviews to newspapers, for example, in addition to writing for popular magazines.

9. Burnham, for example, describes the general attitudes of scientists toward popularization. See John C. Burnham, *How Superstition Won and Science Lost: Popularizing Science and Health in the United States* (New Brunswick, N.J.: Rutgers University Press, 1987).

10. Geoffrey Parsons, "Black Science," *Harper's Monthly Magazine,* June 1927, 106.

11. Daniel J. Kevles, "Robert A. Millikan," *Scientific American,* January 1979, 150.

12. Daniel J. Boorstin, *The Image: A Guide to Pseudo-Events in America* (New York: Harper & Row, 1961) addresses the full range of such activities.

13. May writes that "Bergson's American publisher sold in two years half as many copies of *Creative Evolution* as had been sold in France in fifteen years, and the presses poured out a flood of semipopular explanations." See Henry F. May, *The End of American Innocence, A Study of the First Years of Our Own Time, 1912–1917* (New York: Alfred A. Knopf, 1959), 228. *Everybody's* labeled Bergson "The Most Dangerous Man in the World" because of the controversial nature of some of his theories. (Walter Lippmann, "The Most Dangerous Man in the World," *Everybody's Magazine,* July 1912, 100.)

14. Burnham provides a good summary of the popularization of psychology in this century, and the role of the practitioners in this effort. (Burnham, *Superstition Won,* 85–116.)

15. Samuel George Smith, "The New Science," *The Atlantic Monthly,* December 1912, 803.

16. Jonathan Norton Leonard, "Steinmetz, Jove of Science," Part 2, *The World's Work,* February 1929, 65.

17. Ibid.

18. Ibid. Also see David E. Nye, *Image Worlds: Corporate Identities at General Electric* (Cambridge: The MIT Press, 1985).

19. John Dos Passos, *U.S.A.—The 42nd Parallel* (New York: The Modern Library, 1937), 327.

20. Leonard, "Steinmetz," Part 2, 65.

21. Ibid.

22. Ibid.

23. Ibid.

24. The series included such topics as: Michael I. Pupin, "What I Brought to America," *Scribner's Magazine,* September 1922; and Michael I. Pupin, "From Greenhorn to Citizenship and a College Degree," *Scribner's Magazine,* December 1922.

25. Roy Chapman Andrews, "Explorers and Their Work," *The Saturday Evening Post,* 22 August 1931, 85.

26. Ibid.

27. Ibid.

28. Ibid.

29. Samuel Hopkins Adams, "Leland O. Howard," *The American Magazine,* October 1911, 723.

30. Ibid.

31. At the turn of the century, the popular magazines tended to use such terms as *scientist, inventor,* or *naturalist* interchangeably. An inventor's products were automatically attributed to science, and inventors were assumed to use the methods of science.

32. Edison was repeatedly called a *scientist* or described as doing scientific research, even though he had no formal scientific education.

33. C. Hartley Grattan, "Thomas Alva Edison: An American Symbol," *Scribner's Magazine,* September 1933, 154.

34. For example, these descriptions of Edison. "The vigorous frame, broad in the shoulders . . . fine, rather large head . . . deep and seemingly piercing eyes." (Grattan, "Thomas Alva Edison," 154.) "The forehead is that of a seer, while mouth, chin, and jaw are firm and dominant. . . . The eyes are most noticeable, being luminous and lustrous. At times they blaze, then are tempered into a softened radiance." (Alan Sullivan, "Pioneers of Invention," *Collier's,* 27 November 1915, 36.)

35. See Wyn Wachhorst, *Thomas Alva Edison: An American Myth* (Cambridge: The MIT Press, 1981).

36. Thomas H. Uzzell, "The Future of Electricity," *Collier's,* 2 December 1916, 7.

37. Samuel Crowther, "T. A. E.—A Great National Asset," *The Saturday Evening Post,* 5 January 1929, 6.

38. Grattan, "Thomas Alva Edison," 151.

39. Emil Ludwig, "Edison 'The Greatest American of the Century,'" *The American Magazine,* December 1931, 66.

40. George Ellery Hale, "The New Heavens," *Scribner's Magazine,* October 1920, 387–402; George Ellery Hale, "Giant Stars," *Scribner's Magazine,* July 1921, 3–15; George Ellery Hale, "Cosmic Crucibles," *Scribner's Magazine,* October 1921, 387–98; George Ellery Hale, "Recent Discoveries in Egypt," *Scribner's Magazine,* July 1923, 34–49; and George Ellery Hale, "The Work of an American Orientalist," *Scribner's Magazine,* October 1923, 392–404.

41. Daniel J. Kevles, *The Physicists: The History of a Scientific Community in Modern America* (New York: Alfred A. Knopf, 1978), 183. See also Kevles, "Robert A. Millikan," 148.

42. Robert A. Millikan, "Gulliver's Travels in Science," *Scribner's Maga-*

zine, November 1923, 577–85. Robert A. Millikan, "The Electron and the Light-Quant," *Scribner's Magazine*, January 1925, 75–84.

43. Kevles, "Robert A. Millikan," 148.

44. See Kevles, *The Physicists*, chapters 12 and 13; Kevles, "Robert A. Millikan," 143; Ronald C. Tobey, *The American Ideology of National Science, 1919–1930* (Pittsburgh: University of Pittsburgh Press, 1971), 35–39; and Lance E. Davis and Daniel J. Kevles, "The National Research Fund: A Case Study in the Industrial Support of Academic Science," *Minerva* 12 (April 1974): 207–20.

45. Frank Luther Mott, *A History of American Magazines*, vol. 4 (Cambridge: The Belknap Press of Harvard University Press, 1957), 727.

46. David J. Rhees, "A New Voice for Science: Edwin E. Slosson and the Founding of Science Service, 1921–29," (M.A. thesis, University of North Carolina, 1979).

47. Bruce V. Lewenstein, " 'Public Understanding of Science' in America, 1945–1965," (Ph.D. diss., University of Pennsylvania, 1987).

48. Ibid. Also see Schudson, *Discovering the News*.

49. Neil Eurich, *Science and Utopia: A Mighty Design* (Cambridge: The Belknap Press of Harvard University Press, 1967), 268.

Chapter Four

1. C. G. Suits, as told to Frederic Brownell, "Heed That Hunch," *The American Magazine*, December 1945, 142.

2. Harry S. Hall, "Scientists and Politicians," originally published in *Bulletin of Atomic Scientists*, February 1956; reprinted in Bernard Barber and Walter Hirsch, eds., *The Sociology of Science* (New York: The Free Press, 1962), 269–87; Margaret Mead and Rhoda Métraux, "The Image of the Scientist among College Students," *Science*, 20 August 1957; also reprinted in Barber and Hirsch, *The Sociology of Science*, 230–246. The surveys sponsored by the National Science Foundation are described in the series of National Science Board reports, *Science Indicators* (Washington: National Science Foundation, various dates).

3. J. W. N. Sullivan, "Scientific Citizens," in J. W. N. Sullivan, *Aspects of Science* (London: Richard Cobden-Sanderson, 1923), 101.

4. Suits, "Heed That Hunch," 140.

5. Richard Davies, personal communication.

6. Quoted in Nina S. Purdy, "He Took a Toy and Made It the New Marvel of Navigation," *The American Magazine*, March 1925, 189.

7. Robert M. Yoder, "The Man with the Million-Dollar Nose," *The Saturday Evening Post*, 29 September 1951, 111.

8. Samuel Hopkins Adams, "Leland O. Howard," *The American Magazine*, October 1911, 721.

9. Theodore Roosevelt, "A Naturalist's Tropical Laboratory," *Scribner's Magazine*, January 1917, 46.

10. Robert M. Gay, "The Flavor of Things," *The Atlantic Monthly*, September 1914, 419.

11. Alan Sullivan, "Pioneers of Invention," *Collier's*, 27 November 1915, 21.

12. For example, Peter Clark Macfarlane, "The Conquest of Cancer," *Cosmopolitan*, August 1912, 308; or William Maxwell, "Edison—The 'Original Man from Missouri,'" *The American Magazine*, February 1918, 84 ("the Edison of coldly scientific mind, who reasons ruthlessly and relentlessly . . .").

13. J. D. Ratcliff, "Bad Bug," *Collier's*, 17 May 1941, 54.

14. Suits, "Heed That Hunch," 140.

15. Sumner T. Pike, "Witch-Hunting Then and Now," *The Atlantic Monthly*, November 1947, 93–94.

16. Clarence Woodbury, "Dresses from Chicken Feathers," *The American Magazine*, October 1945, 96.

17. Sullivan, "Scientific Citizens," 36.

18. Herbert Kaufman, "Thomas A. Edison," *Cosmopolitan*, August 1917, 113.

19. George Ellery Hale, "How Men of Science Will Help in Our War," *Scribner's Magazine*, June 1917, 722.

20. Grace Adams, "Titchener at Cornell," *The American Mercury*, December 1931, 446.

21. James J. Haggerty, Jr., "Fastest Man on Earth," *Collier's*, 25 June 1954, 29.

22. George W. Gray, "The Problem of Influenza," *Harper's Monthly Magazine*, January 1940, 176.

23. Robert M. Yoder, "Right With You, Prof. Einstein!" *The Saturday Evening Post*, 25 February 1950, 148.

24. A. Vibert Douglas, "From Atoms to Stars," *The Atlantic Monthly*, August 1929, 158.

25. Maxwell, "Edison," 82.

26. Floyd W. Parsons, "Science in Everyday Life," *The Saturday Evening Post*, 6 February 1926, 14.

27. Julian Huxley, "Will Science Destroy Religion?," *Harper's Monthly Magazine*, April 1926, 538.

28. George W. Gray, "The Riddle of Our Reddening Skies," *Harper's Monthly Magazine*, July 1937, 169.

29. John Burroughs, "Through the Eyes of a Geologist," *The Atlantic Monthly*, May 1910, 590.

30. Ibid.

31. John Wright Buckham, "The Passing of the Scientific Era," *The Century Illustrated Monthly Magazine*, August 1929, 435.

32. Section heading to John Kobler and James Rorty, "Morale in a Test Tube," *The Saturday Evening Post*, 1 November 1941, 27.

33. Sullivan, "Scientific Citizens," 21.

34. Bailey Millard, "A Scientist Who Believes in Religion," *The World's Work*, April 1926, 662–66.

35. Ben Merson, "Mr. Persistence," *Collier's*, 27 November 1943, 24. B. C. Forbes, "Edison Working on How to Communicate with the Next World," *The American Magazine*, October 1920, 10.

36. John A. Craig, "Leo Hendrick Baekeland," *The World's Work*, April 1916, 655. Sidney Shalett, "Look Out—Here Comes a Genius!," *The Saturday Evening Post*, 15 April 1950, 195 [a biography of Robert Sarbacher].

37. Forbes, "Edison Working," 10.

38. Emil Ludwig, "Edison 'The Greatest American of the Century,'" *The American Magazine*, December 1931, 67.

39. Woodbury, "Dresses from Chicken Feathers," 96.

40. Stuart Mackenzie, "The Camera Is the Sherlock Holmes of the Sky," *The American Magazine*, November 1922, 51.

41. C. Hartley Grattan, "Thomas Alva Edison: An American Symbol," *Scribner's Magazine*, September 1933, 151.

42. Henry Ford, in collaboration with Samuel Crowther, "Edison's Life Story," *Cosmopolitan*, August 1930, 48.

43. Kaufman, "Thomas A. Edison," 113.

44. Ford, "Edison's Life Story," 38.

45. Frances Drewry McMullen, "Dr. Florence Reba Sabin," *The World's Work*, February 1926, 417.

46. Edgar C. Wheeler, "Makers of Lightning," *The World's Work*, January 1927, 277.

47. John Janney, "Ten Men in One," *The American Magazine*, December 1935, 35.

48. Wheeler, "Makers of Lightning," 278.

49. Janney, "Ten Men," 35.

50. Millard, "A Scientist Who Believes," 662.

51. Ibid.

52. Wheeler, "Makers of Lightning," 271.

53. Fields of all scientists who were subjects of biographies: physics, 29.7%; biology, 24.2%; chemistry, 16.4%; astronomy, 3.9%; and anthropology or social sciences, 3.1%. Places of employment of all scientists who were subjects of biographies: university, 29.7%; industry, 17.9%; self-employed, 14.1%; government, 11.7%; museum or observatory, 4.7%; private foundation, 6.3%; and other or not identified, 15.7%.

54. Steven M. Spencer, "Born Handy," *The Saturday Evening Post*, 7 May 1949, 31, 153, a biography of Frederick McKinley Jones, Chief Engineer of the United States Thermo Control Company, who was described as a "self-taught Negro scientist"; and Amy Porter, "Anthropological Katie," *Collier's*, 24 February 1945, 68–69, 80, a profile of Katherine Dunham, a Ph.D. anthropologist (see the discussion of this article in Chapter 5).

55. Carl Snyder, "Noguchi—The Man Behind the Contagion Fighters," *Everybody's Magazine*, November 1915, 554–61. This biography of Hideyo Noguchi contained the description: "Dark and oriental in feature, he is obviously a Japanese, though he speaks English without a trace of accent" (p. 555).

56. Edwin Diehl, "How We Made the A-Bomb Shell," *The Saturday Evening Post*, 21 November 1953, 21; Haggerty, "Fastest Man on Earth," 25.

57. Fred C. Kelly, "Pearl—and Provender," *Everybody's Magazine*, August 1918, 57.

58. Ibid.

59. Ives Hendrick, "Conquering Scarlet Fever," *The World's Work*, May 1925, 30.

60. Harris Dickson, "Dethroning King Cotton," *The Saturday Evening Post*, 2 July 1910, 12–13; Alexander McAdie, "Relativity and the Absurdities of Alice," *The Atlantic Monthly*, June 1921, 811.

61. Elizabeth Shepley Sergeant, "Cosmopolite of the Month: Dr. Carl C. Jung," *Cosmopolitan*, January 1939, 15.

62. Sullivan, "Scientific Citizens," 22.

63. George Kent, "Dr. Alexis Carrel Believes We Can Read Each Other's Thoughts," *The American Magazine*, March 1936, 143.

64. Waldemar Kaempffert, "Why Can't We Live Forever?," *The American Magazine*, September 1939, 16.

65. Kent, "Dr. Alexis Carrel," 20.

66. Diehl, "A-Bomb Shell," 21, 101.

67. Ibid.

68. B. C. Forbes, "The Story of a Great Inventor," *The American Magazine*, September 1920, 19.

69. Lorine Pruette, "G. Stanley Hall," *The Century Illustrated Monthly Magazine*, October 1924, 768.

70. Woodbury, "Dresses from Chicken Feathers," 33.

71. Psychiatrists who treat scientists as patients have, in fact, described some of them as "people who wish to flee from the world of uncertainty and seek refuge in a world of exact answers." See Jacqueline Olds and Richard Stanton Schwartz, "The Scientist as Patient," *McLean Hospital Journal*, 4, no. 3 (1979): 109.

72. Ernest Gruening, "Another Germ Bites the Dust!" *Collier's*, 4 October 1924, 30.

73. Ray Tucker, "Noble Experimenting," *Collier's*, 10 November 1934, 23.

74. Kent, "Dr. Alexis Carrel," 21.

75. Mackenzie, "The Camera," 174.

76. Bernard de Voto, "The Timid Profession," *The Saturday Evening Post*, 9 February 1935, 12.

77. R. G. A. Dolby, "On the Autonomy of Pure Science: The Construction and Maintenance of Barriers between Scientific Establishments and Popular Culture," in Norbert Elias, Herminio Martins, and Richard Whitley, eds., *Scientific Establishments and Hierarchies*, vol. 6 of *Sociology of the Sciences* (Dordrecht, Holland: D. Reidel, 1982), 270.

Chapter Five

1. See, for example, Linda S. Dix, ed., *Women: Their Underrepresentation and Career Differentials in Science and Engineering—Proceedings of a Workshop*, Office of Scientific and Engineering Personnel, National Research Council (Washington: National Academy Press, 1987); National Science Board, *Science & Engineering Indicators—1987* (Washington: Government Printing Office, 1987), chapters 2 and 3; and U.S. Congress, Office of Technology Assessment, *Educating*

Scientists and Engineers: Grade School to Grad School, OTA-SET-377 (Washington: Government Printing Office, 1988).

2. Jonathan R. Cole, "Women in Science," in Douglas N. Jackson and J. Philippe Rushton, eds., *Scientific Excellence: Origins and Assessment* (Newbury Park, Calif.: Sage, 1987), 360.

3. Evelyn Fox Keller explained her use of the masculine pronoun in response to a review of one of her books: the pronoun was meant "to underline . . . that the 'founding fathers of modern science' . . . conceptualized science, explicitly and self-consciously, as a specifically 'masculine' endeavor . . ." See Evelyn Fox Keller, "Women in Science" (letter to the editor), *Science,* 1 May 1987, 507.

4. Some magazines published more female authors than others, and editorial practices changed dramatically across the years. No female authors appeared at all in the *Cosmopolitan* issues sampled for 1915–34 and 1945–55; yet in the 1935–44 *Cosmopolitan* sample, women wrote *all* the science articles. One-eighth of the *The Atlantic Monthly* articles for 1910–14 were written by women, but there were no science articles written by women in the remaining sample (1915–55). Almost one-quarter of *The Saturday Evening Post* science authors from 1935 to 1949 were women, but there were none after 1949.

5. See Marion Marzolf, *Up from the Footnote: A History of Women Journalists* (New York: Hastings House, 1977), chapter 2.

6. Ishbel Ross, *Ladies of the Press: The Story of Women in Journalism by an Insider* (New York: Harper and Brothers, 1936), 356.

7. A 1976–78 study of U.S. science journalists identified only three women in a group of twenty-eight journalists who formed the elite "inner club" of the profession. See Sharon Dunwoody, "The Science Writing Inner Club: A Communication Link between Science and the Lay Public," *Science, Technology, & Human Values* 5 (Winter 1980): 14–22.

8. Daniel J. Kevles, *The Physicists: The History of a Scientific Community in Modern America* (New York: Alfred A. Knopf, 1978), 204, 370.

9. In 1920–29, 15.9% of U.S. doctorate degrees in the life sciences were awarded to women; in 1930–39, 15.1%; in 1940–49, 12.7%. See Betty M. Vetter, "Women's Progress," *Mosaic* 18 (Spring 1987): 2.

10. In a sample of 1,131 issues published between January 1910 and December 1923, there were seventy-nine articles written by male scientists and none written by women scientists.

11. Or no more than all the articles published by George Ellery Hale and Robert Millikan in the same sampled issues (see Chapter 3).

12. Out of 687 articles in the sampled issues, 23 (or 3%) were either written by women scientists ($n = 5$) or were biographies of women scientists ($n = 18$); 356 (or 51%) of the aritcles were either written by ($n = 248$), autobiographies of ($n = 7$), or biographies of ($n = 108$) male scientists. One could, of course, also analyze the ratio of references or quotes within articles according to gender—a tedious exercise. Although I did not record them, the references to female scientists within the texts were few and far between. When a journalist included a "roll-call" of famous scientists, he or she frequently listed Darwin, Einstein, and Marie Curie; but direct quotations, such as journalists routinely include in news stories on cur-

rent research, were rarely from women scientists, thereby reinforcing the notion that women were not part of the mainstream of science, not important voices for the research community.

13. See Margaret W. Rossiter, *Women Scientists in America: Struggles to 1940* (Baltimore: The Johns Hopkins University Press, 1982).

14. Ibid., Figures 6.1 and 6.2, pp. 131–132.

15. Vetter, "Women's Progress," 2.

16. As late as 1986, only 3.4% of National Academy of Sciences members were women, and only 2% of the scientists who had by then received the Nobel prize were women. (Cole, "Women in Science," 360.)

17. See Elisabeth Crawford, *The Beginnings of the Nobel Institution* (Cambridge: Cambridge University Press, 1984, and Paris: Editions de la Maison des Science de l'Homme, 1984); and Elisabeth Crawford, J. L. Heilbron, and Rebecca Ulrich, eds., *The Nobel Population, 1901–1937* (Berkeley: Office for History of Science and Technology, University of California, 1987). David Dickson, "Bumps and Falls on the Road to Stockholm," *Science,* 16 October 1987, 264, analyzes the implications of those findings.

18. See John C. Burnham, *How Superstition Won and Science Lost: Popularizing Science and Health in the United States* (New Brunswick, N.J.: Rutgers, 1987), for discussion of this point.

19. These data include an eight-part biography of Marie Curie published in *The Saturday Evening Post* in 1937. That biography series represented over 40% of all the biographies of women scientists published in the issues sampled, but does not alter the overall conclusions, because these issues included at least four major, multipart biographical series on male scientists during the same period.

20. In most instances, the biographies represented less than 10% of all articles on those fields.

21. Maxine Davis, "Modern Miracle Women: Dr. Catherine Macfarlane," *Cosmopolitan,* June 1942, 36–37, 138–39.

22. This visit is described in Kevles, *The Physicists,* 204–20.

23. Quoted in ibid., 205.

24. Elizabeth Shepley Sergeant, "Alice Hamilton, M.D.," *Harper's Monthly Magazine,* May 1926, 767.

25. Eve Curie, "Marie Curie, My Mother," *The Saturday Evening Post,* eight parts, appearing in each issue from 4 September 1937 through 23 October 1937.

26. The book version, *Madame Curie* (New York: Doubleday, Doran, 1938), was published in translation in the United States in 1938 and sold well over a million copies.

27. Sergeant, "Alice Hamilton, M.D.," 763–70.

28. Ibid., 764–65.

29. Ibid., 763.

30. Ibid., 764.

31. Ibid., 765.

32. Barbara Sicherman, *Alice Hamilton: A Life in Letters* (Cambridge: Harvard University Press, 1984), 237.

33. Ibid.

34. "Watchman," *The American Magazine,* March 1940, 86 ("Interesting People" series).

35. Frances Drewry McMullen, "Dr. Florence Rena Sabin," *The World's Work,* February 1926, 417.

36. "Headhunter," *The American Magazine,* September 1935 ("Interesting People" series).

37. "Mrs. Atom," *The American Magazine,* February 1950, 113 ("Interesting People" series).

38. This emphasis coincides with data on how the fiction and nonfiction articles in mass magazines portrayed women in the 1920s—not as the stereotype "flapper," but as most fulfilled in their domestic roles as wives and mothers. See Terry Hynes, "Magazine Portrayal of Women, 1911–1930," *Journalism Monographs* no. 72, (May 1981).

39. Edwin Diehl, "How We Made the A-Bomb Shell," *The Saturday Evening Post,* 21 November 1953, 101.

40. Martha Coman and Hugh Weir, "The Most Difficult Husband in America," *Collier's,* 18 July 1925, 11.

41. James R. Crowell, "What It Means to be Married to a Genius," *American Magazine,* February 1930, 153.

42. Milton Silverman, "Ma Bell's House of Magic," *The Saturday Evening Post,* 10 May 1947, 15.

43. Vernon Kellogg, "The Biologist Speaks of Death," *The Atlantic Monthly,* June 1921, 1.

44. Clarence Hall, "The Man Who Made a Mountain Out of Sex," *The American Magazine,* October 1953, 22 and 112.

45. Cole, "Women in Science," 361–62. Cole writes that women who entered science in this century "were at once rejected by those in the general culture who felt that such activities were inappropriate for women and at the same time were not accepted as full members of the scientific community" (p. 362).

46. Sergeant, "Alice Hamilton, M.D.," 763.

47. Roy Chapman Andrews, "Explorers and Their Work," *The Saturday Evening Post,* 22 August 1931, 84.

48. Ibid.

49. "The unit . . . consists of three professional men technicians and three girls who act as their assistants." (Richard Thruelson, "Laboratory Technician," *The Saturday Evening Post,* 19 February 1949, 124.)

50. Robert M. Yoder, "Buck Rogers Would Love It Here," *The Saturday Evening Post,* 20 October 1951, 126.

51. "Testing the Men," Part 2 of "Man's Survival in Space" series, *Collier's,* 7 March 1953, 56.

52. Thruelson, "Laboratory Technician," 122.

53. Evelyn Fox Keller, *A Feeling for the Organism: The Life and Work of Barbara McClintock* (New York: W. H. Freeman, 1983). Also see, Evelyn Fox Keller, *Reflections on Gender and Science* (New Haven: Yale University Press, 1985).

54. Goodell describes Mead's public reputation at length. See Rae Goodell, *The Visible Scientists* (Boston: Little, Brown, 1977).

55. "Headhunter," *The American Magazine,* September 1935 ("Interesting People" series).

56. McMullen, "Dr. Florence Rena Sabin," *The World's Work,* February 1926, 412.

57. This myth persists in the 1980s. Bruer observes, for example, that "older scientists, both men and women, express the belief that domestic life is incompatible with productive science." See John T. Bruer, "Women in Science: Toward Equitable Participation," *Science, Technology, & Human Values* 9 (Summer 1984): 6.

58. Patricke Johns-Heine and Hans H. Gerth, "Values in Mass Periodical Fiction, 1921–1940," in Bernard Rosenberg and David Manning White, eds., *Mass Culture: The Popular Arts in America* (Glencoe: The Free Press, 1957), 229.

59. Amy Porter, "Anthropological Katie," *Collier's,* 24 February 1945, 68–69, 80.

60. Popular culture sometimes seems like a revolving door—the same topics, the same people, pop in and out of the journalistic spotlight. Perhaps because our images of science as a progressive, not a cyclical, process are so strong, we tend to forget that the same characteristics apply to science journalism.

Even given these circumstances, I was surprised to open *The Boston Globe* one Sunday morning and find a feature article on Katherine Dunham in the magazine section. Dunham has had tremendous influence, as an anthropologist turned choreographer, on folk-based modern dance. Just as the *Collier's* article had in 1945, most of the newspaper article dealt with her entertainment career. And near the end, the author asked Dunham "about the difficulties she encountered as a black woman doing things that no other black—man or woman—had ever done before . . ." " 'Certainly,' she said, 'I was aware of hardships. But somehow, I never felt that they were all directed specifically at me, because I was black, or because I was a woman. Looking back now, I see how many of the problems had the color of racism in them. But I didn't think of it at the time.' " (Sylviane Gold, "With a Shimmy and a Shake," *The Boston Globe Magazine,* 10 April 1988, 65.)

61. Ibid., 84. For more extensive discussion of this idea, see Jonathan R. Cole, *Fair Science: Women in the Scientific Community* (New York: Free Press, 1971), Chapter 6.

62. Cole, *Fair Science,* 298. Jane Butler Kahle quotes from an interview with a typical fifteen-year-old girl who was asked, "What is your image of a scientist?" The girl replied "A scientist's totally involved in work. Therefore, they don't care about appearance. [They] wear white coats, have beards—'cause they're men. They just seem to care only about their science work." See Jane Butler Kahle and Marsha Lakes Matyas, "Equitable Science and Mathematics Education: A Discrepancy Model," in Kahle and Matyas, *Women: Their Underrepresentation and Career Differentials in Science and Engineering, Proceedings of a Workshop* (Washington: National Academy Press, 1987), 30.

63. Norma C. Ware, Nicole A. Steckler, and Jane Leserman, "Undergraduate Women: Who Chooses a Science Major?," *Journal of Higher Education* 56 (January/February 1985): 82.

64. Cole, *Fair Science,* 298. Or as Jane Butler Kahle writes: "Tomorrow's vision [of women in science] begins within today's science classrooms, where new approaches to teaching science stress its egalitarian image and provide equal educational opportunity as well." See Jane Butler Kahle, "Women Biologists: A View and a Vision," *BioScience* 35 (April 1985): 230.

65. Sheila E. Widnall made this point forcefully in her President's Address to the American Association for the Advancement of Science, Boston, Massachusetts, 14 February 1988. (Sheila E. Widnall, "AAAS Presidential Lecture: Voices from the Pipeline," *Science,* 30 September 1988, 1740–1745.)

Chapter Six

1. Carl Sandburg, "Mr. Attila" (1945), in Carl Sandburg, *Complete Poems* (New York: Harcourt, Brace, 1950), 624.

2. William S. Dutton, "Meet Mr. Sherlock Holmes of the Plant World," *The American Mercury,* April 1929, 152.

3. Eugene H. Kone, "Progress in Science," *The American Mercury,* November 1946, 610.

4. Although many scholars have attempted to classify cultural images of scientists, Arthur Koestler's work seems most appropriate to the images I found. He categorized fictional scientists into three types of "Sages": (1) a benevolent "White Magician," whose "conquistadorial urge is derived from a sense of power, the participatory urge from a sense of . . . wonder"; (2) a "Black Magician" who is characterized as having "a monstrous lusting for power" and appears "as the unavoidable component of competitiveness, jealousy, and self-righteousness"; and (3) a Pedant, the "dry, dull, dilligent . . . uninspired, scholarly bookworm or laboratory worker." See Arthur Koestler, *The Act of Creation* (New York: The Macmillan Company, 1964), 257–58.

5. Carl Snyder, "Carrel—Mender of Men," *Collier's,* 16 November 1912, 12–13.

6. Edgar C. Wheeler, "Makers of Lightning," *The World's Work,* January 1927, 269.

7. Frank J. Taylor, "How Your Flowers Are Remodeled," *The Saturday Evening Post,* 1 March 1947, 20, 21.

8. Herbert Kaufman, "Thomas A. Edison," *Cosmopolitan,* August 1917, 76.

9. C. Hartley Grattan, "Thomas Alva Edison: An American Symbol," *Scribner's Magazine,* September 1933, 151.

10. Kaufman, "Thomas A. Edison," 76.

11. Frank Luther Mott, *A History of American Magazines, Volume III (1865–1885)* (Cambridge: The Belknap Press of Harvard University Press, 1938), 119.

12. For example, the Steinmetz biography series: Jonathan Norton Leonard, "Steinmetz, Jove of Science," *The World's Work,* January–March 1929.

13. E. E. Free, "The Electrical Brains in the Telephone," *The World's Work,* February 1927.

14. Wheeler, "Makers of Lightning."

15. Winifred Kirkland, "The Weakness of Psychic Research," *Scribner's Magazine,* December 1920, 705.

16. Floyd W. Parsons, "Science in Everyday Life," *The Saturday Evening Post,* 6 February 1926, 14.

17. Ibid.

18. Paul de Kruif, "Boss Kettering," *The Saturday Evening Post,* 15 July 1933, 5.

19. George Russell Harrison, "The Doctor Consults the Physicist," *The Atlantic Monthly,* May 1939, 649.

20. Charles Lane Callen, "If the Chemist Stepped Out of Your Life—," *The American Magazine,* May 1926, 189.

21. Jeffrey K. Stine, personal communication.

22. Robert Sklar, "Introduction," *The Plastic Age (1917–1930),* ed. Robert Sklar (New York: George Braziller, 1970), 22.

23. Stephen Leacock, "Common Sense and the Universe," *The Atlantic Monthly,* May 1942, 628.

24. Geoffrey Parsons, "Black Science," *Harper's Monthly Magazine,* June 1927, 109.

25. Leacock, "Common Sense," 629.

26. As measured by biographical data, academic degrees, research specialities, publications, and employers. See the table in Appendix 8.

27. Samuel Crowther, "A Scientist's God," *Collier's,* 24 October 1925, 6.

28. "What *Is* Life?," *Cosmopolitan,* May 1920, 26–27.

29. John Ziman, *The Force of Knowledge* (Cambridge: Cambridge University Press, 1976), 126.

30. "In the United States through the 1920s it seemed as though everyone was competing for the honor of thirteenth man." (Daniel J. Kevles, *The Physicists: The History of a Scientific Community in Modern America* [New York: Alfred A. Knopf, 1978], 175.) *Scientific Monthly* stated that "Nearly everybody has sense enough to know that it is hopeless for him to get more than the vaguest notion of what it [the general theory of relativity] is all about." See Fabian Franklin, "Einstein and America," *Scientific Monthly,* March 1929, 279, quoted in Kevles, *The Physicists,* 176.

31. Morris R. Cohen, "Roads to Einstein," *The New Republic,* 6 July 1921, 172–74, quoted in Ronald C. Tobey, *The American Ideology of National Science, 1919–1930* (Pittsburgh: The University of Pittsburgh Press, 1971), 106.

32. Tobey, *Ideology of National Science,* 111–12.

33. Dorothy Giles, "The Wise Men of Science Come to the Manger—Soul Clinics," *Cosmopolitan,* January 1938, 135.

34. Robert M. Yoder, "Right with You, Prof. Einstein!," *The Saturday Evening Post,* 25 February 1950, 25.

35. Ibid.

36. J. D. Bernal, "If Industry Gave Science a Chance," *Harper's Monthly Magazine,* February 1935, 268.

37. Annette M. Woodlief made a similar observation in "Science in Popular Culture," in M. Thomas Inge, ed., *Handbook of American Popular Culture,* vol.

3 (Westport, Conn.: Greenwood Press, 1981), 429–58: "Most Americans throughout history have seen science alternately as creator and destroyer of their more cherished ideals and material progress . . ." (p. 430).

38. Wallace Brett Donham, "Nobody's Business," *The Atlantic Monthly,* September 1940, 371.

39. Charles F. Kettering, as told to Paul de Kruif, "America Comes through a Crisis," *The Saturday Evening Post,* 13 May 1933, 3.

40. Robert C. Merton, "Priorities in Scientific Discovery: A Chapter in the Sociology of Science," in Bernard Barber and Walter Hirsch, eds., *The Sociology of Science* (New York: The Free Press, 1962), 459.

41. See Roderick Nash, *The Nervous Generation: American Thought, 1917–1930* (Chicago: Rand McNally, 1970), 47ff.

42. George W. Gray, "Universe in the Red," *The Atlantic Monthly,* February 1933, 239 (Gray was quoting the writings of Buddha).

43. Edward P. Morgan, "The A-Bomb's Invisible Offspring," *Collier's,* 9 August 1947, 61.

44. Ibid.

45. Stewart Alsop and Ralph E. Lapp, "The Grim Truth about Civil Defense," *The Saturday Evening Post,* 21 April 1951, 36.

46. William L. Laurence, "The Truth about the Hydrogen Bomb," *The Saturday Evening Post,* 24 June 1950, 18, 94.

47. Stewart Alsop and Ralph E. Lapp, "The Inside Story of Our First Hydrogen Bomb," *The Saturday Evening Post,* 25 October 1952, 153.

48. John Lear, "Can a Mechanical Brain Replace *You*?" *Collier's,* 4 April 1953, 58.

49. John Kabler, "You're Not Very Smart at All," *The Saturday Evening Post,* 18 February 1950, 25.

50. Ibid., 113. Kabler is paraphrasing, not quoting, Wiener.

51. Lear, "Mechanical Brain," 58.

52. Ibid.

53. Theodore Roszak, "The Monster and the Titan: Science, Knowledge, and Gnosis," *Daedalus* (Summer 1974): 31.

54. These three types are discussed in Nash, *The Nervous Generation,* Chapter 4, esp. 126–137.

55. Henry F. May, *The End of American Innocence, A Study of the First Years of Our Own Time, 1912–1917* (New York: Alfred A. Knopf, 1959), ix.

56. Title of an article by James Hay, Jr., *The American Magazine,* June 1916, 37 (interview with Alexander Graham Bell).

57. William Maxwell, "Edison—The 'Original Man from Missouri,'" *The American Magazine,* February 1918, 80.

58. Charles P. Steinmetz, "The World Belongs to the Dissatisfied," *The American Magazine,* May 1918, 38.

59. Title of a biography of chemist William Hoskins. Neil M. Clark, "The World's Most Tragic Man Is One Who Never Starts," *The American Magazine,* May 1927, 26.

60. de Kruif, "Boss Kettering."

61. Ibid., 15 July 1933, 5.

62. Kettering, "America Comes through a Crisis."

63. Charles F. Kettering, "Ten Paths to Fame and Fortune," *The American Magazine*, December 1937, 14.

64. Lester Velie, "Bread Within the Waters," *Collier's*, 11 September 1948, 68.

65. Charles E. Rosenberg, *No Other Gods: On Science and American Social Thought* (Baltimore: The Johns Hopkins University Press, 1976).

66. Ibid., 123.

67. Edward Shils, "Faith, Utility, and Legitimacy of Science," *Daedalus* (Summer 1974): 5.

68. Ibid., 8.

69. Fred C. Kelly, "Pearl—and Provender," *Everybody's Magazine*, August 1918, 57.

Chapter Seven

1. Robert Kilburn Root, "The Age of Faith," *The Atlantic Monthly*, July 1912, 114.

2. Hugh Black, "Our Made-Over World," *Everybody's Magazine*, November 1914, 707.

3. Hans Zinsser, "Untheological Reflections," *The Atlantic Monthly*, July 1929, 91.

4. Jim Marshall, "The Big Eye," *Collier's*, 29 November 1947, 22.

5. Ronald Tobey cites as evidence a magazine article by E. E. Slosson, in which the editor calls research "a serious and solemn thing" and labels science as "toil," "drudgery," and "persistent and patient labor." Tobey maintains that the tendency to confuse the scientific method with the qualities and intellectual abilities of the scientist was particularly common in the 1910s and 1920s. See Ronald C. Tobey, *The American Ideology of National Science, 1919–1930* (Pittsburgh: The University of Pittsburgh Press, 1971), 92.

6. Leon Trachtman observes that science is "not at all like the idealized reports of utterly rational and totally inerrant experiments published in the scientific journals" because it is, in reality "tentative, sometimes seeming to take two steps backwards for every one forward, ultimately imprecise in technique and measurement, full of experimental error . . ." See Leon C. Trachtman, "The Public Understanding of Science Effort: A Critique," *Science, Technology, & Human Values* 6 (Summer 1981): 14.

7. Charles F. Kettering with Beverly Smith, "Ten Paths to Fame and Fortune," *The American Magazine*, December 1937, 14.

8. Loren Eiseley, "The Secret of Life," *Harper's Monthly Magazine*, October 1953, 67.

9. Norman Draper, "Electrifying America," *Collier's*, 27 November 1915, 12.

10. Jonathan Norton Leonard, "Steinmetz, Jove of Science (Part III)," *The World's Work*, March 1929, 126.

11. Ives Hendrick, "Conquering Scarlet Fever," *The World's Work,* May 1925, 30.

12. J. B. Rhine, "Things I Can't Explain," *The American Magazine,* January 1949, 42.

13. Hendrick, "Conquering Scarlet Fever," 30.

14. Henshaw Ward, "The Candle of Astronomy," *Harper's Monthly Magazine,* February 1926, 378.

15. Nathan Reingold, "Reflections on 200 Years of Science in the United States," in Nathan Reingold, ed., *The Sciences in the American Context: New Perspectives* (Washington: Smithsonian Institution Press, 1979), 12.

16. Frank J. Taylor, "Big Eye," *The American Magazine,* November 1935, 62.

17. Andrew Hamilton, "Peephole of the Universe," *The American Magazine,* February 1947, 16.

18. Marshall, "The Big Eye," 22.

19. Ira S. Bowen as told to Jim Marshall, "Window to the Universe," *Collier's,* 24 July 1948, 16.

20. Zinsser, "Untheological Reflections," 90.

21. V. K. Zworykin, "You Can Write It Down . . . ," *The American Magazine,* August 1949, 123.

22. Samuel Crowther, "Our Kings of Chemistry," *The World's Work,* February 1921, 349.

23. Ibid.

24. Zworykin, "You Can Write It," 51.

25. Frank B. Stockbridge, "Creating Life in the Laboratory," *Cosmopolitan,* May 1912, 775.

26. Jonathan Norton Leonard, "Steinmetz, Jove of Science (Part II)," *The World's Work,* February 1929, 140.

27. Kettering, "Ten Paths," 14.

28. Zworykin, "You Can Write It," 50.

29. As historian Derek Price once observed, the postwar boom in scientific journal publishing involved not so much an increase in the productivity of individuals as an increase in the proportion of journal articles having multiple authors. (Derek J. de Solla Price, commenting on a paper at the 1977 Annual Meeting of the Society for Social Studies of Science, 16 October 1977, Cambridge, Mass.)

30. Zworykin, "You Can Write It," 123.

31. Ibid.

32. Waldemar Kaempffert, "A New Key to the Unknown," *The American Magazine,* June 1940, 66.

33. "Chicks and Comets," *The American Magazine,* October 1946, 136. Such appreciation of amateurs continues in modern magazines. Prashant Singh, a student in one of my MIT classes, brought to my attention the following quote in a newsmagazine article on Supernova 1987a: "If Las Vegas made book on which amateur astronomer would be the first to spot the next supernova, the odds-on favorite would have to be Robert Evans, 50, a Uniting Church minister from New South Wales, Australia." ("A Super Stargazer," sidebar to Michael Lemonick, J.

Madeleine Nash, Gavin Scott, and Dick Thompson, "Bang! A Star Explodes, Finding New Clues to the Nature of the Universe," *Time,* 23 March 1987, 66.)

34. Floyd W. Parsons, "Man and His 33 Slaves," *The Saturday Evening Post,* 13 February 1926, 138.

35. Clarence Woodbury, "They Called Him *Dumb,*" *The American Magazine,* March 1950, 36.

36. Alan Sullivan, "Pioneers of Invention," *Collier's,* 27 November 1915, 21–22, 37–43.

37. George N. Robillard, "Are We Stifling the Inventors?" *The Saturday Evening Post,* 9 June 1951, 22–23, 111.

38. A number of scholars have written on the contributions of amateurs to American science. For example, Marianne Gosztonyi Ainley, "The Contribution of the Amateur to North American Ornithology: A Historical Perspective," *The Living Bird,* Eighteenth Annual, 1979–80 (Cornell Laboratory of Ornithology, 1 July 1980), 161–77. Also Nathan Reingold, "Definitions and Speculations: The Professionalization of Science in America in the Nineteenth Century," in Alexandra Oleson and Sanborn C. Brown, eds., *The Pursuit of Knowledge in the Early American Republic: American Scientific and Learned Societies from Colonial Times to the Civil War* (Baltimore: The Johns Hopkins University Press, 1976), 33–69.

39. Harold Goddard, "Should Language Be Abolished?," *The Atlantic Monthly,* July 1918, 62.

40. For more on popular news coverage of psychology in the twentieth century, see John C. Burnham, *How Superstition Won and Science Lost: Popularizing Science and Health in the United States* (New Brunswick, N.J.: Rutgers University Press, 1987), especially Chapter 3.

41. Robert H. Kargon, ed., *The Maturing of American Science* (Washington: American Association for the Advancement of Science, 1974), 33.

42. Julian Huxley, "Will Science Destroy Religion?," *Harper's Monthly Magazine,* April 1926, 532.

43. Ibid.

44. John B. Watson, "What Is Behaviorism?," *Harper's Monthly Magazine,* May 1926, 724.

45. Henry Foster Adams, "Psychology Goldbricks," *Scribner's Magazine,* July 1921, 94.

46. Ibid.

47. George Draper, "Psychoanalysis—The Inward Eye," *Scribner's Magazine,* December 1931, 66.

48. Geoffrey Parsons, "Black Science," *Harper's Monthly Magazine,* June 1927, 107.

49. Draper, "Psychoanalysis," 66, italics added.

50. Erwin Schroedinger, "Is Science a Fashion of the Times?" *Harper's Monthly Magazine,* June 1934, 40.

51. Ibid.

52. Huxley, "Will Science Destroy Religion," 532.

53. Henry F. May, *The End of American Innocence, A Study of the First Years of Our Own Time, 1912–1917* (New York: Alfred A. Knopf, 1959), 156.

54. For essays on the political and social conflicts inherent in the postwar funding debates, see Samuel Z. Klausner and Victor M. Lidz, eds., *The Nationalization of the Social Sciences* (Philadelphia: University of Pennsylvania Press, 1986).

55. For discussion of the legislative debate, see House Committee on Science and Astronautics, *Technical Information for Congress,* Report to the Subcommittee on Science, Research, and Development, 92d Congress (Washington: Government Printing Office, revised 15 May 1971), 97–125. See also Daniel S. Greenberg, *The Politics of Pure Science* (New York: New American Library, 1967), 106–11.

56. See Vannevar Bush, *Science—The Endless Frontier* (Washington: Government Printing Office, 1945); J. Merton England, *A Patron for Pure Science: The National Science Foundation's Formative Years, 1945–57* (Washington: National Science Foundation, 1982), 9–10 and elsewhere. Daniel J. Kevles, *The Physicists: The History of a Scientific Community in Modern America* (New York: Alfred A. Knopf, 1978), 347; and Greenberg, *The Politics of Pure Science,* 104–6.

57. House Committee on Science and Astronautics, *Technical Information for Congress,* 105.

58. Ibid., 119.

59. Ibid., 104.

60. Although social science research is supported now at all levels of government, echoes of that earlier debate can still often be detected in the language of official reports or in Congressional statements. When the Reagan administration proposed serious cuts in federal funding for social science research in the 1980s, for example, the "legitimacy" debate was revived, revealing a public image still wary of such research. Critics charged that the social and economic sciences were "esoteric." William Carey editorialized at the time that "the same act of public faith that legitimizes theoretical and applied research in the physical and life sciences has been withheld from the social and economic sciences because the benefits are less amenable to measurement." (William D. Carey, "Affordable Science," *Science* 211 (1 May 1981): 497.)

Chapter Eight

1. L. P. Jacks, "Is There a Foolproof Science?," *The Atlantic Monthly,* February 1924, 231.

2. "There is an inertia of motion, as well as rest. The laboratories have grown so accustomed to doing brilliant scientific work that I suspect they have forgotten how to stop." (E. E. Free, "The Electrical Brains in the Telephone," *The World's Work,* February 1927, 436.)

3. Ibid., 429.

4. Charles F. Kettering, as told to Paul de Kruif, "America Comes through a Crisis," *The Saturday Evening Post,* 13 May 1933, 3.

5. See the discussion of the Bush report in J. Merton England, *A Patron for Pure Science: The National Science Foundation's Formative Years, 1945–57* (Washington: National Science Foundation, 1982), 107–8.

6. See discussion of these attitudes in Denis W. Brogan, *The American Character* (New York: Vintage Books, 1956), 5.

7. See discussion of the debate between social philosophies of private ownership versus "all paths for all people" in relation to restraints on technology in Ian Barbour, *Technology, Environment, and Human Values* (New York: Praeger Publications, 1980).

8. Jacks, "Foolproof Science," 238.

9. Vannevar Bush, "For Man to Know," *The Atlantic Monthly,* August 1955, 33.

10. Jacks, "Foolproof Science," 236.

11. Hugh Black, "Our Made-Over World," *Everybody's Magazine,* November 1914, 710.

12. Vernon Kellogg, "Some Things Science Doesn't Know," *The World's Work,* March 1926, 528.

13. Vernon Kellogg, "The Biologist Speaks of Life," *The Atlantic Monthly,* May 1921, 592.

14. *The New York Times,* 5 September 1927, quoted in Carroll Pursell, "'A Savage Struck by Lightning': The Idea of a Research Moratorium, 1927–37," *Lex et Scientia,* 10 (October–December 1974): 147. Also see Ronald C. Tobey, *The American Ideology of National Science, 1919–1930* (Pittsburgh: The University of Pittsburgh Press, 1971), 150; and Daniel J. Kevles, *The Physicists: The History of a Scientific Community in Modern America* (New York: Alfred A. Knopf, 1978), 180.

15. William McGucken, "The Social Relations of Science: The British Association for the Advancement of Science, 1931–1946," *Proceedings of the American Philosophical Society* 123, no. 4 (August 1979): 237.

16. Robert H. Kargon, ed., *The Maturing of American Science* (Washington: American Association for the Advancement of Science, 1974), 34. Also see discussion in "Can Science Save Us?" *Harper's Monthly Magazine,* December 1945.

17. Pursell, "'A Savage Struck by Lightning,'" 146–61.

18. James R. Newman, "America's Most Radical Law," *Harper's Monthly Magazine,* May 1947, 441, quoting Charles F. Kettering.

19. Fred Hoyle, "The Expanding Universe," *Harper's Monthly Magazine,* April 1951, 90.

20. George W. Gray, "This Earth We Live On," *The American Magazine,* April 1927, 26.

21. For example, Edwin Diehl, "How We Made the A-Bomb Shell," *The Saturday Evening Post,* 21 November 1953, 101. See discussion of this point in Chapter 5.

22. Elsie McCormick, "Death in a Hard Shell," *The Saturday Evening Post,* 15 November 1941, 25.

23. John Burnham has pointed out that this follows the standard formula for heroes, who must overcome some difficulty in order to be a hero. (John C. Burnham, personal communication.)

24. Patricke Johns-Heine and Hans H. Gerth, "Values in Mass Periodical

Fiction, 1921–1940," in Bernard Rosenberg and David Manning White, eds., *Mass Culture: The Popular Arts in America* (Glencoe: The Free Press, 1957), 230–31.

25. Sidney Shalett, "Look Out—Here Comes a Genius!," *The Saturday Evening Post*, 15 April 1950, 195.

26. Edwin E. Slosson, "Science from the Sidelines," *The Century Illustrated Monthly Magazine*, January 1922, 473.

27. Robert K. Merton, "Priorities in Scientific Discoveries: A Chapter in the Sociology of Science," in Bernard Barber and Walter Hirsch, eds., *The Sociology of Science* (New York: The Free Press, 1962), 454.

28. Hugh Black, "The Forces of Unrest," *Everybody's Magazine*, October 1914, 566.

29. Ibid.; and C. E. M. Joad, "Is Man Improving?," *Scribner's Magazine*, August 1935, 112.

30. Marston Taylor Bogert, "The New Marvels of Chemistry in Your Everyday Life," *The American Magazine*, September 1921, 19.

31. Harold Howland, "How Scientists Increase Your Food Supply," *The American Magazine*, February 1925, 44.

32. Victor Heiser, "America's Faces: Scientist," *Cosmopolitan*, April 1945, 21.

33. Clarence Woodbury, "Dresses from Chicken Feathers," *The American Magazine*, October 1945, 33.

34. George Ellery Hale, "Cosmic Crucibles," *Scribner's Magazine*, October 1921, 398.

35. Ibid.

36. Ellwood Hendrick, "How the Dyestuff Crisis Was Met," *The World's Work*, March 1918, 534. An editorial on industrial research declared that every year "it becomes harder and harder to draw the dividing line between pure science and applied science; and rash is he who is ready to declare that any given addition to the body of human knowledge is not, and never will be, of any practical use." ("Science in Industry," *The Saturday Evening Post*, 28 March 1931, 24.)

37. Waldemar Kaempffert, "A New Key to the Unknown," *The American Magazine*, June 1940, 66.

38. Henry Ford, with Samuel Crowther, "The Greatest American," *Cosmopolitan*, July 1930, 193.

39. Ibid.

40. Julian S. Huxley, "Searching for the Elixir of Life," *The Century Illustrated Monthly Magazine*, February 1922, 629.

41. Edgar C. Wheeler, "Makers of Lightning," *The World's Work*, January 1927, 271.

42. George Ellery Hale, "A National Focus of Science and Research," *Scribner's Magazine*, November 1922, 518.

43. A. D. Hall, "The Soil as a Battleground," *Harper's Monthly Magazine*, October 1910, 687.

44. Wheeler, "Makers of Lightning," 270. ("Occasionally science wins a victory at practically no cost at all to the beneficiary." Samuel Hopkins Adams, "Warring on Injurious Insects," *The American Magazine*, July 1910, 302.)

45. James R. Newman, "America's Most Radical Law," *Harper's Monthly Magazine*, May 1947.

46. Joseph Wood Krutch, "Disillusionment with the Laboratory," *The Atlantic Monthly*, March 1928, 369.

47. J. W. N. Sullivan, "Science and the Layman," *The Atlantic Monthly*, September 1934, 335.

48. John Wright Buckham, "The Passing of the Scientific Era," *The Century Illustrated Monthly Magazine*, August 1929, 433.

49. See the discussion in Chapter 2 about McCarthy-era coverage in *The American Mercury*.

50. Robert D. Potter, "Are We Winning the War against TB?," *The Saturday Evening Post*, 15 January 1949, 34.

51. Ibid.

52. Ibid., 74.

53. Howard A. Howe, "Can We Vaccinate Against Polio?," *Harper's Monthly*, April 1951, 42.

54. Ibid.

Chapter Nine

1. John Burroughs, "In the Noon of Science," *The Atlantic Monthly*, September 1912, 327.

2. Daniel Kevles points out: "It was an ambivalence that originated in the extent to which science could be used for destructive purposes, and it was clearly evident in the assault against science mounted in the interwar years. . . . If science had helped win the Great War, it would make the next war catastrophic, particularly, as more than one writer worriedly pointed out, were man to discover the secret of atomic energy." See Daniel J. Kevles, "On the Moral Dilemmas of the American Chemist," in William Beranek, Jr., ed., *Science, Scientists, and Society* (Tarrytown-on-Hudson: Bogden and Quigley, 1972), 10.

3. That is, articles that were intended and presented as critical commentaries on science. This figure does not include any measurement of the appearance of paragraphs or sections of criticism in otherwise positive articles.

4. Harold Goddard, "Should Language Be Abolished?," *The Atlantic Monthly*, July 1918, 61.

5. Arthur D. Little, "The Fifth Estate," *The Atlantic Monthly*, December 1924, 772.

6. E. E. Slosson, "Science From the Sidelines," *The Century Illustrated Monthly Magazine*, January 1922, 471.

7. Henshaw Ward, "A Drop of Water," *Harper's Monthly Magazine*, April 1926, 644.

8. Stuart Mackenzie, "The Camera Is the Sherlock Holmes of the Sky," *The American Magazine*, November 1922, 176.

9. Fred C. Kelly, "Pearl—and Provender," *Everybody's Magazine*, August 1918, 57.

10. Charles Phelps Cushing, "How Much Fresh Air Can a Well Man Stand?" *The World's Work*, February 1917, 404.

11. Charles Phelps Cushing, "Sleep for the Sleepless," *The World's Work,* January 1917, 251.

12. Allan Harding, "Beware of Fear!" *The American Magazine,* December 1922, 37.

13. "Star-Gazer," *The American Magazine,* June 1934, 46.

14. Vernon Kellogg, "The Biologist Speaks of Death," *The Atlantic Monthly,* June 1921, 778.

15. Little, "The Fifth Estate," 772.

16. Hannah Arendt, *The Human Condition* (Chicago: The University of Chicago Press, 1958), 3.

17. Ibid.

18. Ibid.

19. H. P. Sheldon, "Taking the Dust Out of Industry," *The Saturday Evening Post,* 4 September 1920, 46.

20. George W. Gray, "This Earth We Live On," *The American Magazine,* April 1927, 174.

21. Quentin Gulliver, "A New Voyage to Laputa," *The Century Illustrated Monthly Magazine,* July 1929, 352.

22. Robert M. Gay, "The Flavor of Things," *The Atlantic Monthly,* September 1914, 419.

23. Joseph H. Spigelman, "Can Science Make Sense?," *Harper's Monthly Magazine,* May 1951, 54.

24. Vannevar Bush, "For Man to Know," *The Atlantic Monthly,* August 1955, 32.

25. Ibid.

26. Katherine Fullerton Gerould, "The Extirpation of Culture," *The Atlantic Monthly,* October 1915, 454–55.

27. Vernon Kellogg, "Some Things Science Doesn't Know," *The World's Work,* March 1926, 523.

28. Kellogg, "The Biologist Speaks of Death," 778.

29. L. P. Jacks, "Is There a Foolproof Science?," *The Atlantic Monthly,* February 1924, 239.

30. See, for example, discussion of this point in John Wright Buckham, "The Passing of the Scientific Era," *The Century Illustrated Monthly Magazine,* August 1929, 433–35.

31. L. H. Baekeland, "What Is the Matter with the American Chemist?" *Harper's Monthly Magazine,* April 1917, 707.

32. Samuel Hopkins Adams, "The Color Scheme of War," *Collier's,* 7 June 1919, 11.

33. Ibid.

34. Ibid.

35. "The Demobilized Professor," *The Atlantic Monthly,* May 1919, 540.

36. Buckham, "Passing of the Scientific Era," 435.

37. Roy MacLeod, "The Social Function of Science in Britain: A Retrospect," Occasional Paper No. 6 (Queensland, Australia: Science Policy Research Centre, Griffith University, 1980), 6. Also see Roy MacLeod and Kay MacLeod, "The Social Relations of Science and Technology, 1914–1939," in Carlos Chipolla,

ed., *The Fontena Economic History of Europe,* volume 5, *The 20th Century, Part I* (London: Collins/Fontena, 1976), 301–55.

38. Selig Hecht, "The Uncertainty Principle and Human Behavior," *Harper's Monthly Magazine,* January 1935, 238.

39. Aldous Huxley, "The Genius and the Goddess (I)," *Harper's Monthly Magazine,* April 1955, 79.

40. Burroughs, "In the Noon of Science," 323.

41. Ibid., 324.

42. Buckham, "Passing of the Scientific Era," 433.

43. Burroughs, "In the Noon of Science," 327.

44. To Eliot, knowledge only emphasizes ignorance, by showing us what we do not know. "Where," he asks in "The Rock," "is the knowledge we have lost in information?" (T. S. Eliot, *The Complete Poems and Plays, 1909–1950* [New York: Harcourt, Brace & World, 1962], 96.)

45. Julian S. Huxley, "Will Science Destroy Religion?," *Harper's Monthly Magazine,* April 1926, 535.

46. T. S. Eliot, "The Waste Land (I. The Burial of the Dead)," in Eliot, *The Complete Poems,* 38–39.

47. J. W. N. Sullivan, "Science and the Layman," *The Atlantic Monthly,* September 1934, 330.

48. Ibid.

49. Ibid.

50. Huxley, "Will Science Destroy Religion?" 535.

51. See, for example, Joseph Wood Krutch, "The Modern Temper," *The Atlantic Monthly,* February 1927, and Joseph Wood Krutch, "Disillusionment with the Laboratory," *The Atlantic Monthly,* March 1928. Joseph Wood Krutch, *The Modern Temper: A Study and a Confession* (New York: Harcourt Brace Jovanovich, 1957); first published in 1929.

52. Krutch, *The Modern Temper,* xv.

53. In the article "Disillusionment with the Laboratory," Krutch "extended his point that advances in scientific understanding ruthlessly undermined all belief in meaning and value." Roderick Nash, *The Nervous Generation: American Thought, 1917–1930* (Chicago: Rand McNally, 1970), 124, 115–25 for discussion of Krutch. Also see discussion of Krutch and the relations between science and the new humanism in Dumas Malone and Basil Rauch, *War and Troubled Peace, 1917–1939* (New York: Appleton-Century-Crofts, 1960), Chapter 8.

54. Krutch, *The Modern Temper,* 150.

55. "We could no longer trust even our senses," one historian has observed of that period. Nash, *The Nervous Generation,* 124.

56. Krutch, *The Modern Temper,* 9.

57. Ibid., 56.

58. Paul Laubenstein, "The Modern Well-Tempered Mind," *The Atlantic Monthly,* February 1928, 195.

59. Ibid.

60. Ibid., 197.

61. Ibid.

62. Ibid., 199.

63. "We impoverish ourselves by refusing to yield our loyalties to religion . . . because it may contain elements of a type not open to verification by approved scientific methods." (Ibid.)

64. Harry Emerson Fosdick, "Science and Religion," *Harper's Monthly Magazine*, February 1926, 300.

65. Ibid.

66. Patricke Johns-Heine and Hans H. Gerth, "Values in Mass Periodical Fiction, 1921–1940," in Bernard Rosenberg and David Manning White, eds., *Mass Culture: The Popular Arts in America* (Glencoe: The Free Press, 1957), 232–33 and note 9.

67. See, for example, Robert Kilburn Root, "The Age of Faith," *The Atlantic Monthly*, July 1912, 110; R. K. Hack, "Drift," *The Atlantic Monthly*, September 1916, 356; and Albert Edward Wiggam, "The New Decalogue of Science," *The Century Illustrated Monthly Magazine*, March 1922, 647.

68. George A. Lundberg, "Can Science Save Us?" *Harper's Monthly Magazine*, December 1945, 525.

69. John Burroughs, "Scientific Faith," *The Atlantic Monthly*, July 1915, 33.

70. Ibid.

71. Root, "The Age of Faith," 111.

72. Burroughs, "In the Noon of Science," 322; and Burroughs, "Scientific Faith," 32.

73. Such themes are present in many other parts of literature, in poems, films, plays, and novels.

74. Samuel George Smith, "The New Science," *The Atlantic Monthly*, December 1912, 801.

75. Hugh Black, "Our Made-Over World," *Everybody's Magazine*, November 1914, 706.

76. Burroughs, "Scientific Faith," 33.

77. See, for example, the article by Huxley, "Will Science Destroy Religion?" 531ff.

78. Vernon Kellogg, "Some Things Science Doesn't Know," *The World's Work*, March 1926, 529.

79. Ibid.

80. Title and lead notes to Albert Edward Wiggam, "Science Is Leading Us Closer to God," *The American Magazine*, September 1927, 24.

81. Ibid., 196.

82. The case was *The State of Tennessee vs. John Thomas Scopes*. Scopes was found guilty on 21 July 1925 and fined $100. In January 1927, the Tennessee Superior Court reversed the judgment against Scopes on a technicality. See Marcel C. La Follette, ed., *Creationism, Science, and the Law: The Arkansas Case* (Cambridge: The MIT Press, 1983). Also see Dorothy Nelkin, *The Creation Controversy* (New York: W. W. Norton Co., 1983).

83. William G. Shepherd, "Monkey Business in Tennessee," *Collier's*, 18 July 1925, 8.

84. Leonard Darwin, "'You Can't Make a Silk Purse out of a Sow's Ear,'" *Collier's,* 25 July 1925, 11.

85. William Jennings Bryan, "The Bible's Good Enough for Me," *Collier's,* 1 August 1925, 38.

86. Samuel Crowther, "A Scientist's God," *Collier's,* 24 October 1925, 6.

87. Fosdick, "Science and Religion," 297.

88. Elmer Davis, "Notes on a New Bible," *Harper's Monthly Magazine,* February 1932, 294–305.

89. "A new Bible for our time must be at least negatively limited by science," Elmer Davis wrote. (Ibid., 297.)

90. Wiggam, "Science Is Leading Us," 650.

91. Fosdick, "Science and Religion," 296.

92. Ibid., 298.

93. Jon D. Miller, "Science and Religion: The Impact of Religious Tension about Science on Public Attitudes toward Science and Technology," presented to the American Association for the Advancement of Science, Annual Meeting, Chicago, Ill., 14 February 1987, reporting on a survey sponsored by the National Science Foundation.

94. See Marcel C. LaFollette, "Creationism in the News," in LaFollette, *Creationism, Science, and the Law,* 189–207.

Chapter Ten

1. Editor's note to Ella Wheeler Wilcox, "The Madness of Vivisection," *Cosmopolitan,* May 1910, 712.

2. George W. Gray, "The Problem of Influenza," *Harper's Monthly Magazine,* January 1940, 176.

3. A. Vibert Douglas, "From Atom to Stars," *The Atlantic Monthly,* August 1929, 158.

4. J. W. N. Sullivan, "Science and the Layman," *The Atlantic Monthly,* September 1934, 335.

5. House Committee on Science and Technology, *The Regulatory Environment for Science,* Science Policy Study Background Report No. 10, 99th Congress (Washington: Government Printing Office, December 1986).

6. Irwin Edman, "We Superstitious Moderns," *The Century Illustrated Monthly Magazine,* June 1924, 190.

7. Hugh Black, "Our Made-Over World," *Everybody's Magazine,* November 1914, 706.

8. Ibid.

9. Joseph Wood Krutch, "Disillusionment with the Laboratory," *The Atlantic Monthly,* March 1928, 369.

10. Paul Laubenstein, "The Modern Well-Tempered Mind," *The Atlantic Monthly,* February 1928, 197.

11. Ibid.

12. George A. Lundberg, "Can Science Save Us?" *Harper's Monthly Magazine,* December 1945, 526.

13. "Science and the Social Order" (1937), reprinted in Robert K. Merton, *Social Theory and Social Structure,* revised and enlarged edition (Glencoe: The Free Press, 1957), 546.

14. Sullivan, "Science and the Layman," 334.

15. Ibid.

16. Ibid.

17. Vernon Kellogg, "The Biologist Speaks of Life," *The Atlantic Monthly,* May 1921, 593.

18. Laubenstein, "Well-Tempered Mind," 197.

19. Geoffrey Parsons, "Black Science," *Harper's Monthly Magazine,* June 1927, 112.

20. Lundberg, "Can Science Save Us?" 529.

21. Ibid.

22. See, for example, Sumner Welles, "The Atomic Bomb and World Government," *The Atlantic Monthly,* January 1946, 39ff.

23. Harold C. Urey, as told to Michael Amrine, "I'm a Frightened Man," *Collier's,* 5 January 1946, 19.

24. See Richard E. Neustadt and Harvey V. Fineberg, *The Swine Flu Affair: Decision-Making on a Slippery Disease* (Washington: U.S. Department of Health, Education, and Welfare, 1978).

25. Loren Eiseley, "The Scientist as Prophet," *Harper's Monthly Magazine,* November 1971, 96.

26. With the exception of the word *science,* the word *new* was the word (excluding prepositions, conjunctions, and pronouns) that appeared most frequently in the titled of the 687 articles.

27. Edward Arthur Fath, "The Story of the Spirals," *The Century Illustrated Monthly Magazine,* September 1912, 767.

28. Kellogg, "The Biologist Speaks of Life," 592.

29. Historian Paul Ceruzzi has detected less expansive language in the writings of computer pioneers in the 1940s and 1950s and attributes their underestimates of the machines' potential to internal factors related to how the scientists used computers; but these scientists are, I am convinced, exceptions in their modest assessment of the potential of their work. See Paul Ceruzzi, "An Unforeseen Revolution: Computers and Expectations, 1935–1985," in Joseph J. Corn, ed., *Imagining Tomorrow: History, Technology, and the American Future* (Cambridge: The MIT Press, 1986), 188–201.

30. Charles D. Spencer, "Commentary," *Newsletter of the Program on Public Conceptions of Science,* no. 3 (April 1973): 10.

31. Ruth Carson, "Clothes by Chemists," *Collier's,* 24 March 1945, 58.

32. Waldemar Kaempffert, "The World Has Just Begun," *The American Magazine,* January 1940, 42.

33. Wilcox, "The Madness of Vivisection," 714.

34. [author given as "A European"], "Intellectual America," *The Atlantic Monthly,* February 1920, 192.

35. Paul A. Zahl, "New Aids for the Blind," *The Atlantic Monthly,* May 1946, 77.

36. Sidney Shalett, "Look Out—Here Comes a Genius!" *The Saturday Evening Post,* 15 April 1950, 198.

37. J. D. Bernal, "If Industry Gave Science a Chance," *Harper's Monthly Magazine,* February 1935, 264.

38. Elie Metchnikoff and Henry Smith Williams, "Why Not Live Forever?" *Cosmopolitan,* September 1912, 436.

39. For example, Stanley Frost, "Radio—Our Next Great Step Forward," *Collier's,* 8 April 1922, 3; Waldemar Kaempffert, "To-Morrow's Wireless," *Cosmopolitan,* April 1915, 513; Waldemar Kaempffert, "That Boy and the Radio," *Collier's,* 27 December 1924, 7; and M. K. Wisehart, "Hello! Give Me European Long Distance Please!" *The American Magazine,* July 1921, 32.

40. Susan J. Douglas, "Amateur Operators and American Broadcasting: Shaping the Future of Radio," in Corn, ed., *Imagining Tomorrow,* 35.

41. Kaempffert, "To-Morrow's Wireless," 516.

42. Frost, "Radio," 3.

43. Floyd W. Parsons, "The World Does Move," *The Saturday Evening Post,* 14 March 1925, 177.

44. Ibid.

45. See Harvey W. Wiley, "Back to the Farm!" *The Century Illustrated Monthly Magazine,* February 1912, 629; and Leonard Keene Hirschberg, "Making Foods of Chemicals," *The World's Work,* May 1913, 115ff.

46. Bill Davidson, "New Bread from the Sea," *Collier's,* 16 April 1954, 62.

47. Lester Velie, "Bread Within the Waters," *Collier's,* 11 September 1948, 69.

48. Frederick G. Brownell, "How Will You Have Your Weather?," *The American Magazine,* April 1947, 44; and H. T. Orville, "Weather Made to Order?," *Collier's,* 28 May 1954, 25.

49. Eugene H. Kone, "Progress in Science," *The American Mercury,* November 1946, 611.

50. Two excellent books provide comprehensive cultural histories of American images of atomic energy and atomic weapons. See Paul Boyer, *By the Bomb's Early Light: American Thought and Culture at the Dawn of the Atomic Age* (New York: Pantheon Books, 1985) and Spencer R. Weart, *Nuclear Fear: A History of Images* (Cambridge: Harvard University Press, 1988).

51. Charles F. Kettering, as told to Paul de Kruif, "America Comes Through a Crisis," *The Saturday Evening Post,* 13 May 1933, 4.

52. George W. Gray, "Discoveries Within the Atom," *Harper's Monthly Magazine,* March 1934, 340.

53. Illustration caption to R. M. Langer, "Fast New World," *Collier's,* 6 July 1940, 18.

54. Ibid., 55.

55. William L. Laurence, "The Atom Gives Up," *The Saturday Evening Post,* 7 September 1940, 12.

56. John J. O'Neill, "Enter Atomic Power," *Harper's Monthly Magazine,* June 1940, 10.

57. Boyer has given a comprehensive account of the images of atomic energy in popular culture. See Boyer, *Bomb's Early Light*.

58. For the definitive history of the scientists' activities just after the war, see Alice Kimball Smith, *A Peril and a Hope: The Scientists' Movement in America, 1945–47* (Cambridge: The MIT Press, 1970).

59. And public expectations continued to be high. When the Gallup Poll asked in 1949, "Do you think that 50 years from now trains and airplanes will be run by atomic power?," 63% of the respondents said yes. (*The Gallup Poll*, Survey No. 450-K, Question No. 14b, 23 December 1949.)

60. Steven L. Del Sesto, "Wasn't the Future of Nuclear Engineering Wonderful?" in Corn, ed., *Imagining Tomorrow*, 58–76.

61. Atomic testing was also blamed for "fouling up the climate." H. Allen Smith, "Where's That Crazy Weather Coming From?" *The Saturday Evening Post*, 1 August 1953, 30.

62. See discussion of this period in Boyer, *Bomb's Early Light*.

63. James R. Newman, "America's Most Radical Law," *Harper's Monthly Magazine*, May 1947.

64. Ibid., 437.

65. Gordon Dean, "Atomic Energy for Peace," *The Atlantic Monthly*, February 1954, 36. William L. Laurence, "The Promise of Tomorrow," *Collier's*, 23 December 1955, 46.

66. National Science Board, *Science and Engineering Indicators—1987* (Washington: National Science Foundation, 1987), Table 8–21, p. 162. These surveys examined nuclear power in broad definition, confounding attitudes to research with opinions about power plants and nuclear waste. They also did not focus on research related to energy production or weapons development per se. Nevertheless, it seems likely that this double-sided assessment carries over into attitudes toward such research, identifying both its benefits and potential risks.

67. James T. Patterson, *The Dread Disease: Cancer and Modern American Culture* (Cambridge: Harvard University Press, 1987), looks at cancer research up through the early 1980s.

68. Bill Davidson, "Probing the Secret of Life," *Collier's*, 14 May 1954, 78.

69. Holman Harvey, "The Magic Dye of Many Colors," *The American Magazine*, October 1941, 126.

70. J. D. Ratcliff, "Plague Fighter," *Collier's*, 19 August 1944, 46.

71. Robert D. Potter, "Are We Winning the War Against TB?," *The Saturday Evening Post*, 15 January 1949, 34.

72. Clarence Woodbury, "The Race against Pain," *The American Magazine*, January 1950, 128.

73. Ibid.

74. Ibid., 130.

75. Peter Clark Macfarlane, "The Conquest of Cancer," *Cosmopolitan*, August 1912, 306.

76. Louis I. Dublin, "Fighting Cancer," *Scribner's Magazine*, February 1936, 85; and Robert Cook, "Front Line Against Cancer," *Collier's*, 8 February 1941, 46.

77. W. H. Keen, "A Message of Hope," *Reader's Digest,* April 1922, 148 [italics in original]. The article was condensed from an article first published in *Woman's Home Companion.*

78. C. P. Rhoads, "Chemicals for Cancer," *The Atlantic Monthly,* March 1954, 66.

79. "Scientific principles recently discovered may have converted cancer from an unfathomable mystery to a problem susceptible of solution by methods similar to those which have eliminated other incurable diseases." (Ibid., 62.)

80. *The Gallup Poll,* Survey No. 450-K, Question No. 14a, 23 December 1949.

81. Henry Schacht, "Cancer and the Atom," *Harper's Monthly Magazine,* August 1949, 87. As promises such as these continued, they harbored unsuspected irony for a world that forty years later would have scientists predicting increased cancer deaths caused by nuclear power accidents.

82. I am grateful to John C. Burnham for pointing out this possible interpretation.

83. House Committee on Science and Technology, *The Regulatory Environment,* 148. Data are from a contractor's report written for the study by Jon D. Miller.

84. Ibid.

85. National Science Board, *Science and Engineering Indicators,* Table 8–9, p. 150.

86. Analyst Richard Rettig, in Congressional testimony about funding for cancer research, pointed out that a climate of "hyperbole" continually surrounds this issue; "the justification for the expanded cancer effort in 1971," for example, "was based upon inflated public expectations about the progress that could be expected." (Richard Rettig, testimony given in hearings on nutrition and cancer, held by the Senate Subcommittee on Nutrition, Committee on Agriculture, 12 June 1978.)

87. Eiseley, "The Scientist as Prophet," 96–98.

88. R. K. Hack, "Drift," *The Atlantic Monthly,* August 1916, 355.

Chapter Eleven

1. Daniel Yankelovich, *New Rules: Searching for Self-Fulfillment in a World Turned Upside Down* (New York: Random House, 1981), xvi.

2. House Committee on Science and Technology, *The Regulatory Environment for Science,* Science Policy Study Background Report No. 10, 99th Cong., 2d sess. (Washington: Government Printing Office, December 1986), 151. Data are from a contractor's report written for the study by Jon D. Miller.

3. Stephen Withey and Robert C. Davis, "Satellites, Science, and the Public" (Ann Arbor: University of Michigan Survey Research Center, 1959). Also see Stephen Withey, "Public Opinion about Science and Scientists," *Public Opinion,* 38 (1959): 382–88.

4. Karen Oppenheim, "Acceptance and Distrust: Attitudes of American Adults toward Science," (master's thesis, University of Chicago, 1966).

5. In surveys in the 1950s, when asked whether they thought the world "better off" or "worse off" because of science, 83% responded that it was "better off." [Withey and Davis, "Satellites."] In a 1985 survey, 44% thought that the balance strongly favored beneficial results and 24% thought that it only slightly favored beneficial results; 4% thought them about equal; 13% thought that harms slightly outweighed benefits and 6% strongly so. (National Science Board, *Science and Engineering Indicators—1987* [Washington: National Science Foundation, 1987], Table 8–7, p. 148.)

6. National Science Board, *Science and Engineering Indicators,* Table 8–18, p. 159.

7. See Gerald Holton and William A. Blanpied, eds., *Science and the Public: The Changing Relationship* (Boston: D. Reidel, 1976).

8. National Science Board, *Science and Engineering Indicators,* appendix Table 8–12, p. 334. Pion and Lipsey noted this interpretation in a review article: Georgine M. Pion and Mark W. Lipsey, "Public Attitudes toward Science and Technology: What Have the Surveys Told Us?" *Public Opinion Quarterly* 45 (1981): 303–16.

9. "Science Policy Priorities and the Public: A Report on a Pilot Project to Assess Public Attitudes about Priorities and Indicators of Quality for Scientific Research" (New York: Public Agenda Foundation, 1982); prepared for the project on "Assessment of Science: Development and Testing of Indicators of Quality," Harvard University (National Science Foundation grant No. SRS–80–07378; Gerald Holton, principal investigator). For information on availability, write the Public Agenda Foundation, 750 Third Avenue, New York, NY 10017.

10. Pion and Lipsey, "Public Attitudes," 313.

11. Participant in 22 March 1982 focus group; identities of all participants were kept confidential.

12. National Science Board, *Science and Engineering Indicators,* Table 8–19, p. 160.

13. Daniel Yankelovich and Bernard Lefkowitz, "The Public Debate on Growth: Preparing for Resolution," *Technological Forecasting and Social Change* 17 (1980): 100.

14. Ibid., 101.

15. See House Committee on Science and Technology, *The Regulatory Environment for Science.*

16. See Jon D. Miller, "Science and Religion: The Impact of Religious Tension about Science on Public Attitudes toward Science and Technology," presented to the American Association for the Advancement of Science, Annual Meeting, Chicago, Illinois, 14 February 1987, 2, 19, reporting on a December 1985 survey sponsored by the National Science Foundation.

17. Withey and Davis, "Satellites."

18. See discussion also in Pion and Lipsey, "Public Attitudes," 311.

19. The study by Joseph Karjkovich surveyed 933 pupils and teachers in grades seven through twelve in New Jersey schools. ("Pupils' Attitudes on Scientists Surveyed," *Chemical and Engineering News,* 28 August 1978, 7–8.)

20. P. Hills and Michael Shallis, "Scientists and Their Images," *New Scien-*

tist, 28 August 1975, 471–75; also described in Pion and Lipsey, "Public Attitudes," 311.

21. Pion and Lipsey, "Public Attitudes," 311.

22. National Science Board, *Science and Engineering Indicators,* 153.

23. P. M. D. Collins and W. F. Bodmer, "The Public Understanding of Science," *Studies in Science Education* 13 (1986): 98.

24. Ibid.

25. Pion and Lipsey, "Public Attitudes," 306.

26. Polls conducted before and after certain events presumed to affect public attitudes to science have shown less change than expected. Studies of pre- and post-Sputnik attitudes to science, for example, include Withey and Davis, "Satellites." A survey sponsored by the National Science Foundation examined public attitudes following the explosion of the space shuttle *Challenger* and the accident at the Soviet nuclear power plant at Chernobyl; see National Science Board, *Science and Engineering Indicators,* 162–64.

27. "The View after 397 Books and One TV Show: An Interview with Isaac Asimov," *SIPIscope* 17, no. 1 (Winter 1989): 21.

28. R. K. Hack, "Drift," *The Atlantic Monthly,* August 1916.

29. Scientist Salvador Luria once observed that: "It is a fact of life that science has become so expensive that its support can be justified only on the basis of benefits that derive from it, which is to say that science has to be justified by the practical technologies that it generates." (Salvador E. Luria, "The Goals of Science," *Bulletin of the Atomic Scientists* 33, no. 5 [May 1977]: 29.)

30. Hack, "Drift," 355.

31. Irwin Edman, "We Superstitious Moderns," *The Century Illustrated Monthly Magazine,* June 1924, 190.

32. "The responsible scholars of science have not said this, but the facile journalistic camp-followers of science have." (Glenn Frank, "The Seven Lamps of Politics," *The Century Illustrated Monthly Magazine,* April 1924, 939.)

33. Edwin E. Slosson, "Science from the Sidelines," *The Century Illustrated Monthly Magazine,* January 1922, 475.

34. Following the shuttle *Challenger* accident in 1986, many of the journalists who had regularly covered the space program believed that they had failed in their reporting before the disaster and blamed that failure on their placid and friendly relationship with their sources at NASA. See "Media Coverage of the Shuttle Disaster: A Critical Look," transcription of a panel discussion held at the American Association for the Advancement of Science, Annual Meeting, Philadelphia, Pennsylvania, 26 May 1986 (Washington: American Association for the Advancement of Science, 1986).

Selected Bibliography

Because this book draws on the literature from diverse fields of study, I am intensely aware of, and grateful to, many scholars whose work has helped to explain Americans' reactions to science. I have assumed that most readers of this book will be—like the author—expert on or acquainted with some but not all these fields. This bibliography therefore lists some sources for further reading, most of which are representative of hundreds of books and scholarly articles on the same topic.

Chapter One

For background on American culture and politics during the early twentieth century: Henry Steele Commager, *The American Mind: An Interpretation of American Thought and Character* (New Haven: Yale University Press, 1950); Morris Janowitz, *The Last Half-Century: Societal Changes and Politics in America* (Chicago: The University of Chicago Press, 1978); Robert Nisbet, *History of the Idea of Progress* (New York: Basic Books, 1980); Henry F. May, *The End of American Innocence, A Study of the First Years of Our Own Time, 1912–1917* (New York: Alfred A. Knopf, 1959); Roderick Nash, *The Nervous Generation: American Thought, 1917–1930* (Chicago: Rand McNally, 1970); and John Morton Blum, *V Was for Victory: Politics and American Culture during World War II* (New York: Harcourt Brace Jovanovich, 1976).

Frederick Lewis Allen, *Only Yesterday: An Informal History of the Nineteen-Twenties* (New York: Harper & Brothers, 1931); Frederick Lewis Allen,

Since Yesterday: The Nineteen-Thirties in America, 1929–1939 (New York: Harper & Brothers, 1940); Frederick Lewis Allen, *The Big Change: America Transforms Itself, 1900–1950* (New York: Harper & Brothers, 1952); and Mark Sullivan, *Our Times,* 6 vols. (New York: Charles Scribner's Sons, 1926–1935) provide salient contemporary perspectives on American cultural attitudes.

For those unfamiliar with the history of U.S. science, the annual bibliographies published in the journal *Isis* offer a guide. A limited selection is also given in Marc Rothenberg, *The History of Science and Technology in the United States: A Critical and Selective Bibliography* (New York: Garland Publishers, 1982). Useful surveys in the history of American science include: David D. Van Tassel and Michael G. Hall, eds., *Science and Society in the United States* (Homewood, Ill.: The Dorsey Press, 1966); Alexandra Oleson and John Voss, eds., *The Organization of Science in Modern America, 1860–1920* (Baltimore: Johns Hopkins University Press, 1979); Nathan Reingold and Ida H. Reingold, eds., *Science in America: A Documentary History, 1900–1939* (Chicago: The University of Chicago Press, 1981).

Also see: Ronald C. Tobey, *The American Ideology of National Science, 1919–1930* (Pittsburgh: University of Pittsburgh Press, 1971); Charles E. Rosenberg, *No Other Gods: On Science and American Social Thought* (Baltimore: The Johns Hopkins University Press, 1976); and Nathan Reingold, ed., *The Sciences in the American Context: New Perspectives* (Washington: Smithsonian Institution Press, 1979).

For discussion of scientific management, see William E. Akin, *Technocracy and the American Dream: The Technocratic Movement, 1900–1941* (Berkeley: University of California Press, 1977); and Samuel Haber, *Efficiency and Uplift: Scientific Management in the Progressive Era, 1890–1920* (Chicago: The University of Chicago Press, 1964).

Books that focus on the U.S. science-government relationship in the twentieth century include the following: A. Hunter Dupree, *Science and the Federal Government: A History of Policies and Activities to 1940* (Cambridge: The Belknap Press of Harvard University Press, 1957), reissued with a new introduction (Baltimore: Johns Hopkins University Press, 1986); Don K. Price, *The Scientific Estate* (Cambridge: The Belknap Press of Harvard University Press, 1965); and Don K. Price, *Government and Science* (New York: Oxford University Press, 1962).

The contemporary proposals for the organization of postwar science were published in Vannevar Bush, *Science—The Endless Frontier: A Report to the President on a Program for Postwar Scientific Research* (Washington: Government Printing Office, 1945); and John R. Steelman, *Science and Public Policy: A Report to the President* (Washington: Government Printing Office, 1947).

Straightforward histories of postwar federal policy on science include the following: House Committee on Science and Technology, *A History of Science Policy in the United States, 1940–1985,* Science Policy Study Background Report No. 1, 99th Cong., 2d sess. (Washington: Government Printing Office, September 1986); J. Merton England, *A Patron for Pure Science: The National Science Foundation's Formative Years, 1945–57* (Washington: National Science Foundation,

1982); and James L. Penick, Jr., Carroll W. Pursell, Jr., Morgan B. Sherwood, and Donald C. Swain, eds., *The Politics of American Science: 1939 to the Present,* rev. ed. (Cambridge: The MIT Press, 1972).

Books that concentrate on science policy but set that discussion within the context of twentieth-century American society and politics include the following: Jean-Jacques Salomon, *Science and Politics,* trans. Noël Lindsay (Cambridge: The MIT Press, 1973); Daniel S. Greenberg, *The Politics of American Science* (New York: New American Library, 1971); David Dickson, *The New Politics of Science* (New York: Pantheon, 1984), reissued with a new preface (Chicago: The University of Chicago Press, 1988); Jerry Ravetz, *Scientific Knowledge and Its Social Problems* (New York: Oxford University Press, 1971); and Joseph Haberer, *Politics and the Community of Science* (New York: Van Nostrand Reinhold, 1969). Philip Boffey, *The Brain Bank of America: An Inquiry into the Politics of Science* (New York: McGraw-Hill, 1975) specifically chronicles the development of the National Academy of Sciences.

There are many histories of specific scientific fields. The best source on twentieth-century physics is Daniel J. Kevles, *The Physicists: The History of a Scientific Community in Modern America* (New York: Alfred A. Knopf, 1978), which contains an extensive bibliography of sources. Arnold Thackray, Jeffrey L. Sturchio, P. Thomas Carroll, and Robert Bud, *Chemistry in America, 1876–1976: Historical Indicators* (Dordrecht, Holland: D. Reidel, 1985) provides a rich source of data about that field, including a chapter on chemistry and mass culture.

Chapters Two and Three

There is an extensive literature on popular culture in America. Some related books include: Robert W. Rydall, *All the World's a Fair: Visions of Empire at American International Expositions, 1876–1916* (Chicago: The University of Chicago Press, 1984); and Joseph J. Corn, ed., *Imagining Tomorrow: History, Technology, and the American Future* (Cambridge: The MIT Press, 1986).

For the history of the popularization of science, see: John C. Burnham, *How Superstition Won and Science Lost: Popularizing Science and Health in the United States* (New Brunswick, N.J.: Rutgers University Press, 1987); Annette M. Woodlief, "Science in American Culture," in M. Thomas Inge, *Handbook of American Popular Culture,* vol. 3 (Westport: Greenwood Press, 1981), 429–58. Other treatments may be found in Terry Shinn and Richard Whitley, eds., *Expository Science: Forms and Functions of Popularisation* (Dordrecht, Holland: D. Reidel, 1985). A more contemporary view is given in Maurice Goldsmith, *The Science Critic* (London: Routledge and Kegan Paul, 1986). For discussion of the scientific literacy of the American public, see the special issue on "Scientific Literacy," *Daedalus* (Spring 1983).

The history of American magazines up through the early 1950s is amply told in Frank Luther Mott, *A History of American Magazines,* vols. 1–5 (Cambridge: Harvard University Press, 1930, 1938, 1938, 1957, and 1968); Theodore Peterson, *Magazines in the Twentieth Century,* 2d ed. (Urbana: University of Illinois Press, 1964); John Tebbel, *The American Magazine: A Compact History* (New

York: Hawthorne Books, 1969); and James Playstead Wood, *Magazines in the United States*, 2d ed. (New York: The Ronald Press, 1956).

For analysis of newsmaking and the social structure of journalism, past and present, see: Michael Schudson, *Discovering the News: A Social History of American Newspapers* (New York: Basic Books, 1978); and Herbert J. Gans, *Deciding What's News: A Study of CBS Evening News, NBC Nightly News, Newsweek, and Time* (New York: Pantheon, 1979). A good guide to research in communications overall, past and present, may be found in Charles R. Berger and Steven H. Chaffee, eds., *Handbook of Communication Science* (Newbury Park, Calif.: Sage, 1987).

Walter Lippmann, *Public Opinion* (New York: Macmillan, 1960), originally published in 1922, offers a rich interpretation still viable today. Elisabeth Noelle-Neumann, *The Spiral of Silence: Public Opinion—Our Second Skin* (Chicago: The University of Chicago Press, 1984) outlines the connection between public attitudes and political action.

On images and image making: Kenneth E. Boulding, *The Image: Knowledge in Life and Society* (Ann Arbor: The University of Michigan Press, 1961); Daniel J. Boorstin, *The Image: A Guide to Pseudo-Events in America* (New York: Harper & Row, 1961); Roland Marchand, *Advertising the American Dream: Making Way for Modernity, 1920–1940* (Berkeley: University of California Press, 1985).

There are a few good discussions of science journalism, all of them concentrating on contemporary issues: Rae Goodell, *The Visible Scientists* (Boston: Little, Brown, 1977); June Goodfield, *Reflections on Science and the Media* (Washington: American Association for the Advancement of Science, 1981); Sharon M. Friedman, Sharon Dunwoody, and Carol L. Rogers, eds., *Scientists and Journalists: Reporting Science as News* (New York: The Free Press, 1986); and Dorothy Nelkin, *Selling Science: How the Press Covers Science and Technology* (New York: W. H. Freeman, 1987).

Robert H. Kargon, ed., *The Maturing of American Science* (Washington: American Association for the Advancement of Science, 1974) reprints and analyzes selected speeches of the Association's presidents from 1923 to 1970, many of whom discussed science's public relations.

Books on corporate public-relations efforts involving scientists include the following: David E. Nye, *Image Worlds: Corporate Identities at General Electric* (Cambridge: The MIT Press, 1985); Wyn Wachhorst, *Thomas Alva Edison: An American Myth* (Cambridge: The MIT Press, 1981). The journal *Technology and Culture* publishes many articles on the history of industrial research.

Chapters Five–Ten

Recommended histories of twentieth-century women scientists include Margaret W. Rossiter, *Women Scientists in America: Struggles and Strategies to 1940* (Baltimore: Johns Hopkins University Press, 1982); Pnina G. Abir-Am and Dorinda Outram, eds., *Uneasy Careers and Intimate Lives: Women in Science, 1789–1979* (New Brunswick, N.J.: Rutgers University Press, 1987); June Goodfield, *An Imag-*

ined World: A Story of Scientific Discovery (New York: Harper & Row, 1981); Evelyn Fox Keller, *A Feeling for the Organism: The Life and Work of Barbara McClintock* (New York: W. H. Freeman, 1983); Barbara Sicherman, *Alice Hamilton: A Life in Letters* (Cambridge: The Belknap Press of Harvard University Press, 1984); and Richard S. Baldwin, *The Fungus Fighters: Two Women Scientists and Their Discovery* (Ithaca, N.Y.: Cornell University Press, 1981).

For contemporary sociological and political discussion of women in science, see Harriet Zuckerman and Jonathan R. Cole, "Women in American Science," *Minerva* 13 (Spring 1975): 82–102; Jonathan R. Cole, *Fair Science: Women in the Scientific Community* (New York: Free Press, 1971); and the special issue of the journal *Signs* ("Women, Science, and Society," Autumn 1978).

For a history of women journalists, see the following: Marion Marzolf, *Up from the Footnote: A History of Women Journalists* (New York: Hastings House, 1977); Ishbel Ross, *Ladies of the Press: The Story of Women in Journalism by an Insider* (New York: Harper & Brothers, 1936).

Some discussion of cultural images of science, surveys of public attitudes, and analysis of fictional scientists may be found in Gerald Holton, ed., *Science and Culture: A Study of Cohesive and Disjunctive Forces* (Boston: Houghton Mifflin, 1965); Bernard Barber and Walter Hirsch, eds., *The Sociology of Science* (New York: The Free Press, 1962); Gerald Holton and William Blanpied, eds., *Science and Its Public: The Changing Relationship* (Boston: D. Reidel, 1976); and Andrew Tudor, *Monsters and Mad Scientists: A Cultural History of the Horror Movie* (London: Basil Blackwell, 1989).

Discussion, in a cultural-historical context, of such topics as what is or is not science may be found in John Ziman, *Public Knowledge: The Social Dimension of Science* (Cambridge: Cambridge University Press, 1968).

The sociology of science offers a variety of perspectives on science: Bernard Barber, *Science and the Social Order* (New York: Collier Books, 1952; rev. ed., 1962); Everett Mendelsohn, Peter Weingart, and Richard Whitley, eds., *The Social Production of Scientific Knowledge* (Dordrecht, Holland: D. Reidel, 1977); Harriet Zuckerman, *Scientific Elite: Nobel Laureates in the United States* (New York: The Free Press, 1977); Ina Spiegel-Rösing and Derek de Solla Price, eds., *Science, Technology and Society: A Cross-Disciplinary Perspective* (London: Sage, 1977); Jerry Gaston, *The Reward System in British and American Science* (New York: Wiley-Interscience, 1978); G. Nigel Gilbert and Michael Mulkay, *Opening Pandora's Box: A Sociological Analysis of Scientists' Discourse* (Cambridge: Cambridge University Press, 1984); Barry Barnes, *About Science* (Oxford: Basil Blackwell, 1985); and Bruno LaTour, *Science in Action: How to Follow Scientists and Engineers through Society* (Cambridge: Harvard University Press, 1987). The central journals for articles on this topic include *Science, Technology, & Human Values* and *Social Studies of Science*.

The debate over whether to include the social sciences in the National Science Foundation is described in Samuel Z. Klausner and Victor M. Lidz, eds., *The Nationalization of the Social Sciences* (Philadelphia: University of Pennsylvania Press, 1986); and U.S. Library of Congress, Congressional Research Service, *Technical Information for Congress, a Report to the Subcommittee on Science,*

Research, and Development of the Committee on Science and Astronautics, U.S. House of Representatives, rev. ed. (Washington: Government Printing Office, 1971).

On the Scopes trial and the antievolution movements past and present, see L. Sprague de Camp, *The Great Monkey Trial* (Garden City: Doubleday, 1968); Sheldon Norman Grebstein, ed., *Monkey Trial: The State of Tennessee vs. John Thomas Scopes* (Boston: Houghton Mifflin, 1960); Jerry R. Tompkins, ed., *D-Day at Dayton: Reflections on the Scopes Trial* (Baton Rouge: Louisiana State University Press, 1965); Dorothy Nelkin, *The Creationism Controversy: Science or Scriptures in the Schools* (New York: W. W. Norton, 1982); and Marcel Chotkowski LaFollette, ed., *Creationism, Science, and the Law: The Arkansas Case* (Cambridge: The MIT Press, 1983).

On public perceptions of atomic bombs and nuclear power: Paul Boyer, *By the Bomb's Early Light: American Thought and Culture at the Dawn of the Atomic Age* (New York: Pantheon, 1985); and Spencer R. Weart, *Nuclear Fear: A History of Images* (Cambridge: Harvard University Press, 1988), which includes an extensive bibliography of sources on atomic and nucler power research and policy. The policy to use the bomb and later public reactions are described through contemporary documents in such collections as Barton J. Bernstein, ed., *The Atomic Bomb: The Critical Issues* (Boston: Little, Brown and Company, 1976); and Paul R. Baker, ed., *The Atomic Bomb: The Great Decision* (Hinsdale, Ill.: The Dryden Press, 1968). Subsequent policy and public attitudes are discussed in Steven L. Del Sesto, *Science, Politics, and Controversy: Civilian Nuclear Power in the United States, 1946–1974* (Boulder, Colo.: Westview Press, 1979); and William R. Freudenburg and Eugene A. Rosa, eds., *Public Reactions to Nuclear Power: Are There Critical Masses?* (Boulder, Colo.: Westview Press, 1982).

For discussion of cancer research and policy, see James T. Patterson, *The Dread Disease: Cancer and Modern American Culture* (Cambridge: Harvard University Press, 1987), which contains rich bibliographic notes; Mark E. Rushefsky, *Making Cancer Policy* (Albany: State University of New York Press, 1986); Kenneth E. Studer and Daryl E. Chubin, *The Cancer Mission: Social Contexts of Biomedical Research* (Beverly Hills: Sage, 1980); Stephen P. Strickland, *Research and the Health of Americans: Improving the Policy Process* (Lexington, Mass.: Lexington Books, 1978).

Chapter Eleven

One of the best reviews of public attitude surveys on science is still Georgine M. Pion and Mark Lipsey, "Public Attitudes toward Science and Technology: What Have the Surveys Told Us?" *Public Opinion Quarterly* 145 (1981): 303–16. Also see Jon D. Miller, *The American People and Science Policy: The Role of Public Attitudes in the Policy Process* (New York: Pergamon Press, 1983); Jon D. Miller, Robert W. Suchner, and Alan M. Voelker, *Citizenship in an Age of Science: Changing Attitudes among Young Adults* (New York: Pergamon Press, 1980).

On political and social regulation of research: House Committee on Science and Technology, *The Regulatory Environment for Science*, Science Policy Study

Background Report No. 10, 99th Cong., 2d sess. (Washington: Government Printing Office, 1986); also published as Office of Technology Assessment, *The Regulatory Environment for Science* (Washington: Government Printing Office, 1986). Other contemporary overviews of research regulation include: Paul A. Fruend, ed., *Experimentation with Human Subjects* (New York: George Braziller, 1969); Murray L. Wax and Joan Cassell, eds., *Federal Regulations, Ethical Issues and Social Research* (Boulder, Colo.: Westview Press, 1979); Keith M. Wulff, ed., *Regulation of Scientific Inquiry* (Boulder, Colo.: Westview Press, 1979).

INDEX

References to figures and tables are printed in boldface type.